GRAIG STREET

L.B.
P.H.

EBENEZER STREET

Chap.

B.M.68·1

MARINER STREET

High Street Station

Patent Fuel Works

Pot
Bra
(Su

NEW STREET

Urinal

63 IVEY PLACE

313

A N D R A   W A R D

P.O.

Bl. Gd.

Swansea Wharf

Stage

TUDOR COURT

62

Chap.
B.M.62·1

COLLEGE ACADEMY

Well

QUARRY

STREET

Institute

Sun. Sch.

Tank

SP

Mooring Posts

Public Library

PLEASANT STREET

RICHARD'S PLACE

ORCHARD STREET

Sch.

KING STREET

MORRIS LANE

51

STRAND

PH

SP

NORTH

DOCK

PLACE

SOUTH PROSPECT

THE

Miner

M.Ps

Chap.

Slip

314
7·883

15
6·497

ALBION
C

Ward Bdy.
C. Dock

Cr

STRAND ROW

Und.

47

WELCOME STREET

L.B.

COLLEGE STREET

CASTLE BAILEY STREET

WORCESTER PLACE

G.W.R.

M.Ps

B.M.43·3

MERT STREET

COAT STREET

SOUTH DOCK BRANCH

Wharves

M.Ps

M.P

Draw Bridge

WATERLOO

ARCADE

B.M.

51·1

TEMPLE STREET

P.O.

SQUIRES PLACE

ley's Yard

CASTLE

SP

315
(19·650

Cr

Jubilee Swansea

THE TOWN AND ITS PEOPLE
IN THE 1890S

VOLUME II

GERALD GABB

(1999)

Introductory

This is not a very serious history book. It is about people and places in Swansea a hundred years ago, and is written in the hope that some Swansea people of today may find it interesting. Like "Jubilee Swansea" Volume I, it does rather meander, so there is a detailed contents list opposite and a long index at the end. There is a street map inside the front and back covers. Also near the end you will find a list of sources.

Gerald Gabb 1999

Acknowledgements

The book owes a great deal to help, advice and information from Dr. Ronald Austin, Stuart Batcup, Susan Beckley, Dave Beynon, Mike Collier, Richard Davies, Rosalyn Gee, Gary Gregor, Helen Hallesy, Joan Harding, Suzanne and Dick Hart, Mike Lewis, Dr.Peter Lloyd Jones, Bernard Morris, John Radford, Paul Reynolds, Jennifer Sabine, Carl Smith and Sandra Thomas. That you are now looking at the finished product says a great deal for the skill and patience of Mike Evans of Designprint.

I am grateful to my colleagues in the museums service and to the staff at the West Glamorgan Archives Service for repeated help over a long period, and again I owe a lot to the staff at Swansea Reference Library for their patient help with consulting the marvellous collections there. It is invidious to single people out, but, being unsure what that word means, I will single out Gwyn Davies for all the documents he has put in front of me, and Dorothy Jenkins for her most knowledgeable guidance.

Pictures

The images which punctuate the text are very much part of the story, as well as hopefully making the book look nicer! The museums, the archives and the library have been the main sources. Bernice Cardy, Jennifer Sabine, Susan Beckley and Marilyn Jones have helped greatly over these. Others have been gratefully received from Gareth Mills, Jeff Long, Andre Scoville and Arthur Strick. Nigel Clatworthy took some of the modern photos. Some are my own. These individuals and institutions retain ownership of copyright.

A few were copied by Howard Jones some while ago. My thanks to him. Most have been done more recently by Graham Matthews, promptly and at a difficult time.

ISBN 0 9527151 1 2

Above: The town from Clifton Hill, showing what was called the Free Library, opened by Gladstone in 1887, before the Art Gallery was built across the road and the police station was joined on the end. Notice Holy Trinity church to the right.
The cover picture shows Constitution Hill and its tramway (see page 40).
The photograph on the title page is High Street, from its junction with College Street.

Contents

R.J.D. Burnie
MP for Swansea Town 1892-5.
Meet him on page 104.

William Williams, MP for Swansea District 1893-5. Meet him on page 10.

A warning about the middle classes

This second book about the town in the 1890s fills some of the gaps left by the first...but a huge amount still remains unsaid. When you strive to write about ordinary people, it soon dawns upon you that there were quite a lot of them, and most rather active. Imagine trying to describe the city today in the same way! The picture which emerges is bound to be influenced by the author, just in choosing what goes in and what is left out. After that, though, the people of Swansea are usually left to tell their own story, without much comment. For example, an early passage describes the vanishing higgledy-piggledy Oxford Street which had grown up over perhaps 60 years. We might talk about its charm, but that thought would be very foreign to the dominant "mind set" of one hundred years ago — the journalist in 1900 calls it *"hideous"*. So, the following pages will give you a picture of some aspects of our town as it was, in the way people saw it then......just think your own thoughts!

One unavoidable slant must be pointed out, though. This book tries very hard to be about people, where they lived and worked, and what they did and said. The information has been gathered from all over the place, but in one respect it is pretty uniform — it is from newspapers, directories, scrapbooks, letters, albums and guidebooks put together at the time by middle class people. They were a wide and varied grouping, but obviously a minority, and we tend to see ordinary, poorer Swansea people of the time only through their eyes. In October, 1892 a reporter for "the Cambrian" newspaper put together nearly a column and a half on *"The Poor Children of Swansea"*. This is an example of an article about some of the poorest in the town, and as you read it, remember it was written by a professional journalist for a literate and comfortable readership.

> *"'Wax lights! Penny a box...' These were the cries uttered by a boyish voice last Saturday night as I sauntered leisurely home."* (The reporter bought the last box of five dozen that day. The lad had *'a pale sunken face'*.)

> *'I went home to my cosy room in front of the fire and as I watched the dying embers burn my thoughts wandered out into the cold streets. It was cold, very, on Saturday night last...let me ask my readers a question. Do they in the happiness of their houses ever think of the poor little outcasts who day after day, night after night, are wandering hungry, hopeless, uncared for...scantily covered...even here in Swansea? No. Then they ought to."*

(Some, he said, were driven from their homes by parental brutality, often made worse by drunkenness. They took to the streets in infancy, and were there for life. He reckoned charity, the churches and the schools made some difference, but thought that society should do a lot more. Even orphanages ignored the poorest. *"These children of the streets are taught nothing and entirely neglected"*. Costermongers — street sellers of fruit and vegetables — would employ some. Many went through a set sequence — first errand running, then parcel carrying, horse holding and street trading in matches or fusees— smokers' matches.) After that *"It is Poverty — grim, gaunt Poverty — which teaches him to steal. The lad is hungry; he has not the wherewithal to buy a basin of soup or a hard biscuit; he haunts the coffee tavern doors, and watches the people eat with envious eyes. The proprietors try to drive him away. He sneaks slowly in, he spies a hunch of bread, or a bit of meat, or a potato left on a table, and before one can say 'Jack Robinson' he dashes for the food..."*

The writer befriended just such an eight year old, with a *"dirty face and unkempt hair"*, giving him food from his coffee tavern table (this looks like the Waverley, next to the Cameron Arms in High Street), and found him honest in running errands. Then there was a spell when the journalist ate elsewhere, and on return he found the lad thinner and the cafe staff hostile. He had begun to pilfer, and seemed *"bolder and more impudent"*. Meeting him in the street, he was about to give him a penny when the lad ran off down Welcome Lane — *"he had espied a detective"*. Soon he was before the police court, charged with stealing from a market stall. Later came another offence, and the writer never saw him again.

The top of Welcome Lane today, then usually called Welcome Street.

If this sounds like a piece of Dickens, and certainly there is a pinch of sentimentality in the style of writing, picture for yourself that boy running for survival down the steep hill beside our Argos store, perhaps to hide and eventually sleep under one of the dark railway arches which then ran along the edge of what we call Parc Tawe. Imagine for yourself, as our writer might say, the cold, dark and hunger, and the coal trains rumbling past overhead. If you want names, in January 1890, Patrick Cullin, Timothy Teag and Richard Sullivan, all aged 6, were before the police court for begging in the freezing cold of Temple Street. They were filthy, Patrick had no shirt, and when Detective Morris went to his home in Grove Street, Mrs.Cullin was *"...beastly drunk...[had]...not washed herself for some time...[and the]...stench in the passage was enough to knock anyone down..."*

The writer mentions orphanages. These words are from a report of the Industrial Home for Orphan and Friendless Girls in Longlands Place, which took 7 to 16 year olds —

"...at 16...they are furnished with a complete outfit and sent to service, and if any girl retains her first situation for two years, she receives...the reward of £1..."

He spoke also of charities. By 1899, there was a Swansea Charity Organization Society. Between January and July that year it helped 63 *"cases"* with emigration, bedding, loans, medical assistance and employment.

"A start is being made in pension work, and we have recently organised a weekly allowance for an old Lady who was on parish relief".

This was hardly a large scale operation, and perhaps anyway this was a middle class lady, fallen on hard times. However, there were ideas about, like those of Miss Brock, probably the daughter of the former minister of the Unitarian chapel in High Street, which were drifting from practical philanthropy towards a sort of middle class socialism –

"As for the workhouse test, she thought it a horrible thing. The very bad person did not feel any disgrace in going into the Union. A person who had tried to live a good life came to the House and was offered a means test. She would not take it...There were a great many people who had done nothing to deserve their poverty, and poverty was no more discreditable to them in many ways than wealth was creditable to many people who had inherited it without moving a hand to make it...there were thousands of people living in clubs and hotels in London...who had never paid a farthing to the rates..."

The Cambrian Institution for the Deaf and Dumb dominated the skyline above Cradock Street. The original building of 1855 was extended by stages — the west wing was added in 1864, the east in 1874. It was demolished in 1997.

But the workhouse remained the backbone of "social insurance". In October, 1898, little Edith Phillips was begging, pale and thin, in the town centre. Her mother, Susan, had just one piece of bread in their house, in Bond Street in the Sandfields. Her father, Eugene, had once been assistant manager of the Deaf and Dumb Institution, the great gabled building on the hill, in line with your eyes if you looked up from outside the Albert Hall in Cradock Street. Afterwards he worked in Lambert's Copper Works, near the Prince of Wales Dock, but these days he lay in bed until 11.00 and merely wrote begging letters. An N.S.P.C.C. inspector prosecuted him, and the magistrate (J. Viner Leeder) gave him a year's hard labour, and advised Susan to take Edith into the workhouse.

Don't forget Susan and Edith as we journey to the luxuries of Ffynone, to baronial Maesygwernen or to princely Penllergaer.

A changing town

As the old century expired, an anonymous Swansea reporter wrote:

> *"...Oxford street, once hideous because of low irregular buildings and the hoardings which covered the walls of the old Market, has come to quite a Metropolitan appearance...and will soon be a serious rival to High street...*
>
> *The New Empire...is amongst the finest music halls in the provinces, and its facade to Oxford street is quite worthy of the splendid interior...*
>
> *Opposite the Great Western Railway Station there used to be a block of small shops...They have now given place to a more commodious and handsome building..*
>
> *In Wind street...the new post office is still in the process of erection..."*

Daniel Sugrue was an Irishman of "a little fire", who managed the Swansea street tramways from 1884, and very successfully. In 1900 he left for a London job, commenting —

Daniel Sugrue.

Oxford Street, Swansea

The new grander buildings are on the right — John Brown's (the only one still standing), the Empire Theatre, and then the towers of the 1897 market with David Evans store (1899) in the distance.

The New Empire Theatre, opened 10th December 1899.

The Wind Street Post Office was completed in 1901, so the carved "V.R." on the Green Dragon Lane wall is just about in order.

"...although an Irishman by birth...he might still consider himself a Swansea man...who would look back with pride on the position the old town had acquired for herself, solely through the efforts of her own sons — not nurtured by 'belted earls' or men of high degree with long purses..."

While Cardiff was prospering as never before, "Abertawe", the little rivermouth market town was becoming grander too. The copper industry which had first fuelled this growth was now wilting in the face of American competition. The Vivians, the largest copper owners, had diversified. At the Hafod Isha Works, for example, they refined cobalt and nickel, but, by 1894 when Henry Hussey Vivian, Lord Swansea, died, this enterprise had lost £45,000. In the following January, it was suggested:

"His late lordship was...never so wealthy as he appeared in public... (and rather unfairly)...The only things which seemed to succeed were the ventures his father had begun...Lady Swansea has already thrilled the servants' hall by giving notice to very many old and faithful servants...Even the old folk who keep the lodges are under notice to quit..."

Henry Hussey Vivian in 1893.

In June, 1898, Singleton Abbey, the palatial family home of the Vivians was empty, and a year later was let to Louis Nott, a dock contractor. The great names of the copper ore trade were disappearing — by 1890 Henry Bath & Sons, copper ore merchants, were based first and foremost at New Broadstreet in London, and Richardson & Co. stopped trading in February, 1897. Henry Hussey Vivian had told the Chamber of Commerce in January, 1893, about "the very serious reduction" in the local copper industry —

"Swansea had its origin in the prosperity of the Cornish mines...The quantity of copper [ore] produced in Cornwall last year did not exceed 350 tons. I am old enough to remember when it produced more than that in a fortnight...I remember when we used to export copper to America; but now America is the greatest copper producing country in the world, and sends enormous quantities to England..."

Colonel Pike, who became mayor in November 1893, summed up the changes like this —

"...the copper trade has now almost entirely passed away... anthracite...[is]...the coal of the future...Swansea, by virtue of her geographical position, must be the centre for its export...streets are crowding upon one another in parts of the town which in my boyhood were looked on as ruralistic retreats...in all directions the town is spreading, until there are now no less than 16,000 houses..."

The anthracite trade was certainly growing and so was patent fuel manufacture. But the prosperity and confidence indicated by the growth and enshrined in the fine new buildings of Swansea came from a different source...and a one word answer to this puzzle would be **tinplate**.

Colonel Pike. By 1898 he was a director of the Langland Bay Hotel, and lived nearby.

PIC: SWANSEA MUSEUM.

A Morriston Wedding

In April, 1892, Dr. Arnallt Jones married Alice Williams at St. David's Church, Morriston — it was quite an event. Visiting reporters set the scene —

"the prosperity of the last couple of decades is now rapidly transforming the somewhat irregular streets of old, and small houses, into fine urban thoroughfares, lined with grand places of public wor-

St.David's Church, Morriston.

ship and fine shops...Woodfield Street with its Congregational cathedral (Tabernacle) and other temples...is the very centre of the life of Morriston..

(everything) looked unwontedly gay...with festoons of bunting and triumphal arches of evergreens...one with the motto 'Duu a Digon' (God and Plenty)...”

The bride wore an Empire style gown of duchesse satin with a full brocaded train and her nephew, *“pretty little Jack Edwards”*, was pageboy *“in a Lord Fauntleroy suit of electric plush with court shoes and white felt hat with plumes...”* Apart from an endless list of prominent guests — Sir John and Lady Jones Jenkins, Edward Rice Daniel, David Glasbrook, Ben Evans — *“...the whole population thronged the streets..it was pleasant to see the large number of neatly dressed workmen assembled to witness the ceremony”.* When the guests moved off to what one newspaper called the “at House” held at the bride's home, along what must have been quite a country lane, they found *“from every cottage gaudy bunting fluttered, and those of the cottagers who had no bunting hung out their gaily coloured coverlets”,* — perhaps patchwork quilts. Maesygwernen was —

“a handsome and commodious new house situated on some of the most fertile farmland...sufficiently remote from all the metal manufactories to be wholly free from all the effects of those blessed but blighting fumes...the Hall itself is built of warm red brick, with soft grey Forest of Dean stone dressings. From its large square windows, and from its well kept grassy lawns, are to be caught glimpses of fine stretches of country...the extensive lawn on the south front of the mansion was bright with flowers...two large marquees were set aside for refreshments, solid and liquid, teetotal and alcoholic...”

Catering was by Mr. Chester Row of the Royal Hotel, High Street, Swansea, (*“...first class chef...Specially prepared floor for Dancing”*), the bridal trousseau by Ben Evans, and her flowers by Tom Barron, who ran nurseries at Blackpill and Lilliput, and a shop at 7 Oxford Street. The couple went off to the junction station at Landore for a train to Bath, en route to the Isle of Wight, while their guests repaired to the billiard room to view the hundreds of presents, including a diamond star, necklace and bracelets for Alice from her parents, a silver crumb spoon, an ivory paper knife, Dresden ornaments and a framed pair of scripture texts.

The Royal was on the Western side of High Street, opposite the Bush.

The groom was an Aberafan G.P., son of the Vicar of Abergwesin. He had made a name for himself by his unceasing efforts at the site of the recent Morfa colliery explosion. But the pomp of the occasion owed nearly everything to William Williams, father to the bride.

William Williams and Edward Rice Daniel

William Williams became M.P. for Swansea District in 1893, and was said to be a millionaire. His mansion in *“the alderwood fields”* (“Maesygwernen”) was near Cwmrhydyceirw, on the hillside above Morriston, and some of the smoke in the valley issued from his own Upper Forest and Worcester Tinplate Works, just north of the Wychtree bridge. He had built the house in 1886-7, on the site of Maesygwernen Farm, which he bought in '85. Together with stables and a coach house, it had a walled kitchen garden, vinery, hothouses, conservatory, boiler house and lodge. William had started as a cold roll boy at Upper Forest, but, losing his leg in an accident, was given a wooden leg and a job in the pay office. By 1868 he

Maesygwernen today — still impressive.

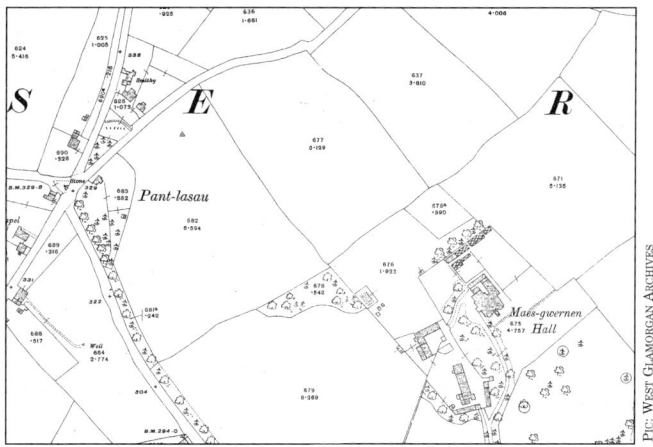

The area in the 1890s. The house now forms part of Morriston Hospital, whose buildings sprawl across the adjacent fields.

PIC: WEST GLAMORGAN ARCHIVES

had enough money to build the Worcester Works and in 1878 he bought the nextdoor Upper Forest from Edward Bagot. He was mayor in 1884. By 1892, he was *"one of our most successful and popular Captains of Industry"*, employing more than 2,000. Like his workforce, he was a nonconformist (an Independent) and a Welsh speaker. His election to the Commons as a Liberal was unopposed — Sir John Jones Jenkins (Unionist) and Tom Phillips (Labour) both withdrew. At the announcement, a big crowd from Morriston came to meet him at the Mackworth Arms, (the original one in Wind Street), unhitched his horses as was the custom, and pulled him manually the five miles to his home. The labour leaders were invited to ride in the same carriage, and after the speeches on the lawns of Maesygwernen, even Tom Phillips spoke of —

"...an extraordinary example of how a man might rise from the ranks..."

PIC: ANDRE SCOVILLE

Left: The Worcester Tinplate Works (two views. both from the west).

PIC: SWANSEA MUSEUM

PIC: SWANSEA MUSEUM

Tinplate had been hugely profitable for more than ten years, but when this changed with the McKinley Tariff William Williams closed the works for a spell, laying off all his men in September 1892, and again, giving just one week's notice, in March, 1896. His partners disputed the need, and he seems to have sold out to them in 1898 for £96,200. At the time of the sale it was described as *"the largest combined steel and tinplate works in the kingdom"*. In October, he hosted a crowded *"valedictory meeting...cyfarfod ymadawol"* at Hebron chapel where he spoke at length:

> *"I was the son of a poor working man — a good one...after my accident I was determined not to be a burden to society...a tie, in force for so many years, creates affection and love...I had intended that this meeting be a sort of family meeting, a sacred meeting..."*

and it ended with a Welsh hymn.

Even his enemies conceded that William Williams was open, straightforward and a good employer, but they suggested that he talked about giving money for hospitals, libraries and public baths, rather than actually doing it. (An exception was the site of the Teachers' Training College on Townhill, which he gave in 1900). Like other tinplate owners, he was of humble parentage, and it could be that the singlemindedness which gave him success was very hard to relax when he had achieved it. In March 1896, after Upper Forest had been closed for 3 months and the Worcester for 15, he had decided on limited production *"as soon as the machinery could possibly be got ready and the brickwork and masonry had properly dried"* even though *"his warehouses were full of tinplates [and] ...he had not a single order..."* He urged the men to be thrifty. When he finally broke his links with the Worcester in October, 1898, he parted from some of his old workmen, saying *"he would still be their neighbour"*. Unemployed rollermen cannot have viewed too happily the gates of their works, so often locked, when their families had little to eat, and the Williams family lived in plenty at Maesygwernen. One newspaper put it more harshly in 1896 —

> *"...the men of the Worcester Works, the oldest of Mr. Williams's workmen, are literally starving...the works are idle and for sale...Mr. Williams is recruiting his health on the continent..."*

(The family, though, had its misfortunes. William's wife Margaret died in April 1893, just a year after the wedding, aged only 44, and William himself aged 64 in April 1904).

Edward Rice Daniels.

Edward Rice Daniel had been manager or owner of Cwmfelin Tinplate since at least 1883. He had been mayor in 1882-3. In 1893 he was described as a mining engineer linked for example with Alfred Sterry's Mountain Colliery at Gorseinon, and estate agent and valuer to, for instance, the Earl of Cawdor. His business address was 6 Worcester Place. He was brother-in-law to John Jones Jenkins, the acknowledged champion of the port and industry of Swansea, and in interviews he gave to the press in October 1892 and May 1896, you can see a similar mixture of attitudes. He could be very realistic, full of common sense, but still positive and open minded. He visited the States, and came back impressed with its rivers and lakes, railways and shrewd, enterprising people.

"They are beyond us in many things — in architecture, science, machines..as far as American demand is concerned ....they will soon provide themselves with all the tinplates they need. We must open up fresh markets entirely...the tinplate trade has gone to America to stay...but the world is open to us as it is to them. China may be opened out..."

Terneplates (tinplates on which the tin was alloyed with lead) were being used for roofing on new Swansea buildings — the Market, the Metal Exchange in Fisher street, the Grand Theatre, but

"...Mr. Daniels observed he did not think much of it himself. He was afraid that we in Wales were too much wedded to slates."

Yet this practical, clear sighted man expected his own employees to operate Cwmfelin at reduced capacity, and of course reduced wages, while he lived at Cwmgelly House.

This was close enough to the mines and works of Landore, but *"pleasantly situated in its own grounds"*; it was where the reporters *"waited on him"* in 1892. The second interview ended —

"In compliance with the advice of his doctor, who had recently accompanied him to Madeira, he was not at present doing much in connection with the management of the Cwmfelin works for the past twelve months [sic]. *It had not been given up by him"*.

There were two worlds. In March 1896 Edward Rice Daniel and Sir John Jones Jenkins had asked their workforce of more than 1,000 to take a 25% wage cut. They refused and walked out. The following month they sold Cwmfelin. Edward Rice Daniel was to retire as councillor for St. John's Ward in June 1897. He died in 1905, aged 76. His widow was still living at Cwmgelly in 1919, aged 94.

The McKinley Tariff

Morriston was the centre of British tinplate production. Most was exported, the majority to the United States, about half being used to can fruit and meat. By October, 1890, a duty to deter Welsh imports, proposed by William McKinley, was being debated in Congress. William Williams was one of those who visited the U.S. to consider opening mills there, but he concluded, *"...I should not embark any capital..."* Attitudes to American ambitions varied. There was great hilarity when it was found that the campaign badges of Ohio republicans bearing McKinley's face and the slogan "American Tin " were made of Swansea tinplate. At a time when Britain was easily the largest coal producer in the world (mining three times as much as Germany, its nearest rival) and owned more than half the world's steamships (5,792 of 9,969), there was a tendency to be patronising:

William McKinley

"Because Cousin Jonathan thinks proper to try on his 'prentice hand' at tinplate making, why should there be all this fuss and bother?.."

This complacency came to have a hollow ring very quickly. Henry Morton Stanley the explorer of Africa spoke to a crowded Albert Hall in May 1896. He could remind Swansea:

"You who listen to me well remember the boast you used to make in South Wales that the Americans would never rival you in the manufacture of tinplate.."

He pointed to British

"insular conceit...love for old fashioned ways..laziness...trade unions...[and even suggested]*...there are intelligent people who maintain that education should largely be in Welsh; as though there were countries abroad where the knowledge of Welsh would be an advantage to their sons."*

There was some hissing, but he was generally listened to and applauded. And he was probably right about the dislike of change. Daniel Edwards of the Dyffryn Tinplate Works, for example, invented a machine to dip the plates, and tried to bring in mechanisation of other processes, but in 1890 his men, understandably perhaps, struck to resist this. Some industrialists had long foreseen trouble. As early as 1890, Henry Hussey Vivian thought the American market *"precarious"*. Welsh owners felt that American capitalists had been stupid enough to produce copper on a massive scale, and so bring down profits, and

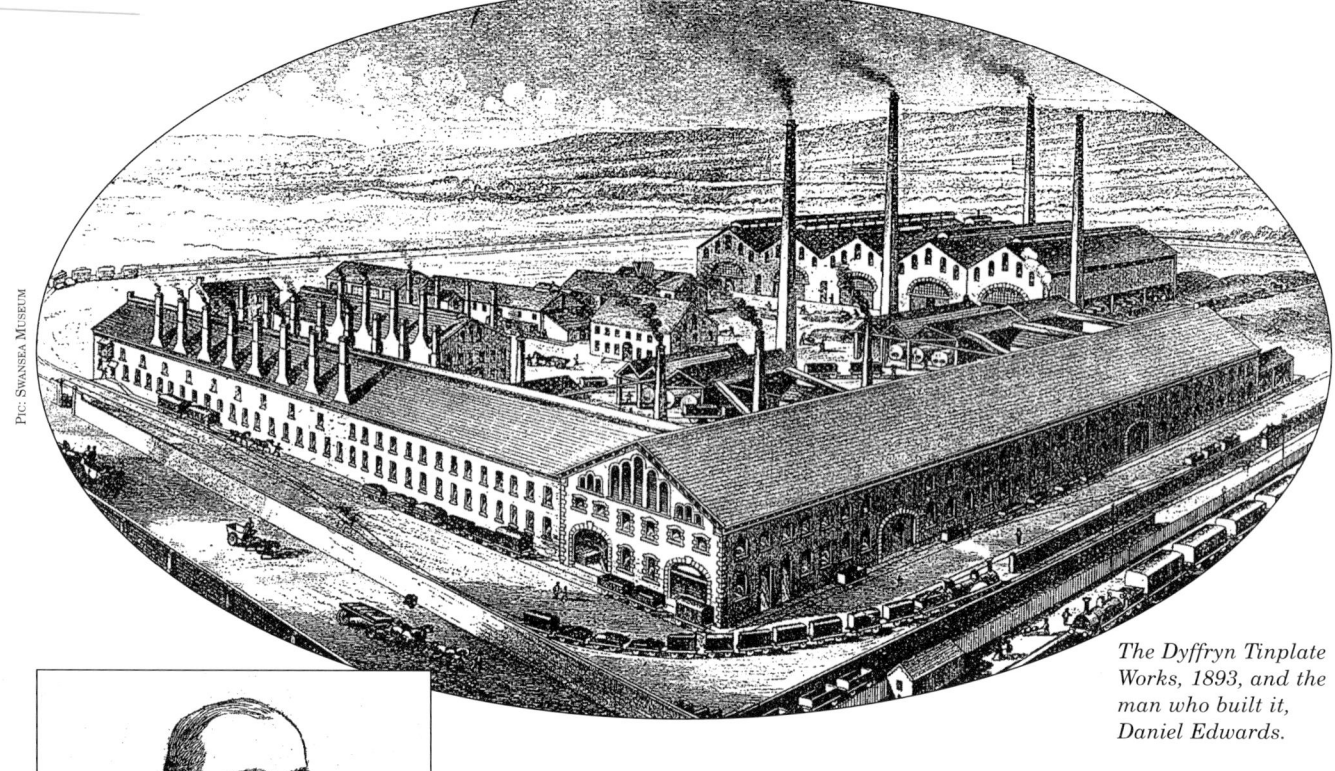

Pic: Swansea Museum

The Dyffryn Tinplate Works, 1893, and the man who built it, Daniel Edwards.

Pic: Swansea Museum

feared that they might do the same with tinplate! Of course, the U.S. industry could not immediately take up the slack — by March, 1892, it had just 52 mills, about the same as Morriston — but in November, 1897, this had risen to 206, with 85 under construction. Their workers were now paid double the Welsh rates, produced 52 boxes per 8 hour shift compared with the home limit of 36, and were discarding working practices they had used just 5 years before, while Morriston kept faith with the established methods of generations past. This was the message of a local journalist —

"There is yet possibly time for the Welsh tinplate makers and workmen to pull themselves together by straining every nerve to reduce the cost and to improve the quality of Welsh tinplates before they inscribe over the doors of every Welsh tinplate works 'Ichabod. The glory is departed.' "

The Boom...

At the Prince of Wales Dock, the five months up to Saturday, June 13th, 1891, were like this:

"....the fine fleet of ocean-going steamers of four powerful companies have never, even for a single hour, permitted the possibility of a vacant berth...Day and night it has been the scene of constant operations, and one round of ceaseless delivery from the spacious warehouses, vans, carts and coasters to the splendid vessels which were bound for the opposite shores. Notwithstanding this steady delivery there was not until this last week or so any appreciable impression made upon the bulk which was sent by an unbroken line of carts, averaging 250 per diem, from the neighbouring works, in fact the inward rush of traffic for 3 months out of the 5 considerably exceeded the export, although in January alone no less than 13 steamers left the port each with their Plimsolls kissing the surface of the water.."

This wild panic was an attempt to get plates to the U.S. before the McKinley Tariff became operational on 1st July. Even in late June, some were rushed by rail to Liverpool to catch fast American steamers. Week after week, the port was *"fuller of ships than ever it has been before"*, and this was a vindication of

The dockside sheds piled high with boxed tinplate.

Pic: Swansea Maritime and Industrial Museum

Pic: Swansea Museum

The crowded Prince of Wales Dock, looking west.

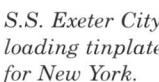

S.S. Exeter City loading tinplate for New York.

Pic: Swansea Museum

The eastward extension of the Prince of Wales Dock under construction

Complete, and ready to let the water in.

The opening, 11th March, 1898.

the farsightedness of the Harbour Trust from the time the Prince of Wales Dock was begun in 1879 — Swansea had become the tinplate port of Britain. Regularly, *"the largest steamer yet to enter the port"* passed through the lock — in July, 1890 it was the "British Queen", capacity 6,500 tons. At the town end of the dock, the Midland Railway coal wharf was taken over for tinplate. Plates were packed in boxes made from birch, elm and other hardwoods and in June, 1891, W.H. Stone was leased 800 square yards of land on the shore side of the South Dock to build a new saw mill in a bid to meet the demand. The Trust's tinplate department was run by Mr. Thurgood until May, 1891, when he seems to have started his own firm, based in Exchange

Buildings — his replacement was H.D. Randall. A new office was built for them, beside the dock, in April. New storage buildings had to be provided very hurriedly on the seaward side of the Prince of Wales, near the galvanised sheds built in the eighties. They were complete by the end of February, 1891:

> *"...a wooden structure, roofed with felt...30,000 square feet...providing storage room for 100,000 boxes of tinplates...increased storage room at the East Dock by 50%...erected in 4 weeks, Peter Holloway contractor...80-100 men involved..."*

It is important to remember people in the midst of events. Mr. Holloway died in March, 1892. Another man who worked in these tinplate sheds for some years died in May, 1899. Edwin Jones, born in North Wales, was brought up in the U.S.. A bookbinder by trade, he sang for 10 years in the chorus at Covent Garden. When he first came to Swansea he became the agent for Howe's sewing machines, from an office on the corner of Waterloo Street and Oxford Street. He sang in the choir of St. David's Roman Catholic church, and in locally produced light operas, where songs were specially written to suit his *"fine bass voice"*. He died at the Salisbury Club in Wind Street, of which he was a life member.

After the boom...

In fact, the immediate disaster that some feared was postponed. The duty on unfinished "blackplate" was still low, and exports to America were substantial until this loophole was closed in 1894. However, the fever of '91 had repercussions. Tom Phillips ("Twm Phil", a leading tinplate union official and one of the defeated candidates in 1893), speaking as late as 1896, reckoned:

> *"American markets are stocked today with tens of thousands of boxes of tinplates exported in 1891...which were absolutely useless...the masters had ruined the trade by turning out plates of inferior quality and rushing them into the market...they swept the warehouses of all the wastes they could find, in order to satisfy their own greed..."*

An ordinary tinman put it like this:

> *"Our manufacturers...sent all kinds of old stock...120,000 boxes were fit for nothing but to cast into the sea...making small fortunes in the course of six months...twelve hundred pounds a week...(and we)...worked like niggers through the heat and dust of summer with...the usual rate of wages..."*

Unbiassed observers tended to agree. Also, in the frenzy of 1890-1, the masters borrowed to put in more mills, and the heavy interest payments made their costs much higher. In August, 1891:

> *"...considerable orders are reported but the prices offered are so low that makers...will not touch them..."*

Tinplate owners had always reacted to trade fluctuations by laying off workers — smaller works like those at Cwmbwrla, Birchgrove or Penclawdd were specially subject to sudden expansions followed by instant closures. Birchgrove was one that closed for good, with an on site sale of all the plant and

T.R.W. Mason.

Pic: Swansea Reference Library

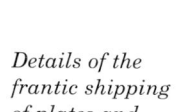

Details of the frantic shipping of plates and portraits of some leading shipping agents.

Messrs. M. JONES and BRO., Swansea.
Messrs. Mark Whitwill, Son, and Judge, London & Swansea, The "Great Western Steamship" Line.

1891.	Vessels' Names.	Reg. Tonnage	No. of Boxes Tinplates Shipped.	Net Weight.	Ports of Discharge.	Loaded at Prince of Wales Dock, Swansea, by
January	State of Alabama	1511	26489	1536	New York	
February	St. Oswald	1781	30278	1889	,,	
Do	Inflexible	1489	36314	2094	,,	W. B. Westlake, Mount-st., Swansea, Stevedore and Contractor to the Swansea Harbour Trust.
Do	Bengore Head	1619	48613	2685	,,	
April	Lord Lansdowne	1815	48791	3028	,,	
May	Lord Londonderry	1565	56870	3340	,,	
Do	Marston Moor	1566	34399	2027	,,	
June	Connemara	2166	54656	3553	,,	

Messrs. T. R. W. MASON and Co., Swansea,
Messrs. Anderson, Anderson, and Co.'s Line, London.

1891.	Vessels' Names.	Reg. Tonnage	No. of Boxes Tinplates Shipped.	Net Weight.	Ports of Discharge.	Loaded at Prince of Wales Dock, Swansea, by
January	Enskar	1995	7801	417	Philadelphia	
February	Bidar	1891	49016	2618	,,	
Do	Ed King	1418	14764	1042	New Orleans	
Do	Fonar	1975	28787	1710	Philadelphia	
Do	Kingdom	1413	18963	1175	New Orleans	W. B. Westlake, Mount-st., Swansea, Stevedore and Contractor to the Swansea Harbour Trust.
March	City of Lincoln	2103	11846	825	,,	
Do	Holkar	2140	34664	2315	Philadelphia	
Do	Federation	1578	8177	579	New Orleans	
Do	Enskar	1995	38266	2412	Philadelphia	
April	Fonar	1975	55503	3514	,,	
May	Holkar	2140	50943	3058	,,	
Do	Red Sea	2112	36191	2230	New Orleans	
Do	Enskar	1995	44124	2492	Philadelphia	

Messrs. WILLIAMS, TORREY, and FEILD, London & Swansea,
The "Atlantic Transport" Line.

1891.	Vessels' Names.	Reg. Tonnage	No. of Boxes Tinplates Shipped.	Net Weight.	Ports of Discharge.	Loaded at Prince of Wales Dock, Swansea, by
January	Mississippi	2388	31098	1946	Philadelphia and Baltimore	
Do	Montana	1804	33521	2127	,,	
Do	Missouri	1858	25816	1566	,,	
Do	Minnesota	2079	9400	701	,,	
Do	Maine	1690	29742	1877	,,	
Do	British Crown	2065	22620	1294	,,	
February	Memphis	2051	50126	2932	,,	
Do	Michigan	2383	30240	1928	,,	
Do	Lord Lansdowne	1816	38471	2413	,,	
Do	China	1410	26250	1473	,,	
March	Montana	1804	29655	1957	,,	
Do	Missouri	1858	27309	1946	,,	W. B. Westlake, Mount-st., Swansea, Stevedore and Contractor to the Swansea Harbour Trust.
Do	Minnesota	2079	33362	2037	,,	
Do	Lord O'Neil	1816	45600	2836	,,	
April	Maine	1690	48710	2977	,,	
Do	Maryland	1650	23985	1476	,,	
Do	Michigan	2383	31340	2026	,,	
Do	Mississippi	2388	49717	3016	,,	
Do	Missouri	1858	23104	1554	,,	
Do	Montana	1804	44474	2596	,,	
May	British Crown	2065	31129	2066	,,	
Do	Minnesota	2079	26929	1697	,,	
Do	China	1410	42525	2406	,,	
Do	Memphis	2035	61339	3732	,,	
June	Maryland	1650	34867	2116	,,	
Do	Michigan	2383	—	—	,,	
Do 13th	Mississippi	2388	—	—	,,	

Messrs. BURGESS and Co., Swansea.
Messrs. Charles. Hill and Sons, Bristol, The "City" Line.

1891.	Vessels' Names.	Reg. Tonnage	No. of Boxes Tinplates Shipped.	Net Weight.	Ports of Discharge.	Loaded at Prince of Wales Dock, Swansea, by
January	Wells City	1136	16735	979	New York	
Do	Jersey City	1261	17657	1039	,,	
Do	Mineola	1581	19871	1125	,,	
Do	Port Stanley (ship)	2186	6299	384	San Francisco	
Do	Llandaff City	1258	18886	1045	New York	
February	Exeter City	1434	19266	1047	,,	
Do	Brooklyn City	1122	12250	737	,,	
Do	Well City	1136	15885	909	,,	
March	Jersey City	1261	21951	1243	,,	W. B. Westlake, Mount-st., Swansea Stevedore and Contractor to the Swansea Harbour Trust.
Do	Mineola	1581	24182	1472	,,	
April	Exeter City	1434	24776	1536	,,	
Do	Brooklyn City	1122	16928	1159	,,	
Do	Wells City	1136	18410	1182	,,	
Do	Llandaff City	1258	22472	1354	,,	
May	Mineola	1581	26907	1649	,,	
Do	Jersey City	1261	26098	1535	,,	
Do	Llandaff City	1258	25660	1508	,,	
June	Exeter City	1434	24952	1559	,,	
Do	Brooklyn City	1122	19577	1246	,,	
Do	Wells City	1136			,,	

Pic: Swansea Reference Library

Pic: Swansea Museum

J.H.Burgess.

George Shaddick (of Burgesses).

Boxed plates in number one tinplate shed by the Prince of Wales Dock.

Pic: Swansea Reference Library

Pic: Swansea Reference Library

machinery in November 1899 — there were buyers from as far off as Manchester and Wigan, though local dealers C.E. & H.M. Peel took a lot. (They had a yard and offices alongside Quay Parade, adjoining Forester's Iron Yard — the premises ran right up to the bridge over the lock between the North Dock and Weavers Basin). As early as April, 1891, the masters had decided to close all plants for 28 days from July 1st, and by October all William Williams's men were idle. One answer was to look for other markets. There was still Germany —

"They sent Tinplates and Backplates into Germany, and they got them back in the form of toys..."

S.S."*Glaucus*" loading tinplate.

lead-painted ships, trains and soldiers, some of them clockwork. Plates were shipped direct to San Francisco for the Californian canning industry. Packing Indian tea in tin boxes was considered. There was hope of a market in Natal and Cape Colony, for roofing and for canning South African fruit. China was thought to have huge trading potential; the first direct shipment was 1,300 tons in the "Chin Wo" in June 1897. By 1902, Shanghai was taking 271,832 tons. At this time, oil was shipped from oil wells to refineries in tinplate drums — as early as 1887, 5,124 tons of plates went to the Russian oilfield at Batoum on the Black Sea. A danger on this front was the appearance of S.S. "Caucase" in the Prince of Wales dock in January, 1891 —

"a steamer of somewhat unusual construction, being built with tanks for bringing oil from Batoum..."

This early tanker was loaded with tinplate for its return voyage! John Jones Jenkins, Chairman of the Harbour Trust, wrote to "The Times" like a latter day King Canute, to protest against permission given

"to carry petroleum in bulk through the Suez Canal in tank steamers...the petroleum trade is now and has been since the discovery of the valuable petroleum wells at Batoum, conducted safely in tin cans...easily distributed to the consumers at the receiving stations...nearly all the tinplates used for this purpose are made in this neighbourhood..."

He did not prevail! By 1897, the Globe Dry Dock, which lay beside the South Dock lock, was specialising in *"oil ships"*, having repaired the largest tanker then afloat — that year their engineers and boilermakers demanded double time for the filthy work on these vessels!

The empty site of the Cwmfelin Works today, looking from Cwm Road towards Manselton.

One Swansea newspaper suggested the *"princely Manufacturer"* would be hit quite as hard as the *"artisan"*. It was quite obviously not true. Some men crossed the Atlantic. William John was an Upper Forest man who emigrated to work in Anderson City, but died within a year — William Williams's sons visited his grave when they went to meet the Welsh tinplaters of Indiana in 1898. As early as 1893 *"ten of the best tinplaters in Morriston"* were seen off by 200 friends from Victoria Station, en route for Liverpool and the

States. Some moved to other industries. Richard Grove of Penfilia, a furnaceman at Cwmfelin, moved to the Swansea Smelting Company's zinc works in Llansamlet, and died there in 1897, perhaps from blood poisoning. In November, 1896, the whole Cwmfelin plant had been closed for eight months — in many of the households of Cwmbwrla it was said *"voices cry for bread"*. Local ministers went from family to family and found, for example:

> *"Case No.3 Nine in family; all children are small, and the father has not been able to obtain more than a fortnight's work these last seven months...*

> *Case No.7 Seven in family; most of the furniture has been sold to buy food and pay the rent...*

> *Case No.9 Eleven in family and the children are small, the father is laid up with severe illness...lack of proper nourishment...*

> *...an affectionate mother has gone into service in order to earn something for...her family. Her husband, since the stoppage, a meal has cost him many a walk, and many a walk in search of work has been in vain..."*

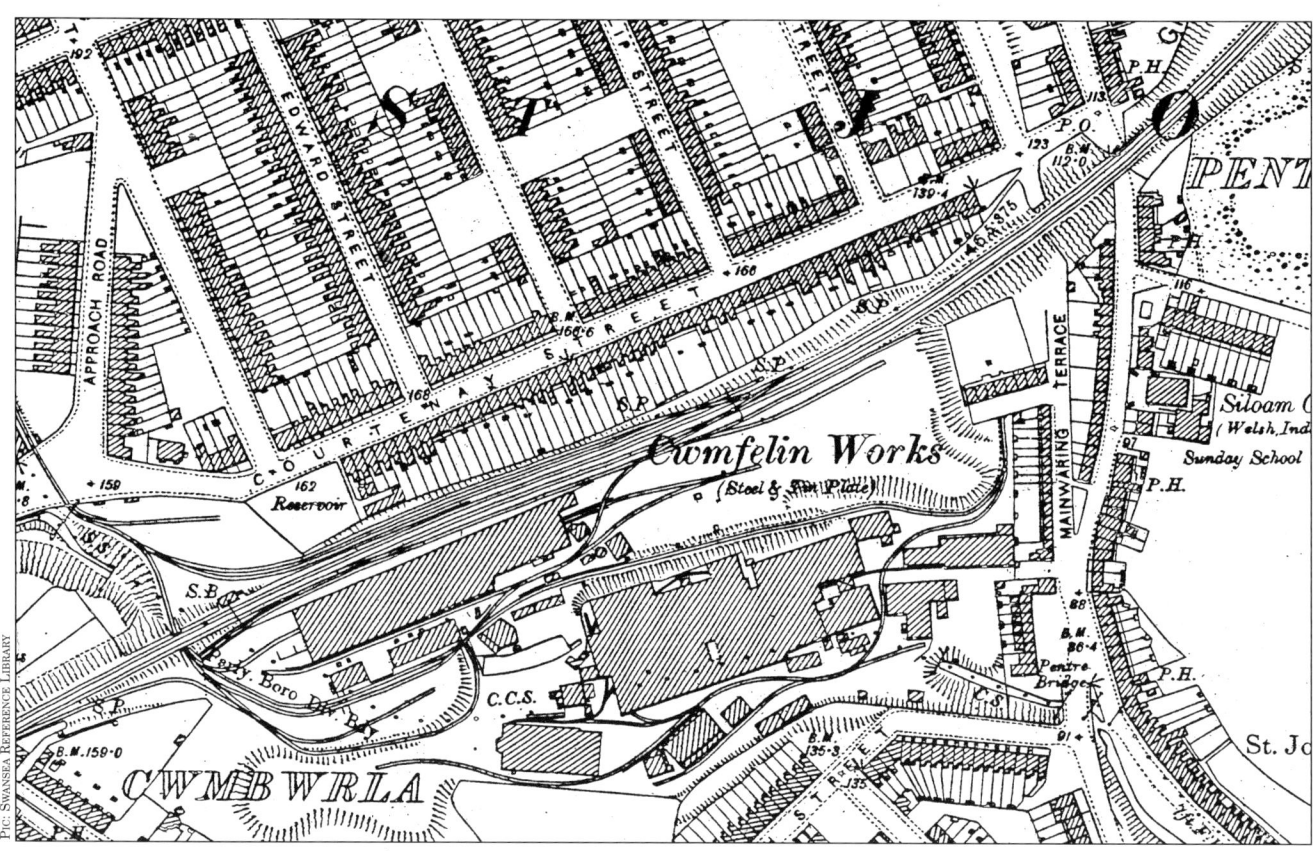

Cwmfelin Tinplate Works in the 1890s, hemmed in by the houses of Cwmbwrla, Manselton, Pentre Estyll and Greenhill.

In Morriston, Rev. Emlyn Jones had not seen such hardship in 28 years —

> *"There was a family of 12, the youngest 5 weeks old, and to stave off the pangs of hunger, one of the children, aged 3, was found eating orange peel picked off the street..."*

Hardship, they said, was lessened a little by employers sharing out available work, by shopkeepers putting food on the slate and landlords waiving rents. Sir John Talbot Dillwyn Llewelyn of Penllergaer *"out of sympathy with the great suffering and distress in the neighbourhood"* gave cash to enable steel-making at Cwmfelin to restart in the December. Otherwise a little money came from the Central Relief Fund (organised by the mayor, Frederick Bradford, in 1896), and from local collections with weekly contributions by those in work (Landore Steel works, £1/6/6), by congregations (Zoar chapel, £1/4/8), by the rich (William Williams, 5 guineas) and others (Mr. Yeandle, 1 sack of baking flour, John Guppy & Son, 1

guinea — Mr. Guppy was, among other things, a butter merchant living in Ivey Place, opposite the station.)

The basis of wage payments for the tinmen was "the List of 1874", a code of general rates fixed following a strike in that year. As time went by, particularly after McKinley, employers disregarded this agreement; at the Morriston, Midland and Beaufort works in 1896 for example, the men were asked to take a 15% reduction. This sort of practice led to a strike for "the List" which lasted through November. There was some bitterness reflected in the union paper "Industrial World":

"...the telephone has been largely in use this week by Makers...to call into account backsliders in the league of oppression...

When workmen are out of work, penniless, comfortless, standing near a crossroad or some other place, and see So-and-So dash by in their carriages, brightly bournished, and with high stepping horses...

Ministers of the Gospel express their indignation against the attractions of the football field and of the theatre, the public bar and the room of amusement... But...why not raise their voice against the starvation policy adopted by the Masters?..when will such men realise that it is their duty to preach the truth as it is in Christ, and not construe it to meet the views of certain Capitalists that may be in their midst?

In our towns there are noble buildings erected where thousands meet to worship the lowly Jesus. However there is evidence the pulpit is gradually losing its hold upon the masses."

The editor of this paper, John Hopkin John, had started as a copper worker at Morfa, at the age of 13, and in 1877 became a tinman at Forest. He had played a leading role in unionism in local tin works, and so there was now a journal which expressed the views of the men. Straightforward class hatred was limited by men of moderation on both sides, but younger masters like W.H. Edwards, who was mayor in 1895, had perhaps grown away from their roots in the local community. He ran the Dyffryn, which had eight mills over a 10 acre site, and employed about 400 men and women. In December, he told a deputation that he would close for up to 6 months, would employ whoever he liked, and workmen would just have to suffer. The newspaper commented:

W.H.Edwards. He died in 1919, aged 59. In his later days he lived at Hendrefoilan House.

"The great object of the capitalist is to make money. What cares he if, in the making of it the men he employs breathe an unhealthy atmosphere, over strain their bodies, and that at an early age the toiler is carried to his grave, and that a wife and family is left to mourn his loss? What cares he? All he troubles about is to get another fool to abuse his body in the same way, so that he may still make money."

Edwards was accused of using *"the starvation weapon relentlessly"* until his father, Daniel, emerged from retirement to push him (it seems) into compromise. At Cwmfelin in April, Edward Rice Daniel persuaded the men to take a cut of 15% to keep production going, but two weeks later his son Llewelyn pressed them for 22% and Cwmfelin closed. Again the younger man had less fellow feeling. By the new year, the "List of '74" had been accepted across the industry.

John Hopkin John.

From the seventies to the nineties, tinplate union meetings were held at the Oddfellows Hall at the "Bird in Hand", 217, High Street, just below the station. Such pub meetings were criticised by temperance members:

> *"The Tinplate Millman...in mid winter..is bathed in perspiration; his lot in this broiling weather is truly pitiable...*
>
> [There is a] *general impression that the Millman is fond of his pint....the old boys were never so happy as when dividing a 'fetching' or meeting together at their favourite public to — 'yfed ato' — drink the health of a fellow workman..*
>
> *A custom long practised by members of Friendly Societies was to pay for the use of a room to hold meetings by paying for so much drink..."*

An immense jug of beer might be placed on the central table, and if some were absent, others would get drunk,... using up the *"Club Beer"*.

Tinplate Workers

The main owners were prominent men — we meet them as mayors, and leaders in church and chapel. The lesser partners and managers are more shadowy figures. David Owen is one. Up to 1892 he ran the Midland Works at Tyrcanol, Morriston, in partnership with David Mansel Glasbrook. David Jones is another, manager of the Swansea Tinplate Works at Cwmdu, he died in 1890, and was buried at Oystermouth cemetery. John Williams is more shadowy still. Thirty one in 1891 he lived at 3, Henrietta Street — a Landore man, he is just described as "Manager of tinplate works". So is Arthur Wolfe of 14 Somerset Place, son of the priest who ran St. Nicholas's seaman's chapel in Gloucester Place.

The men are even less discoverable. We can find their names. The newspapers tell us about them when they were injured or killed, and then not always by name —

> *"Whilst a workman at the Cwmfelin Tinplate Works was engaged in the annealing house...a large pile of plates, weighing about half a ton, fell on him. Death was instantaneous..."* (7th October, 1898)

A trawl of Llansamlet, Cwmbwrla or most certainly Morriston at the time of the 1891 census would produce streets full of tinplate men. Oddly, though, even the town centre had its share. Perhaps, with the frantic boom in full cry, housing nearer the works was at a premium.

Evan Long tinman of 16 Gam Street
Thomas G. Sherlock boarding at 16 Wind Street, born at Ascot, foreman of shipment of tinplates.
James Beynon, born in the U.S., at 67, High Street, porter in tinworks
Thomas John Coutts, 15 years old, tinplate worker, at 4 Wassail Street
William Phillips, 49, tinplate sampler, born Gloucester, at 28 Rutland Street
Thomas Thursfield (from Salford) and Benjamin Hancher (Wolverhampton) tinplateworkers, both lodging at 3 St.Mary Street.
At 19 St.Mary Street: William Williams and David Joseph, Morriston tinworkers, Thomas Davies rollerman, William Jones doubler and four other lodgers.
Richard Oxenham from Tunbridge, harbour clerk, tinplates, at 50 Garden Street.
Fred Crabbe tinman at 17 Oxford Street
Charles Moggridge, 16, tinplateworker at 2 Ferryside
John Kent, apprentice tinman (14 years old) at 11 Wellington Street
Lewis Evans, clerk in tinworks at 6 Glamorgan Street
Alfred Ridd, chargeman tin, at 24 Bond Street...and many more.

By the way...
"The Swansea Gazette & Shipping Register"

PIC: SWANSEA MUSEUM

Robert Capper.

A great deal of the information about the tinplate boom is from "The Swansea Gazette & Swansea Shipping Register". It was founded in 1877 at the suggestion of Robert Capper, then the superintendent of the docks. The senior partner was J.C. Manning, but from 1883 it was run solely by William Morris Vaughan, who had been only 23 when it started. Vaughan was a nephew of William Morris ("Gwilym Tawe"), who for years carried on a printing concern at the Old Stamp Office — Howell Watkins, Mayor of Swansea in 1896-7, was apprenticed there. By the nineties, the paper came out on Wednesdays, at a penny an issue, or 6/6 quarterly.

He ran it from offices at 47/8 Wind street, not far from the New Theatre, — there were very regular reviews of the plays there! But most space went to a full list of vessels in all three docks and in the river, arrivals and departures, and messages from Swansea ships all over the world. There are accounts of sinkings, sales of ships and maritime legal cases. Updates on the docks from John Dixon and later William Law are regularly included. Meetings of the Harbour Trust and Chamber of Commerce are always well covered. Like most editors of the time, he was driven to include quite a lot of "infill" — "bits from books", extracts from the "Western Mail" and London papers, recipes, amusing stories, and large adverts for his own services! For, like several Swansea papers, he used his presses to run a general printing firm — order books, billheads, programmes (for balls, concerts, athletics meetings), annual reports and balance sheets. Also, from 1888, he published a Yearbook and Tidetable — there is a great deal in these on the early use of telephones in Swansea, clearly an interest of his.

In 1897 it seems that his premises were demolished as part of the clearance made for the new Metropole Hotel. He moved around the corner into Salubrious Place, where he opened on 5th January, 1898. He died at his home, 12, Page Street on 8th November, 1900, aged 46. On August 25th, 1903, W.J. Rees auctioned 1-7 Salubrious Place, including Vaughan's Printing Works, with its machine room, engine room and stores at street level, and a *"light and lofty compositor's room and office"* upstairs.

A SWANSEA SHIPPING CASE.

At the Glamorganshire Summer Assizes held at the Guildhall, Swansea, before Mr. Justice Lawrence, Frank Chapman claimed damages from Messrs. Jones Bros., of Swansea, for personal injuries caused through negligence. Defendants are the brokers for a line of steamers trading between Swansea and Glasgow, and when some sacks of sawdust were being discharged the donkeyman was alleged to have suddenly started the engine, the sacks were lifted, and the defendant fell into the hold and sustained serious injuries, dislocating both his wrists. The defence was that the stage was not too narrow, and that the accident would not have happened if the donkeyman had not wound up the sling. It was subsequently stated that the engineman was in the same employ as the plaintiff, but not in authority, so the doctrine of common employment applied. Judgment was given for the defendants, but they did not ask for costs.

Swansea Harbour.
Shipping Intelligence.
NORTH DOCK.

Annie 75, Crosby, Wexford
Alletha 191, Wilce, Falmouth
Ariel 79, Jones, Chester
Adria s 521, Wilmot, Bordeaux
Alf 300, Svensen, Antwerp
Antares, 137, Guillo, Tremblade
Ada 73, Withers, Bridgwater
Buron 267, Bounvery, Bordeaux
Bess Mitchell 98, Davies, Dublin
Blue Grit 62, Stafford, Arklow
Caroline 80, Edmunds, Runcorn
Convivial 93, Lewis, Shoreham
Cambria 39, Chichester, Barnstaple
Creek Fisher 118, Forshau, Limerick
Copious 58, Poole, Bridgwater
Commerce 55, Lee, Bridgwater
Charles 56, Price, Gloster
Doris 79, Bennett, Bristol
Ellen Catherine 118, Phillips, Limerick
Emily Burnyeat 93, Gregory, Hayle
Forth s 312, Anderson, Escombrera via London
Henry s 652, Grinton, Messida
Hinda 442, Jones, Port Nolloth
Hilda 65, Thomas, Chester
Helen 68, McCarthy, Queensferry
Inverleith s 743, Grey, Glasgow
Jules Courdert s 931, Courllandear, Liverpool
Julie 38, Lobb, Gloster
Lydia 30, Braughton, Arcklow
Lizzie R. Wilce 155, Peters, Plymouth
Lady Chandos 79, Crocker, London
Lionel s 681, McNulty, Cork
Mary Peers 132, Garrett, Chester
Pan s 675, Schenly, Dunkerque
Pleiades 86, Hay, Gloster
Rebecca Mary 79, Hughes, Carnarvon
Sarah Ann 74, Walters, Brussel
Speedwell 60, Guy, Bridgwater
Telegraph 40, Pitaway, Watchet
Tyne s 421 Bewen, Trouville
Trio 72, Bruford, New Ross
Viola 121, Bennet, Chester

ARRIVED

June 16. p.m
Kate 25, Taylor, Newport (Pem)
Pluvier 134, Annis, L'Orient
Jane Gwynne 79, Robinson, Clare Castle

June 17, a.m
Morfa s 237, Mitchell, Belfast

SAILED

June 10, a.m
Abraham Sutton s 174, Taggart, Newry
Hereford 46, Phillips, Bridgwater
Vanguard s 322, Pike, St Johns, N.F

PIC: SWANSEA REFERENCE LIBRARY

The "Gazette" painted a detailed picture of the thriving port.

Published Officially.   Established 1877

THE
Swansea Gazette
and Daily Shipping Register.

Containing a List of all Vessels in Port, Where Stationed, Registered Tonnage, Where From, Together with all Sailings up to the hour of Publication.

"Swansea, you may depend upon it, is destined to become the Ocean Port of England."—Sir H. Hussey Vivian, Bart., M.P.

| 4117 REGISTERED FOR TRANSMISSION ABROAD | WEDNESDAY, JULY 22, 1891 | PRICE—ONE PENNY DAILY Or 6s 6d, per Quarter |

PIC. SWANSEA REFERENCE LIBRARY

William Thomas of Lan

One man hit by the tinplate crisis was William Thomas of Lan. In 1890 he was already 74, and his great days were done. Over 20 years as a councillor he had fought with tenacity, fire and passion for "open spaces", as housing spilled out from the town's riverside core. Llewelyn's Park, Brynmill, Cwmdonkin, Victoria Park and others were his legacy. He was strongly aware of

> "...the dull monotony of the lives of the poor people...particularly the women and children...in the sombre surroundings of Greenhill, Hafod or the Strand..."

He wanted " People's Parks" rather than *"a place where people could play croquet, cricket, or games of that sort..."* He had the drive and self-confidence to push his vision forward in the face of vested interests and unimaginative money-savers — *"such a question should not be one of money..."* And he succeeded. Victoria Park, for example, was created out of *"a waste of sandheaps"*, a street layout for which had already been devised. Who, asked Mayor Howell Watkins in 1897, would suggest building on that ground now?

William Thomas as mayor in 1878 — a hint of Henry VIII!

Still in the nineties he was bursting with schemes for parks on Townhill and at Morriston, and for converting the whole area between the Singleton Estate and Blackpill ("Gipsy Common") into public playingfields. His aim was to continue *"as long as I have breath"*, but after a two year absence caused by ill-health and lack of funds, he retired from the council in November 1894. Not that he had felt at home there since 1890, when the guildhall started to administer a much larger area, including most of Morriston, and council meetings were of *"forty nine wise men instead of twenty four"*. With a wider franchise, councillors like George Nancarrow, manager of the Morfa Copper Works, and William Thomas were seen by some as rich folk elected to "represent" working men. Councillor John Hopkin John, the newspaper editor, was a real pioneer, being elected in 1890 as a Liberal-Labour candidate in Morriston. (David Jones, Labour, won in the Victoria ward the same year.) He believed council meetings should be held at 6.30 p.m. not 11.30 a.m., so that the working class could "represent" itself. There had always been lively debates, but the club atmosphere and leisurely practices of the council chamber were now undermined by less courteous language and less respect for convention. Some of those responsible cared deeply

PIC: WEST GLAMORGAN ARCHIVES

Brynmill Park, model boats on the lake, the school in the background, about 1905.

PIC: WEST GLAMORGAN ARCHIVES

Cwmdonkin Park in the snow, about 1905.

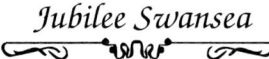
about people and issues, though, as ever, some were there to make a name. At meetings in 1892, Walter Monger called senior members *"worthless and inactive"* and referred to two who

> *"pretended to feel very much for the poor, but it was all assumed, and better actors he did not think could be found around the table.."*

William Thomas saw no need to take sides. He thought of himself as open-minded and practical. In 1891, he gave a wholehearted welcome to William Usher's radical plans for the council to build houses to replace the town slums. In June that year he took part in a meeting at Hermon chapel which protested over the appalling roads, lighting and drainage at Plasmarl and on Graig Trewyddfa above. He blamed local landlords *"with the honourable exception of Hussey Vivian"*. (That same year, Charles Mannesman, one of the German brothers who owned the nearby tubeworks, was asked to give his impression of the town — he was very critical, and thought Landore *"beyond description"*.) In his speech at the opening of an Anglican mission church in Plasmarl William Thomas said:

> *"He did not trouble himself about creeds and orthodoxy…and had always tried to encourage every good object. Nothing was more important than that people should honour God…and in that connection they owed much to the Nonconformists.."*

He criticised older councillors as *"worse bores than the young bloods"*. After one meeting in March, 1891 (4 hours, 172 speeches) he lamented,

> *"the flow of talk went on as usual in one weak, washy, everlasting flood…not the veriest old village gossip could exceed the gentlemen in garrulity."*

The new men he wrote off as just "economists"(money savers) and grumbled quite openly at being given a place on only four committees, when others were *"packed with men who knew nothing about the work."* There were hardly any party labels and political positions could get very muddled. Consider that Walter Monger mentioned above. Like his father and grandfather, he lived rent-free in a house in the Hafod, where a street was named after the family. He was an Anglican who wanted to dis-establish the church. On Sunday closing, he thought rich men's clubs should be shut, just like public houses. In 1892 he attacked Hussey Vivian for not allowing his tenants to take out a mortgage with a building society without paying a guinea to the estate (on threat of eviction), and he stood for Parliament against him. When criticised for turning against his patron and former mentor, he replied that he was a Liberal Unionist who refused to agree with Gladstone (and Vivian) over Home Rule!

Thomas of Lan was harder than most to pigeon-hole. His social idealism was strong. When first elected to the School Board in 1870

> *"he believed one of the chief duties of the Board would be to sweep children who never went to school at all…from no sins of their own…Street Arabs, gutter children, waifs of society…into school"*

However, he had a great respect for the Vivians, and especially for John Talbot Dillwyn Llewelyn, a very considerable landowner, whose father, John Dillwyn Llewelyn, the pioneer photographer, gave the land for Llewelyn's Park on Trewyddfa. Then, as later, it was country pursuits that formed the bond between William Thomas and the squires of Penllergaer. Through these, he tended to be thought of as conservative. A suggestion that he be knighted in 1886 came from C.H. Glascodine than whom no councillor was further to the right! When William was suggested as a prospective Tory M.P. in the eighties, he preferred to support J.T.D., who was in fact elected in 1895.

Cwmgelly Cemetery

The municipal cemetery at Danygraig had opened in 1858, though only after a long quarrel with the bishop of St. David's. Until 1891, northern Swansea used Llangyfelach churchyard for burials, but then it was closed. One ratepayer suggested this would halve the trade of the village's three pubs, describing

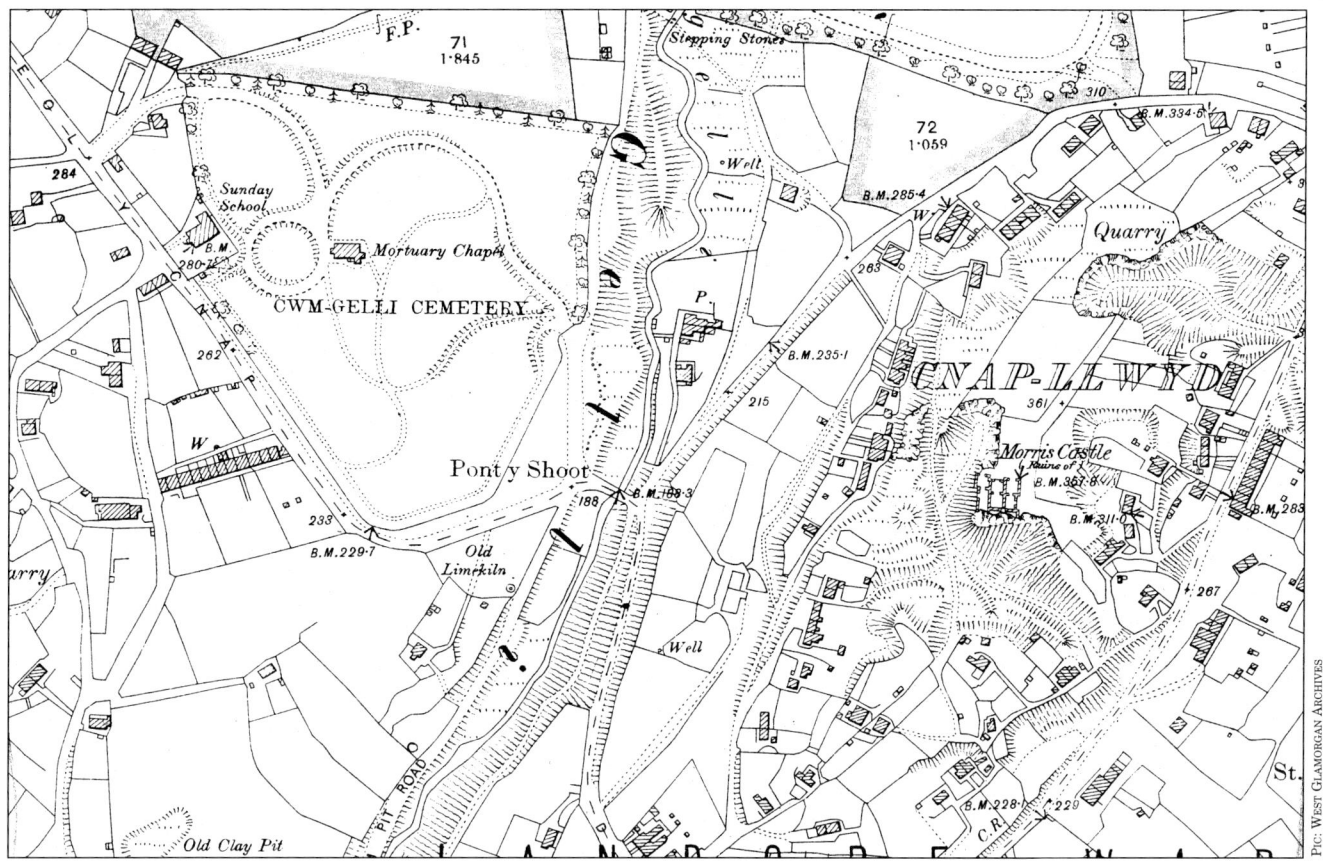

The walled cemetery a hundred years ago - for the Gelli valley and "Cnap-Llwyd" beyond, see the photograph overleaf.

how *"after large funerals, the village was a scene of drunkenness and riot"*. In January, 1892, the council proposed building a new cemetery at Cwmgelly, but the Home Office refused a £4,950 grant unless part of it was consecrated for Anglican use. This would give the vicar rights there, including the ability to charge fees. Nonconformist councillors were furious. Alderman Richard Martin told of an old collector of customs charged £5 for the right to put a stone over his sister's grave. Alderman Chapman, the High Street photographer, protested that he had had to pay more to the vicar for the right to put a headstone over his mother than for the rest of the funeral expenses put together. The affair dragged on and William Thomas described it as:

> *"..sentimental rubbish...people are made to trudge in all weathers to the Cemetery at St. Thomas because of the nonsense of a few councillors..."*

For once this was unfair. Eventually the council applied for the grant in its role as a Sanitary Authority, a trick devised by Morgan Tutton, one of the more talkative members. Cwmgelly opened in September, 1895.

Cwmgelly Cemetery today, still trim. Go there and admire the curving stonework of the outer wall.

Pic: Swansea Museum

Pic: Swansea Museum

Pic: Swansea Museum

Pic: Swansea Museum

Pic: Swansea Museum

The Squire of Lan

High on Trewyddfa, above Cwmgelly, was the fine house of Lan where William Thomas lived. With servants and a carriage his life had a certain style. He looked the squire, and loved to shoot and fish on his 122 acre estate at "Cwmwysk" near Defynnog until 1901. He had once been shy in company, telling tales of an early engagement where he had avoided speaking by hiding under a table before slipping off back to Lan. In later life, he always seemed *"bright, cheery and optimistic"*, and had come to love the limelight. His style of oratory was entertaining, bluff and no-nonsense with an ability to startle and amuse. When William, son of Sir J.T.D. Llewelyn, came of age in February, 1890, Thomas of Lan was invited to make the main speech — and stood on a chair at Penllergaer to do it! In November, the Harbour Trustees were entertained on the Beaver line steamer "Lake Ontario" in the Prince of Wales Dock. After sherry and bitters and a sumptuous luncheon, he rose to speak — quite at the wrong time! — was typically rumbustuous and was greeted with laughter and applause. His comment on the Mckinley Tariff, then drawing uncomfortably near, was

"he hoped Captain Campbell would drive his ship right through it."

Last Days

In fact, the tariff sank William. Twenty years before he had been able to distribute 11,833 buns and 2,951 new pennies to children. By 1894 he was privately searching for *"ways and means to sustain myself with some degree of ease of comfort"*. His problems were due to *"the cloud hanging over my affairs at Landore."* He had been a director of the Landore Tinplate Works since it was formed in 1851. He had also had a share in the Millbrook Engineering Works next door, which produced machinery, particularly, of course, for the tin works. At one time the Landore Works was probably the largest in the world, employing 1,000.

PIC: SWANSEA MARITIME AND INDUSTRIAL MUSEUM

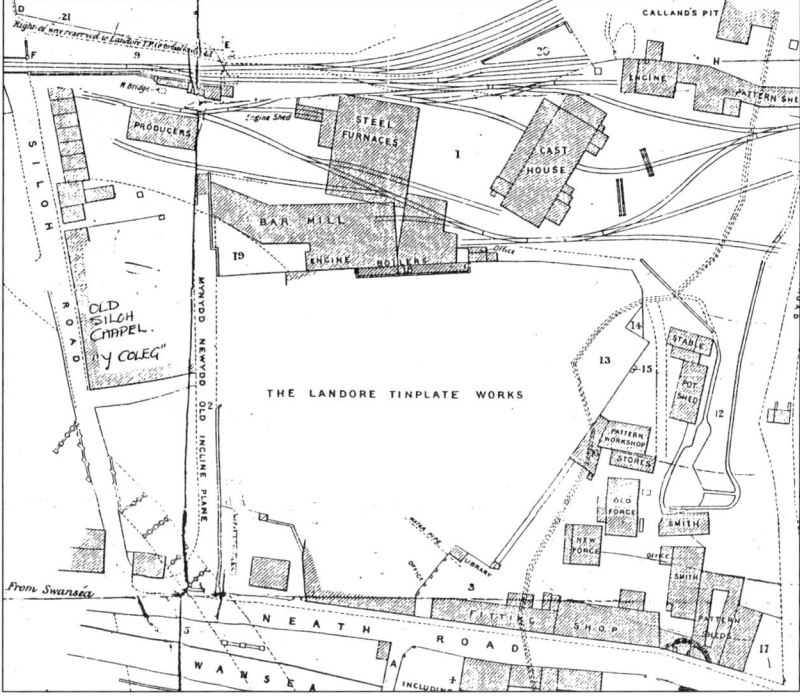

MAP: SWANSEA MUSEUM

PIC: SWANSEA MARITIME AND INDUSTRIAL MUSEUM

PIC: SWANSEA MARITIME AND INDUSTRIAL MUSEUM

Top: The valley of Cwmgelly, with the cemetery to the left, the Millbrook and Landore Works to the right. Morris Castle is on the summit of Trewyddfa. 1880s?

Middle left: The shaded buildings are the Millbrook Works.

Middle right & bottom left: Machinery produced at Millbrook.

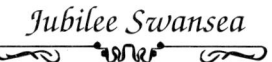

By 1888 it was down to 700, and by 1893 450. Final closure came in 1901, it was in ruins by 1903 and demolished in February, 1906. His partners in the firm were —

John Powell, (probably from Waunarlwydd), Richard Hughes of Rock House, Morriston, a councillor and leading member of Tabernacle, who died in 1903, aged 86 and George Lockwood Morris, who lived at Machen Lodge, Sketty — he was only 32 in 1891. It was Morris who promised to help over money as far as possible, but eventually lack of cash seems to have forced William out of Lan, and he moved to 7, Finsbury Terrace. This is the long hill which takes you from St. Helens Cricket Ground to Uplands. At least, it was said, he was not far there from *"the joyful shouts of children"* in his own Victoria Park.

By the way — Thomases and Morrises

For about 100 years from the 1720s three generations of the Morris family were at the centre of the coal and copper industries in the area. In the 1790s, Sir John Morris founded Morriston. He was also a pioneer of agricultural improvements on his Clase estate. William Thomas's grandfather, who died in 1817, aged 84, worked at Clase farm

"for nearly fifty years....and had the management of very extensive agricultural improvements"...

Of William's father, who died in 1837, the second Sir John wrote, *"we were bred up together from childhood.."* William was the third of his family to act as agent to the Morrises. Another link was through the works at Landore. The Millbrook developed out of the Nantrhydyvilias Air Furnace Foundry which opened in about 1804, owned by the Bevans, another family to work with and for the Morrises. The swingbridge which carried the main road across the Tawe from 1851 to December 1897 was a Millbrook product. By the nineties the Millbrook was supplying tinplate works with its own patent pickling and tinning machines and mill engines, producing agricultural machinery, and exporting. George Lockwood Morris of Landore was the son of George Byng Morris, who died at Danygraig, Bridgend on 2nd December, 1899, aged 83. He was the second son of the second Sir John. The Lockwood family intermarried with their industrial partners the Morrises during the 18th Century.

The Statue of William Thomas

An appeal for funds to commemorate his achievements was launched in March, 1891, but the impetous died, and the money in the National Bank of Wales mysteriously vanished. The idea was revived in 1896. Preparations for the queen's Diamond Jubilee in 1897 slowed things, but in August that year a well attended meeting was held at the Guildhall. Among those who spoke, wrote or donated were R.D. Burnie, Fred Rocke, E.E. Rowse, James Buckley Wilson, David Lewis, Braham Freedman, Phillip Rogers, Ben Evans and D.F. Sugrue. A Mr. G.M. Pritchard sent 10 dollars from Baltimore and local schoolchildren raised nearly £40 on St. David's Day, 1898.

All the same, the total had reached only £50 that June, and it seemed they must be satisfied with a bust on a pedestal. Enthusiasm waned. It seems that John Thomas, the Town Clerk, was against the whole thing. However, the movement revived in 1903, the fund reached £400, and Swansea sculptor Ivor J. Thomas took on the commission. It was unveiled on 22nd September, 1906.

PIC: SWANSEA MUSEUM

The cheaper option as drawn in 1897.

PIC: SWANSEA MUSEUM

Ivor Thomas, 1907.

PIC: SWANSEA MUSEUM

Unveiling the statue at last, 1906 (Victoria Park).

Ivor J. Thomas came to Swansea in 1887. By 1906 he had sculpted local men like W.H. Spring and J. Allan Smith, as well as being commissioned to carve a lifesize statue of Queen Victoria to stand in Karachi. He also made statuettes — one certainly exists of H.A. Chapman. But Ivor Thomas probably made most of his income as a monumental mason. It is said that all monumental sculptors in Swansea in 1900 could be traced back to Phillip Rogers who had a yard at the back of Coleridge House and later one in Wassail Square. He died in the sixties and his son, also Phillip Rogers, retired in 1873. The second yard was sold as the site of the Swansea United Brewery. By the time the son died in 1902, aged 92, the monumental masons of Swansea were William Morris of Rutland Street and William Copus of St. Helens Road, both his pupils, William Brown and Ivor Thomas, who both learnt from Copus.

Ivor Thomas was very short — *"he's little but he's wise, a terror for his size."* He was a great worker at the hospital carnival, and a lover of music and painting as well as sculpture.

A.C. Wright

Arthur Cooper Wright was the secretary of the fund, the man who kept things going from beginning to end. A photograph of 1904 shows a thickset alert man, with a neat beard, greased hair, and a loose spotted bow tie. In 1889, he acted as agent for the Royal, Union and Crown Insurance Companies, but he was first and foremost a printer. He worked from a *"printing and publishing works at the back of 131, St. Helens Avenue"* — he called it "Leamington House". He compiled and published directories of Swansea and nearby towns — his publication on Swansea and Llanelly for 1889-1890 is an amazing accummulation. By 1894, this had become "Wright's Annual Reference Book, Tide Table and Almanack". From 1896, he was also bringing out a yearly tourist guide to Swansea and Mumbles, 3d from booksellers, 4d by post. His football annual, which was first issued in 1891, was on rugby — fixtures, *"photo portraits of prominent players"* and so on.

PIC: SWANSEA MUSEUM

A.C.Wright.

In addition, he took on *"Books, Magazines, Pamphlets, Schedules, Concert Bills, Tickets, Programmes, Billheads, Letterheadings, Invoices...Photo block and colour printing a speciality...High Class Work...Moderate Prices."* In fact he seems to have been a middle of the market printer. Taking his 1906

Guide, for example, you see a nice varied use of typefaces and of attractive sketches by W.T. Pearce. Some of the photographs, though, are poorly reproduced, and the guide concludes with 40 pages on the career of William Thomas!

Mr. Wright's flagship publication was "The South Walian" (called "The Swansea and South Walian" from July 1896 and "The South Walian and Swansea Advertiser" from February, 1902.) It was a small format monthly magazine which he owned in partnership with J.C. Manning, known as "Carl Morgannwg". Manning was a freemason who wrote the words of the Oddfellows Jubilee song "Here's to the Old Craft" in 1895. He had once been landlord of the Carmarthen Arms in Castle street. He was a longtime admirer of William Thomas and an experienced journalist. When he attended the opening of Llewelyn's Park in 1874, it was as local editor of the "Western Mail". He had also owned and edited a journal called the "Swansea Boy". In 1885 he wrote a seven stanza poem on William Thomas, and in the glossy pages of the "South

When in doubt as to where and how to advertise ask a policeman to direct you to Wʀɪɢʜᴛ's Printing and Publishing Works, 131, St. Helen's Avenue, Swansea.

Walian", Manning and Wright wrote constantly of *"open spaces"* and the man who had championed them.

There are also articles in "the South Walian" which show Mr. Wright was a proud family man. In 1897 we learn that his son Albert Edward Manning Wright married Florence Morgans of Argyle street in St. Gabriel's Church. In 1907 another son, F.E.C. Wright, heroically saved a shipmate who fell overboard from the "Gael" at Newcastle, New South Wales, *"notwithstanding* (writes the proud father) *the presence of three sharks"*!

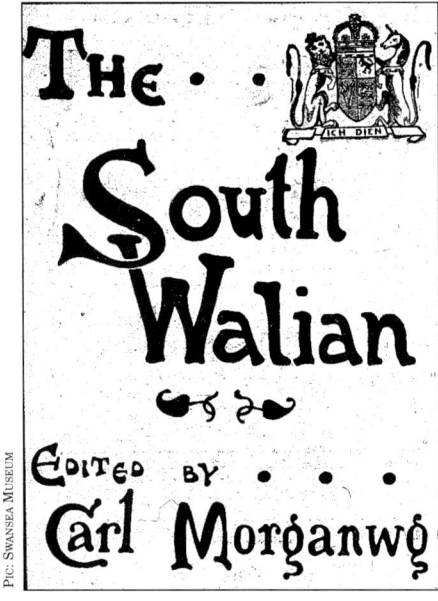

William Henry Spring

W.H. Spring took over the mantle of Thomas of Lan with enthusiasm. A councillor since 1889, he became chairman of the Open Spaces committee in 1896, and was said never to miss a meeting. By this time parks expenditure had reached £1,353/16/10 a year, but he pushed hard for more parks, and organised entertainment in those that existed — in 1900, a hundred deck chairs were bought from Ben Evans at 3/8 a piece for people to listen to the bands in Cwmdonkin in comfort! He was mayor in 1904. He was born in Gloucester in 1827, and came to Swansea as an employee of the South Wales Railway (afterwards part of the G.W.R.). He seems to have set up in business in 1853, and by the nineties ran W.H.

Spring and Son, Wholesale Potato Merchants and Shipping Contractors. Railway arches alongside Quay Parade carried a line from a junction at the bottom of the Strand across the North Dock and the Tawe en route for Neath. His fruit and potato stores were under the first and fourth stone arches, and it was probably no coincidence that vessels were unloading very close at hand — they may well have delivered stock as well as being customers. For some years he had a monster loaf of bread baked, using a whole sack of flour, for the harvest services at St. Mary's — it was afterwards given to the poor.

He seems to have been a racehorse owner in his younger days, running his "Alice Grey" on the course on Crymlyn Burrows. He was a freemason, and also an Oddfellow, having a lodge named after him which met in the Vernon Arms, Caer Street, and afterwards at the Exeter Hotel on the corner of Dillwyn and Oxford Streets. He lived at 28 Wind Street, next but one to the Borough Arms, and a mere minute away from his business premises. At the meeting in August 1897, he ended his speech with —

> *" The Swansea Parks for beauty*
> *There I find delight*
> *And our bay so magnificent*
> *Oh, what a charming sight!"*

Perhaps his poetry did not quite match his enthusiasm.

Victoria Park was to shrink a great deal when the Guildhall was built in the thirties — an old entrance arch stands oddly beside the baths — but the statue survives.

John Dixon, 1896.

John Dixon moves on

John Dixon haled from Northumberland, the same part of the country as the Edens who were managers for the Vivians and the Hedleys who were *"in anthracite coal"*. He was 49 in 1891, and living at 68, Walter Road. He had been Dock Superintendant or Harbour Master all through the mayhem of 1891 and 1892. But that July it was announced he had got the job as manager of Southampton Docks. He began there in October. Though he had only been in charge since 1888, there was quite a series of farewells, starting with a banquet arranged by the Sea Pilots on 7th September — their sense of loss seems very sincere. On 6th October, he was presented with a silver inkstand on behalf of the clerks and officials of the Trust by William Hoskins of the

Pic: Swansea Museum

William Hoskins, 1896.
(He began as Harbour Master's
clerk in 1859).

Accounts department, the oldest of their number. Dixon shook hands with them one by one as they left the offices. The next evening he was entertained at the old Mackworth Hotel in Wind Street. The festivities, chaired by the mayor, Albert Mason, were, trusted Dixon, *"positively the last!"*

In more than one of the speeches he made over these weeks, he put forward very clear schemes for improving the port. Like John Henry Vivian in the 1830s and Henry Hussey Vivian in the 1870s, he wanted to "float" the whole river, with a lock and a wier at its mouth. This would give thousands of feet of quay space, and allow lighters, barges and even *"small import steamers"* to ply from works well upstream to any dock, without obstruction.

"Bristol was talking of spending a million, Cardiff had a big scheme, and Barry also had one..."

They must not be timid any longer!

Floating the river

This old scheme was often pushed during the nineties. Councillor Walter Lewis, a mining engineer who lived in St. Thomas, wrote a series of letters to the press in 1891, and these were published as a pamphlet in 1894.

> *"...it would have been well for our town if Mr. Vivian's able advice had been carried out...[in 1831]...Swansea would then have had a great start in advance of the other Bristol Channel ports..."*

He thought the South Dock had been a failure — the river should have been floated, business confined to its banks, and *"the western side of our town should have been kept and fostered for marine residences..."* Colonel William Pike, mayor in 1893, was a convert — *"...every foot of frontage at the Prince of Wales Dock has now been taken up."* A working man like John Hopkin John spoke in favour. So did Rosser Rosser.

Walter Lewis.

Sometime in the mid-nineties, Rosser Rosser retired to Westbury Villas, Walter Road, where he died in 1901 after a long illness. But in 1891 he was 55 and lived at 15 Somerset Place (as he long had) with his wife Mary and two children. The house faced the Guildhall yard, with its railings, its statue of John Henry Vivian, and its cannon captured during the Crimean War. He had gone to sea as a lad, becoming a master mariner and then a leading tug owner. Latterly he managed the steamships of Frank Strick and Company. In 1892 he was given permission to run a ferryboat from the North Dock steps to the slope of the Prince of Wales Dock. He represented the Castle ward from 1891 to 1895, succeeding Henry Maliphant. Despite being *"very regular in his attendance...he never had much to say in public...a silent member"*. A reticent man then, but steeped in the life of the port, his views were not to be lightly disregarded. He advocated building a central jetty between the East and West Piers, so that two sets of lock gates could be built between the piers at their seaward end.

Councillor William Westlake was not reticent. In February 1891 he took a reporter down to the harbour entrance and explained his scheme in detail and with great enthusiasm. There was to be a *"by wash"* or wier beside the lock gates, set a little landward of the ones in Captain Rosser's scheme, with the Prince of Wales Dock keeping its own separate entrance. "Freshets", sudden floods of water caused by heavy rain upriver, would be dealt with by opening sluices at the rivermouth, warnings being given by telegraph—

> *"It takes a dead dog or a log of wood something like four hours to travel down with the swiftest flow...from Ystalyfera.."*

At the same time mud and gravel would be scoured from the riverbed. He had grand visions:

"...there would be one long lake, and penny steamboats might run continually from the Town Hall quay to Hafod, to Landore, to Morriston...instead of using trams, trains, cabs and carriages...and the system might be extended to local canals...the whole aspect of the district would be changed for the better from the point of view of health and pleasure as well as of trade...by floating the whole of the area of mud which is now exposed at the recession of each tide, much of the offensive exhalation which now arises would be obviated...

Moreover, if the overflow water at the dam....were properly utilised to turn...three powerful turbine wheels, we should have for nothing or next to nothing, sufficient power to light the whole of the docks, and perhaps the whole of the town as well."

He was not to prevail. At an Oddfellows meeting at the Bird in Hand, High Street, in May 1891, he spoke at great length in the same strain, putting the cost of his scheme at £200,000. The chairman of the meeting and chairman also of the Harbour Trust was John Jones Jenkins, he listened politely,... and then changed the subject. By 1896, the decision had been made. William Law, Dixon's successor, and A.O.Schenk, the Docks Engineer, had examined the question —

"The decision to let matters rest is based on the hard fact that to dockise the river would cost a fair and square half a million...and...the possible revenue...by no means justifies the outlay...There is only one road to prosperity...keeping the harbour rates as low as possible..."

The new men were not *"timid"*. In every other way they were confidence and enterprise personified. Perhaps without a McKinley Tariff there would have been a Tawe barrage before 1900, but before we pass on, let us learn a little more about Messrs. Rosser and Westlake.

Rossers and tugmen

Rosser is a surname found all through the story of the port, and it would be a life's work to relate them all, one to another. Rosser Rosser's father was a shipowner who once kept the Vivian Arms, probably on the corner of Ferryside and Bath lane. When Rosser was buried at Danygraig, his brothers Joseph and Richard followed the coffin. Another brother, "Captain John", had been deputy harbour master from 1856. Latterly a martyr to sciatica, he was never missing from his little office near the North Dock entrance; retiring in the May, 1890, he died in July. In 1889, he seems to have lived in Bryn Road. His brig, the "Llewelyn" went to his son, B.J. Rosser of Adelaide Street. A Captain George Rosser retired through ill health after a brief spell as deputy harbour master in January 1892 — he had worked for the Harbour Trust for 32 years.

John Rosser's son, also John, became a freeman of the borough, inheriting the status from his father, as he had before him. (Even a son-in-law could still inherit). Perhaps the same Joseph Rosser mentioned above, a lifelong member and senior deacon of Trinity (Welsh) Methodist Church, was said to have personified the local temperance movement, having held office in Swansea anti-drink groups since 1840. He was Chairman of the Swansea School Board in 1899- the Calvinist representative. Thomas Rosser was a painter and plumber of Somerset Place who died of 'flu in December, 1891, aged just 39. By 1903, the oldest teetotaller, in town was William Rosser, a retired sea pilot of 4 Pier Street — in 1891 he shared the house with his grandson William Henry and his grand daughter Annetta. Almost certainly it was his son William Henry, a shipbroker, and daughter in law Annetta, with four more of their children, who were at 9 Langdon place, on Oystermouth Road. Twelve years later the old man was reckoned to be 95 and:

"...resting quietly, peacefully waiting to meet his Pilot face to face....His length of years, his physical and mental health, his cheery, serene and benignant presence, make him a telling example....So lately

as May of this year he might have been seen in his room on the sunny side of the street...reading his Bible with the unassisted eye..."

Pier Street was a narrow run of small terraced houses hemmed in by chandlery workshops and warehouses; number 4 faced towards Cambrian Place and the South Dock beyond.

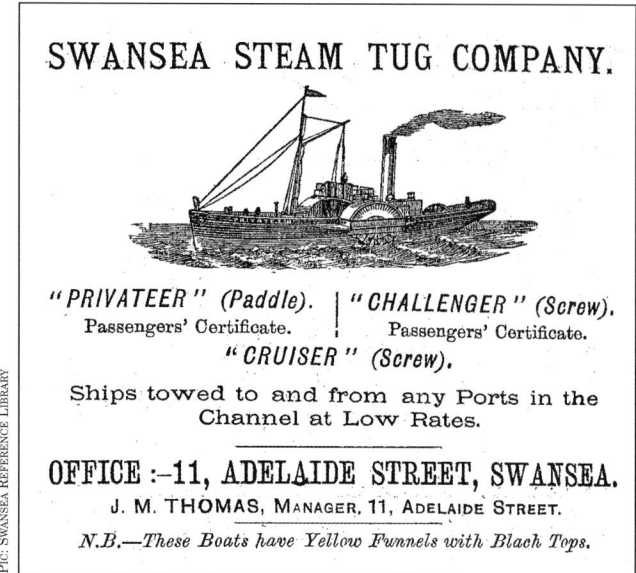

SWANSEA STEAM TUG COMPANY.

"PRIVATEER" (Paddle). | "CHALLENGER" (Screw).
Passengers' Certificate. | Passengers' Certificate.
"CRUISER" (Screw).

Ships towed to and from any Ports in the Channel at Low Rates.

OFFICE :–11, ADELAIDE STREET, SWANSEA.
J. M. THOMAS, MANAGER, 11, ADELAIDE STREET.

N.B.—These Boats have Yellow Funnels with Black Tops.

Rosser Rosser had once owned more tugs than any other Swansea man — he *"served the requirements of the port for some time"*. Three were "Flying Scud", "Flying Cloud" and "Pero Gomez". By 1888, his interests were probably vested in the Swansea Steam Tug Company, manager Peter Rousey, with *"commodious offices"* at 11 Adelaide Street, opposite the Royal Institution. The previous manager had been Barnstaple born William Phillip Ching, who died in April 1888. Rosser Rosser was still secretary in 1894....he was followed by J.M. Thomas. They owned "Pero Gomez", "Pioneer" and "Privateer", "Edward Finch", "Cruiser"and "Challenger". These last two were built for them by Messrs. Cox of Falmouth in 1897.....but there must have been an earlier "Challenger", which, for example, towed the barque "Ashlow" into the lee of Mumbles Head during a great storm in January 1890, while "Privateer" and presumably an earlier "Cruiser" pulled the Newcastle steamship "Ethel" into the Prince of Wales Dock when her engines broke down. In 1892 "Cruiser" found wreckage near Mumbles Head with "M.M." on it. Sometimes tugs doubled as trawlers while idle, having been fitted with the necessary gear, but this caused anger. In December 1895, a sparsely attended meeting of the Glamorgan Sea Fisheries Committee passed a bye-law banning steam fishery in Swansea Bay. There was no mention of proper steam trawlers, just off-duty tugs — the "May" and Captain Gurning's "Defiance". To let this continue would, it was said, *"render useless a fleet of boats valued at £4,700..."*

Telegrams : " LINK, SWANSEA."

"Conqueror" from the stationery of the "Swansea Steam Tug Owners".

"Challenger" near the North Dock entrance.

In 1888, there were ten screw tugs at the port and also ten paddlers. In 1890, the paddle tug "Digby" was sold off as a trawler *"to the port of Shields"*. In 1892, there were just two paddle tugs left, and by 1893 "Privateer" was the last. A registration document for "Privateer" shows that she was built as late as 1883 by T.& W. Toward of Newcastle, sloop rigged, clinker built, round stern, 96 feet by 18, gross tonnage 103. Ownership of even so small a vessel was divided into 64ths, and only 2 out of more than 30 shareholders listed held 8 shares or more. Nearly all are Swansea people, among them William Pike, livery stable owner, Henry Hoskins of Uplands House, Councillor James Jones, a prosperous grocer, William Dewsbury steamboat captain, John Dyer, flour merchant, George John Mansfield of Longfields in Norton, Charles Arkele an outfitter, Henry Broughton a High Street watchmaker and even Ann

Evans, *"widow, Llansamlet."* It was probably during the eighties that Collins captain of the "Privateer" also ran the Gloucester Arms in the Strand, and used the tug to run Saturday afternoon pleasure trips to the Scarweather lightship, or even Ilfracombe.

Possibly "Fawn", owned in the nineties by W. Morris of St.Thomas, bought by the Dewsbury family in 1902. Probably towing barges in this picture.

At 10 Quay Parade, on the corner of Mount Street, opposite the railway arches, was the office of Peter Whiteside. He owned the "Stag" (25h.p.) and "Staghound" (30). In May 1892, he took delivery of a new 65 foot screw tug "Gazelle", built by John Payne of Bristol. He boasted that his crews were hand picked because of their *"intricate and dangerous"* duties. He lived in Trafalgar Terrace, Oystermouth Road, and, most unusually for the time, was a committed Conservative. In May 1890, the mate of a 100 ton French dandy quarrelled with the captain and deserted him, which left him quite alone! The crew of the "Stag" hoisted the sail for him, and watched the boat disappear towards Bideford. Charles Hammond, also listed as a marine surveyor, was another tug owner, based at the Exchange Buildings and later Adelaide Chambers. At various times he had "Searchlight", "The Times" , "Alpha" and "May". He was a Devon man who, in 1891, lived at 3 Cleveland Terrace on Mount Pleasant. Harris Brothers who owned dry docks on the riverside had their own tugs — "Cambrian" and "Gwalia" in 1892. The "Gwalia" rescued a hobbler called Burton in the bay in 1890 when Phillip Michell, a pilot off the "Grenfell" was lost. In May, 1892, the "Gwalia" left for Constantinople, sold to a Turkish firm. In April, 1891, the tug "Fawn" was towing the "Carl", (Captain J.M. Jensen, 379 tons), with 600 tons of coal for Rio. The ship's steering went awry, and she ran aground on a stoney bank which stretched out from the East Pier. A number of tugs tried to pull her off, but she was soon described as —

"...already fast breaking up; her mast broken short off and lies over the side; men are engaged in removing her copper plates, and heeled over on one side she presents a picture of desolation..."

In October 1890, William McGibbon a customs man fell off the rail of the "Fawn" while sitting there smoking. He drowned.

It was normal for Swansea tugs to cruise around looking for work; it was called "seeking to" or "dodging". In 1896, "Britannia" (63 tons, 80 feet long) was caught doing this without lights to elude other tugs, and was prosecuted. On 20th April, 1895 the steamship "Severn" had just cleared Mumbles Head en route for Scotland. Like "Avon", "Ettrick", "Solway", "Medway", "Tweed", "Teviot" and "Yarrow" she belonged to William Sloane and Co. of Glasgow. The local agents were M. Jones Brothers (established 1852) who ran weekly services to Glasgow and Belfast, thrice a month to Antwerp, Rotterdam and Amsterdam, fortnightly to Rouen and Dieppe, and occasionally to New York, from Number 1 Shed, South Dock.

STEAM TUGS—PADDLE.

FLYING SCUD.—Master: W. Harvey. Horse Power: 60. Owner: Rosser Rosser, Somerset Place.

PRIVATEER.—Master: W. Day. Horse Power: 70. Manager: J. M. Thomas, 11, Adelaide Street.

STEAM TUGS—SCREW.

CAMBRIAN.—Master: J. Phillips. Horse Power: 25. Owners: Harris Brothers.

CHALLENGER.—Master: B. Pengelley. Horse Power: 70. Manager: J. M. Thomas, 11, Adelaide Street.

CRUISER.—Master: W. Tanner. Horse Power: 60. Manager: J. M. Thomas, 11, Adelaide Street.

FAWN.—Master: W. Bate. Horse Power: 25. Owner: Morris.

KATIE.—Master: W. Stribbling. Horse Power: 25. Owner: Fender.

STAG.—Master: R. Elliott. Horse Power: 25. Owner: Mr. Peter Whiteside, Jun.

STAG HOUND.—Master: J. Edwards. Horse Power: 35. Owner: Mr. Peter Whiteside, Jun.

THE TIMES.—Master: John Morgan. Horse Power: 25. Owner: Captain Hammond.

WASP.—Master: R. Jones. Horse Power: 25.

GLEANER.—

The Owners will not be responsible for any accident that may occur, or any damages that may be caused whilst their Tugs are Towing.

At 3.16 A.M. "Severn", off Langland, hit a tug which crossed her bows, just aft of the funnel — it sank in 30 seconds. Boats from the steamer and the tug "Cambrian" searched for the crew for two hours without success. Obviously much shaken, the master of the "Severn", McDougall, returned to port, where, by a process of elimination, the casualty was identified as "Wasp". She had been owned by the men who worked her. James Jones, the "engineer" or "driver" was from Pell Street, near Mount Pleasant chapel; he is buried at Danygraig. Harry Beynon, master mariner, the mate, had lived in the same street, but now, newly married, he had moved to Western Street. His wife fainted when the news arrived. David Morgan was the "fireman". "Wasp" had left port "seeking" on a beautifully fine night and she met her end just off the Mixen sands. The wreck was raised, and "Wasp" seems to have returned to service, as the next story shows.

Thomas Milward who lived in Bryn Road owned the tug "Antelope". In November, 1898, she was lying by the East Pier when "Llandaf City", a steamship in the American trade, ploughed into her, smashing in her bow plates and carrying away her mast. "Antelope" had to be towed away by the "Wasp".

The Harbour Trust had their own tug, "Princess". In December 1892, William Westlake suggested alleviating unemployment, which was then very bad, by bringing slag from the works tips at Landore, and using it to make rough extensions to the piers, thus improving the flow of the river. The men would load the six 500 ton hopper dredge lighters, then lying idle in the South Dock, and "Princess" would tow them to the pier heads. Apart from anything else, this reminds us that tugs were used in the river, probably towing barges of copper ore from the North Dock yards to the Hafod and other smelters.

The tugs were part of the town, not always to their benefit, as the master of the "Britannia" found when his binoculars were stolen from his cabin in 1898. And tugmen were part of the town, again not always beneficially — John Godbeer, tug engineer, lost his knife, tobacco box and 1 shilling and twopence, when Dorcas Carr ran off with his coat in 1890....a lady *of ill fame* and 52 previous charges, she was given 6 weeks prison with hard labour.

William Westlake and Constitution Hill

In 1891, William Bondfield Westlake, his wife Elizabeth, and their eight children lived at 19 Northampton Place, at the town end of St.Helens Road. Daniel Westlake, a contractor, lived with his daughters Ann, Ada and Sarah in a cottage near the Graigola Fuel Works, which stood near the top end of the North Dock, where the Cambrian Pottery had once been. In 1890 he took out a patent for inventions in making patent fuel, his address being "Pentreguinea". William was 53, Daniel 51, both were born in Ottery, Somerset — they may well have been brothers.

William was the one who hit the headlines. His Low Level Haulage and Storage Company had their offices on the corner of Mount Street, (tel 103), facing Coleridge House, and perhaps took their name from the street level railway track which passed the side wall. He supplied loam, sand, gravel, white lime, Aberthaw Pebble lime, etc.. He was a haulier by road, rail and canal, hiring out locomotives, steam barges and lighters. In 1890 he opened a new patent fuel works at the north west corner of the Prince of Wales Dock and advertised:

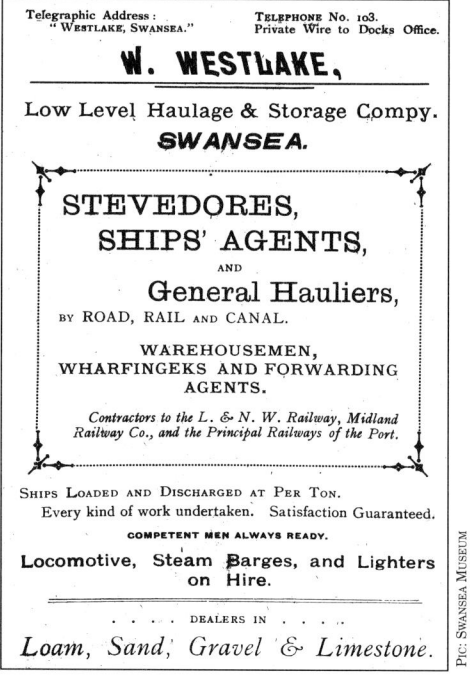

"The Fuel of the Future, Westlake's new patent compressed caloric, in blocks for household use, now being produced at New Inland Fuel Works, East Dock...handy sized...produces a greater heat...cleaner than coal..."

By May 1891, he had sold out to a Cardiff based firm, Fisher, Renwick & Co, but William, who had thirty years experience of the industry, continued as manager, took out patents in his own name, and built a fuel works for a firm in Manchester. Perhaps he returned to production in his own right, for in 1897 he was boasting of his "Carbon Farina" brand.

On the census, he called himself a stevedore, and he offered *"Ships loaded and discharged at per ton"* (sic). In 1890, he had the contract to work the ships, cranes and railways at the Prince of Wales Dock. In May a new hydraulic hoist was completed for tipping wagons of Rhondda coal into the ships below, and in January, 1891 S.S. "Cleveland" lay below it for just two hours while

"Mr. Westlake's men put 350 tons into her— a feat which will take some beating."

Then, in August, John Jones Jenkins was elected to be chairman of the Harbour Trust in place of the ailing George Burden Strick....and Mr. C. Rowland, just retired as the port's traffic manager, got the haulage contract for the next three years. This seems to have included Westlake's dock work for the Midland Railway as well. Perhaps the trustees indulged in favouritism — certainly Phillip Jenkins the Castle Street draper got the contract for supplying uniforms to harbour officers year after year, despite questions — and possibly Sir John was not a Westlake fan. He was not crushed though. In 1893 he was still manager of what was

now called the Pacific Patent Fuel Company, and managing director of the nearby Mersey Engineering works. He was contractor to the London & North Western Railway and the Grovesend Steelworks, near Gorseinon. And he had an office in Dearborn Street, Chicago! He has all the hallmarks of a flamboyant and volatile character, whose career is likely to have peaks and troughs. By 1896 he was the leader of a group of businessmen who wanted to build a tramway up Constitution Hill.

At a meeting in August, 1891, the slums of the town were heartily damned by Councillors David Jones and Fred Rocke:

"disgraceful hovels....not fit for animals to live in...the way the people were huddled together in the various back streets and alleys...was a disgrace to civilisation..."

Gwilym Morgan referred to

"the bad way in which houses had been arranged along Carmarthen road and up Mountpleasant. Why not do what had been done in Manselton, and give the working men encouragement to build on their own land?"

Some present were worried about the expenditure involved, but William Usher put forward an inspirational solution —

"159 acres of land at Town Hill...ripe for building purposes...(for) artisans' dwellings..(each with) a little bit of ground...In order to make the hill get-at-able, they could erect..a line running up from High Street near Waun Wen...and a tramline up Constitution Hill..."

The idea dates back at least to 1883, when Samuel Clearstone Gamwell, editor of "the Cambrian", responded to an idealistic speech by Thomas of Lan with:

"What splendid sites for building does the Town Hill estate offer! The only difficulty...is that of an easy approach...with a small reservoir placed on the estate an 'hydraulic' lift could carry people up and down Constitution Hill..."

By October 1894 William Thomas was writing of the *"lift project now taken in hand by Councillor W.B. Westlake..."* In December, 1896, the council gave approval as long as there was a waiting room at the bottom, and by the next November, while carriage construction at Loughborough had been slowed by a strike, it was pronounced nearly ready, due to Westlake's energy. In July, 1899, the estate agent J.M. Leeder was advertising a

"Detatched Freehold Residence, No.68 Terrace Road, close to the Constitution Hill Railway Terminus."

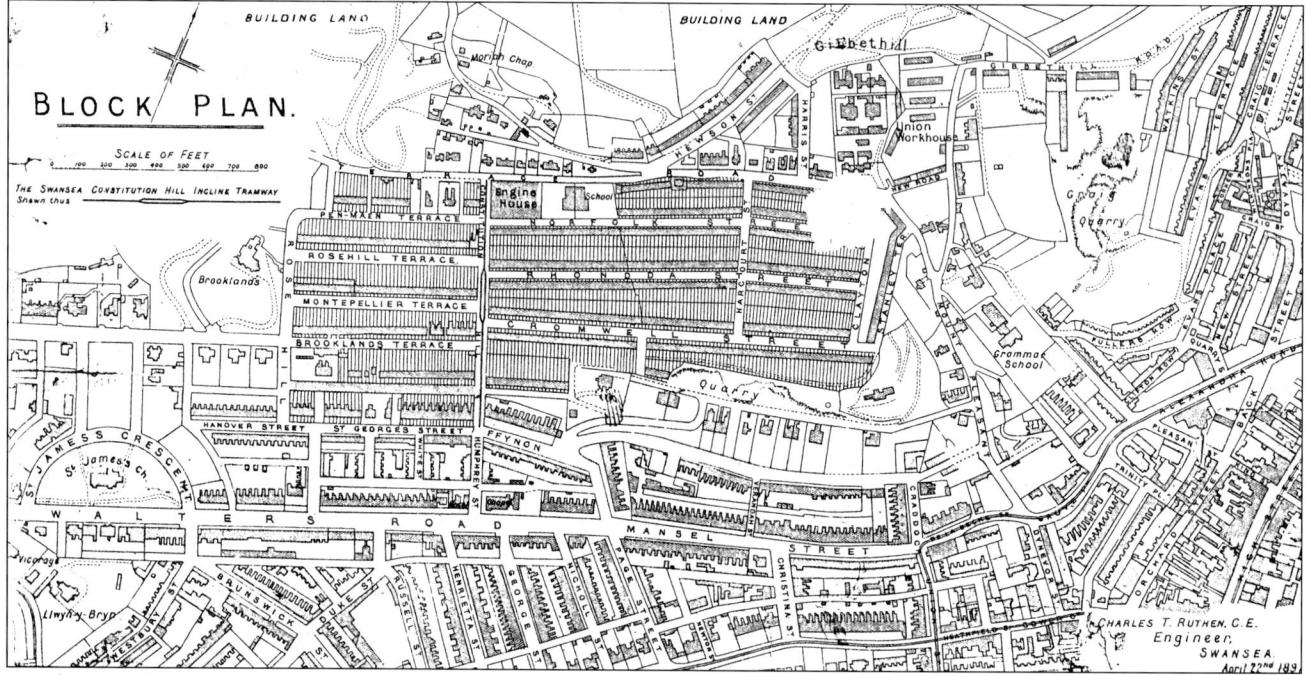

Mr.Ruthen's plan — notice the "building land" earmarked further up the hill.

A very clear photograph, taken from the further side of Walter Road, with the tramway drawn in.

But what looked like an enterprising and successful venture ended as a flop. The basic problem was the Hill, which rose 185 feet in less than a quarter of a mile, at about 1 in 5. The serried terraces across the face of Mount Pleasant probably maximised the builders' profits, but a long diagonal access road would have made transport far easier. All the same, by April 1898, what was called *"the Cliff Railway"* was ready. Water power was rejected, it seems, because an accident might lead to drownings! A gas engine was housed at the top, built into the hillside, hauling a 1" diameter steel cable, which was permanently attached to the 4-wheel carriages. Both the floors and the reversible seats were angled to make the ride more comfortable. The engineman controlled everything, but the cars balanced each other to an extent, and also had their own brakes, which gripped the rails like vices.

John T. Harris who carried on the ship repair firm, and his brother William Edwin, solicitor.

Ruthen, who later designed the Carlton Cinema, Mond Buildings, the Exchange and houses on Mayhill

Then came the first disaster. The Board of Trade inspector, Colonel Yorke, refused the line a certificate.....because the carriage brakes would fail if the cable snapped and there was not enough friction on the cable with one car full and the other empty. New men came to the fore — William Pike, George Lennard, a Whitby born owner of steamships trading to the Mediterranean and Henry Coles, an electrical engineer. All were Swansea residents. The engineer throughout was Charles Tamlin Ruthen, who later made a considerable name as an architect. At this stage he was keen on floating the Tawe — he published a pamphlet and drew the map showing Westlake's scheme. The secretaries were David Meager and then William Edwin Harris of Meager and Harris of 15 Castle Street, which became the company offices — the second was the son of John Harris, of Harris Brothers, ship repairers. (W.E. Harris became a solicitor in 1890. He was a School Board member from 1894 to 1902. He was said to be *"of a cheery and courteous disposition"*.)

A new "Scotch" brake was installed. In August, 1898, a car loaded with two and a half tons of iron was stopped by this in 10 feet, and the tramway was allowed to open three weeks later. But it ran only until

The tramway in operation. The cars on the right are passing near the junction with Montpellier Terrace.

the end of 1901, when it closed forever, and in 1903 it was removed for scrap. The problem now was money. In its first 14 months it carried 200,000 passengers at a penny each, but it had to support a staff of 5 — an engineman, and a driver and conductor in each car — running continuously for 12 hours (11 a.m. to 11.15 p.m.), six days a week. It seems that while houses were being built in the vicinity the line was run at a loss, to encourage buyers, and the downhill fare was even reduced to a halfpenny. But when the council refused to buy it for just £150 the end came.

William Westlake had built it. He contracted to do so for £8,212.....but the inspection failure cost him more than £2,000 of this, and even when he withdrew from the picture at that stage, the company had the right to charge him for the necessary alterations. It is hard to imagine them not doing so.

Houses and Builders

The stone frontage of Terrace Road School from Norfolk Street and the red brick of St.Thomas School from Windmill Terrace.

A good indicator of the spread of housing was school construction. St. Thomas School, for example, was like a red brick giant among the pigmy terraces — the foundation stone was laid on 14th January, 1896 by Alderman David Harris. Manselton Elementary School, was completed in 1900. They were very big places, built to take up some of the town's rocketing population. In a similar way, a right turn at the top of the Constitution Hill tramway took you, in seconds, to a school opened in 1888....a large enough building to rise from Norfolk Street to Terrace Road (which it was named after), from one "ledge" to the next, and still look massive at the higher level. As early as 1889 the Swansea School Board, meeting at their offices in Fisher Street, was told

> *"The number of houses in the locality, and the attendance in the school, was increasing at so rapid a rate that Terrace Road School would probably have another hundred pupils before the end of the year."*

By 1894, 123 infants were crammed into a room built for 70. The school itself cost £5,000. By 1897 Bennet Brothers, whose yard was very close, were building an £11,000 extension! St. Helens in the Sandfields, an older school in quite an established area, was being swamped by the

> *"large population...springing up between Victoria Park and Brynmill Lane.."*

The new school at Brynmill, proposed in 1888, was not opened until 10th September, 1896 by Sir George Kekewich. It was another monster, with space for 1086 and provision to extend for 315 more...and by 1899 it needed an annexe!

Builders prospered. The Burman Street yard, a hundred yards or so from the bottom of the tramway, was behind those fine houses in Walter Road known as Walters Terrace. In 1893 this belonged to **Goskar, Price & Griffiths**, builders and contractors. By June 1896 they had steam sawmills working

Manselton School, early twentieth century.

The brick gables of Brynmill School from Le Breos Street.

there, and the firm was now Goskar & Price. By November, it was just William Price. In 1901 **John Davies**, builder, had premises in Humphry Street, which joins Constitution Hill to Walter Road, though 4 years before his yard was off the main street — Walters Road Yard he called it. He lived nearby at 29 Henrietta Street.

Harcourt Street links Terrace Road with Cromwell Street, cutting through the terraces of central Mount Pleasant. In 1896, **Bennet Brothers**, builders and contractors, telephone 181, had their yard there. William Bennet lived at 94 Terrace Road by 1899, John Bennet at 9 Hewson Street, (between the Workhouse and St Jude's Church).

In 1893 they laid the sewers in Cwmbwrla. They won one of the plum jobs of the nineties, rebuilding the market. By 1898 they were also builders' merchants, and had moved to what they called Heathfield Yard, a wedge of space between the houses of Carlton Terrace and the back of Ffynone Street — later called Calvert Terrace. This had been owned by **T.P. Jones** in 1892 —

"Lath Render...brick, tile and slate merchant...dealer in Plaster of Paris, plasterer's hair...London Portland Cement Company's depot"

Before that again the yard was **Aaron Boundy's**.

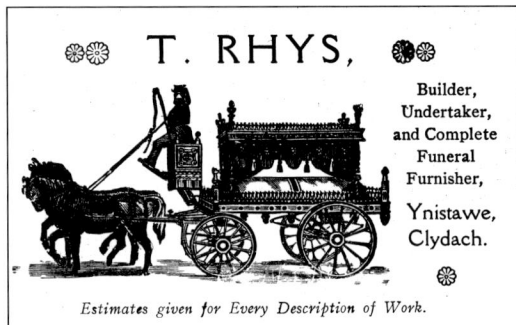
(These "yards" are interesting. They probably began as supply dumps for materials and spaces for cutting up timber, in among the growing maze of terraces, and became formalised into permanent walled and gated premises).

Lloyd Brothers who built Brynmill school worked from a "steam joinery works" in Argyle Street, probably on the town side, backing on to the Arsenal by the Vetch field.

In 1897, 18 Lower Oxford Street was the business address of **W.J. Marles**, son of J. Marles of 5 Richardson Street. He was a builder & contractor who hedged his bets — *"Special attention given to the Undertaking branch"*. There are also references to builders called J. Marles & Son of Richardson Street Yard and Argyle Street, Charles Marles of 84 Oxford Street and T.A. Marles of 6 Henrietta Street.

Thomas Davies had the £3,000 contract to build the Metal Exchange in Fisher street — he was based at the Francis and Clarence Yards, presumably near Victoria Park and the gasworks respectively.

Thomas Richards *"encaustic tiling and concrete flooring a speciality"* ran the Northampton Yard at the back of Northampton Place.

Joseph Gwyn of Sketty built St.David's Church in Morriston, the scene of the wedding which began this book. The foundation stone was laid on 2nd January, 1890 by Lady Llewelyn. He also constructed an *"unusually large coffin"*, 7'4"x 2' x 23"deep, in May 1887, for the burial at Llangyfelach of John Glasbrook, a big man in more ways than one.

Thomas, Watkins & Jenkins were the leading builders and contractors in town. Established in 1856, they had a large yard at 67, Brunswick Street (telephone 89) with *"a fine suite of offices"*, sawmills, workshops, stables, stocks of *"English and foreign timber"* and all kinds of building materials. They also had premises by the South Dock (tel 90). By 1899 they could boast of having worked on nearby Swansea Hospital, the Union Workhouse on Mount Pleasant, the Swansea Music Hall (the Albert Hall), the Pavilion (later the Palace Theatre), the Globe drydock (beside the South Dock lock), and "Alltyferin House" (the Carmarthenshire mansion of Charles Lambert, the wealthy copper owner, and later of Edward Bath), the original Terrace Road School and Brecon College. They built many congregational chapels in South Wales, including Walters Road, Ebenezer and Zoar in Swansea. Watkins was a deacon at Castle Street Congregational for many years. All freemasons — they were initiated on the same night — they seem to have built the Masonic Hall in Caer Street in 1874. They had a large workforce and even owned ships, like the 550 ton "Vigil", a former tea clipper acquired in 1862 and the 537 ton barque "Coronel" sold to a Mr. Grove of

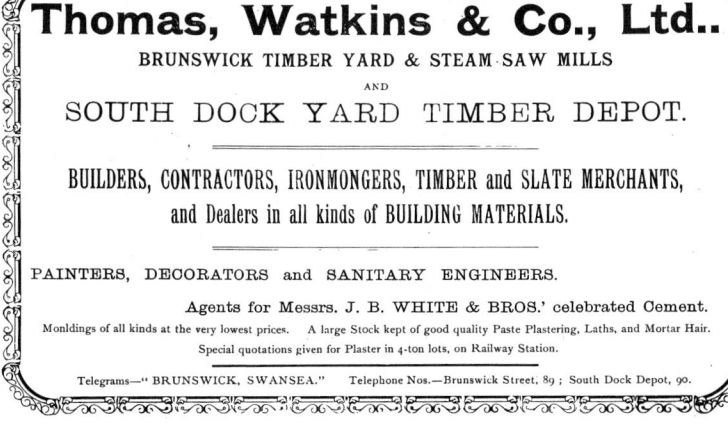

Murton in 1892. Wonderfully nick-named "the Firm", they lived in adjacent houses in Ffynone — David Jenkins, "Llwynhelig", William Thomas, "Cilwendig", William Watkins, "Ashleigh".

William Watkins was the most prominent locally, a J.P., and mayor in 1890 and 1900. From the mid eighties, he diversified, as chairman of Clayton Tinplate, Pontardulais, director of the Villiers Spelter at Llansamlet, of the Swansea Model Laundry and the Albert Hall. When he became

William Watkins

His daughter who acted as his mayoress in 1900. His wife died in 1894.

mayor in 1899, he remembered the town of 1856 — less than 40,000 people and 7,000 houses — now grown to a population of 102,000 in 19,000. "The Cambrian" described the huge role the Firm had in the expansion of Swansea. Their first contract was for two shops by the Bush in High Street. And then...

The Firm were "freeholders of a large estate between the Graig and Poppet Hill". Here it is laid out for building, with the start of Terrace Road on the right, the line of Clayton Street running off to the left, and Norfolk Street off that.

"The development of the Sand Fields was initiated by Thomas, Watkins and Jenkins, on one occasion plans for upwards of 200 houses passed in 1856. In 1856, Swansea, to the West of Dynevor place, was as rural as any part of Gower today. Many of our readers will probably recall Page's Fields. They are now Page Street, Nicholl Street, Henrietta Street and Russell Street, and were developed by the Firm, who also erected a large number of houses in Mansel Street, Walters Road and Brynymor.

Thomas, Watkins and Jenkins were the freeholders of the large estate between the Graig and Poppet Hill. Today it is covered with houses almost all of which were built by them."

In 1892, David Jenkins broke away, basing himself at "the Oxford Joinery Works" in Beach Street in the Sandfields. One early advertisement seemed to be looking towards a smaller specialist market — *"Greenhouses, conservatories, etc, made to order at shortest notice..."* but there is plenty to suggest that it was he who often took the biggest contracts — the enormous Ben Evans extension (1893-4), Weavers flour mill (1897), the Post Office in Wind Street (1898-1900). Mr. Jenkins died on 24th August, 1905 and was buried at Oystermouth Cemetery. The remainder of the original company, which was Watkins, Thomas and Co. by 1900, built, for example, a jetty in the half-tide basin of the Prince of Wales Dock in 1897 for £5,000. William Thomas was dead by 1899.

When Masters & Co. of 18-19 Castle Street — *"Terms CASH. One Price. Every article marked in plain figures"* — rebuilt their premises, they employed Thomas Evans of Brynhyfryd. During the school Christmas holidays, 1895-6, there were improvements at the new Intermediate School (Dynevor), including new fives courts with concrete floors, and at what had until then been the Grammar School on Mount

Pic: Swansea Museum

A much later photograph. The residences of Thomas, Watkins and Jenkins are in the top left hand corner.
Their legacy can be seen in the tall terraces of Mount Pleasant at the top and the streets of the Sandfields, either
side of the Vetch Field, at the bottom.

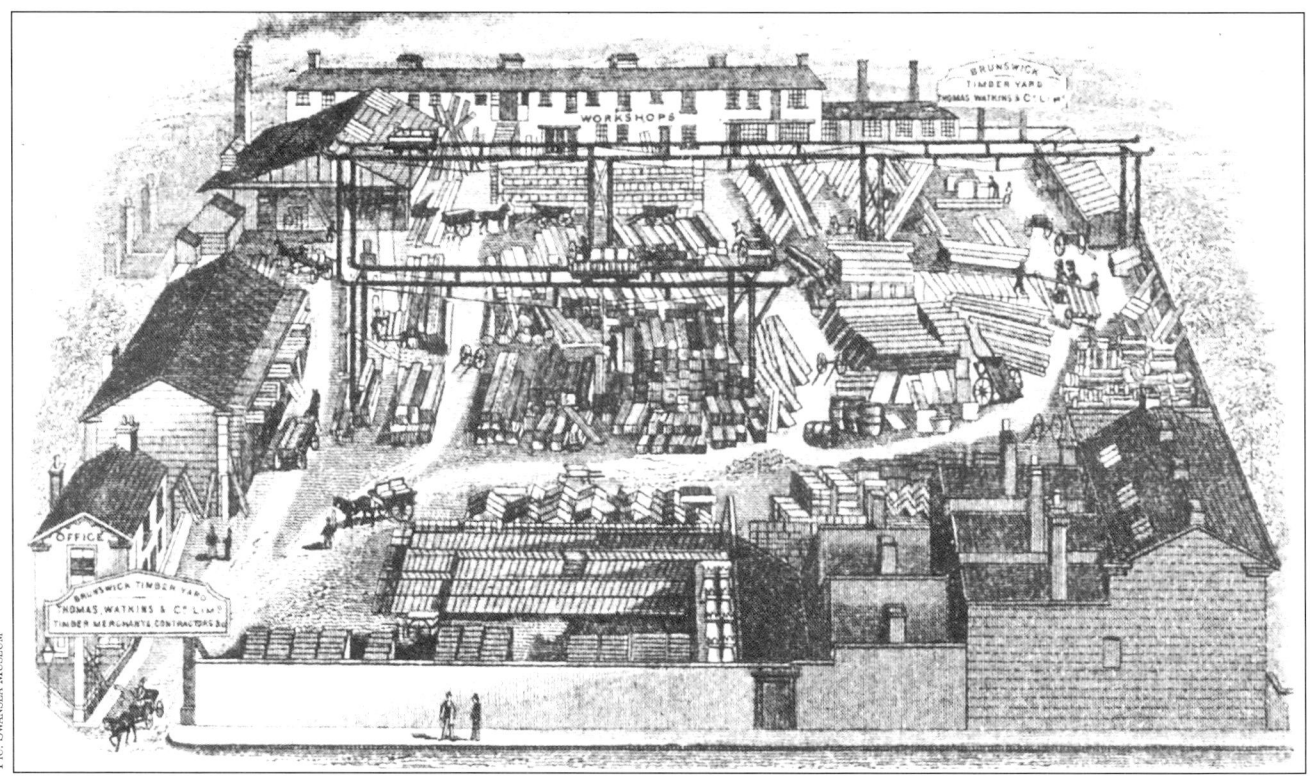

Pic: Swansea Museum

The "Firm's" yard at Brunswick Street was to become the South Wales Transport Company's first Swansea headquarters
in 1914, and is now the site of flats and offices.

Pleasant hill. The work was done by J. & F. Weaver, *"well known Manselton builders"*, of Approach Road, Cwmbwrla. A year earlier they had built a "Lecture Room, Art Gallery and various offices" on to the back of the Royal Institution building. Gustavus Brothers had the Carmarthen Road Saw Mills and Steam Joinery Works at 1 Sea View Terrace, a lofty ledge supported by high stone retaining walls above Dyfatty, their yard looking across to the top of Greenhill and way on up the valley. The brothers seem to have been Charles and George. They were contractors for the nearby vicarage at St. Mark's, Waun Wen, for the arcade constructed to link Goat Street and Waterloo Street, and for the conversion of the warehouses around the Beaufort Basin into Weavers first mill — all these in 1892! George Gustavus stood for the Victoria ward in 1897 and in the same year they were employed to put up a large block in High Street, *"next to Madame Fletcher's premises"*. By March, the old buildings there were being demolished, and

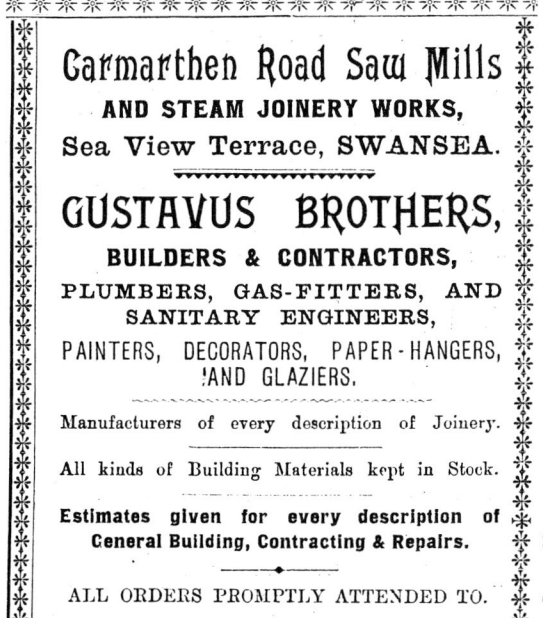

the plan was for 4 floors on a sixty foot frontage, 140 foot depth, with three shops on street level, dining rooms and coffee rooms above, and 60 bedrooms with private sitting rooms on the top three storeys. Each would have a fireplace and *"American radiator"*. All floors were to have "lavatories, bathrooms and water closets". The facade was to be

"of red bricks with Bath stone dressings and stone mullioned windows, terminating with stone gables."

Decorators

This section is a small reminder of all the other trades involved in building. For decoration, you might use **J.B. Edwards** of St. Helens Road, in an area particularly thick with chapel buildings, hence his speciality. Or you might go to **Sidney Clarke** in Waterloo Street — it surely must be him in the elegant pale bowler hat, standing with his staff in the doorway of the fine shop, with flagpole, and characteristic advertisement painted on to the side wall. In 1891, Richard Webborn, a *"furniture broker"*, and his

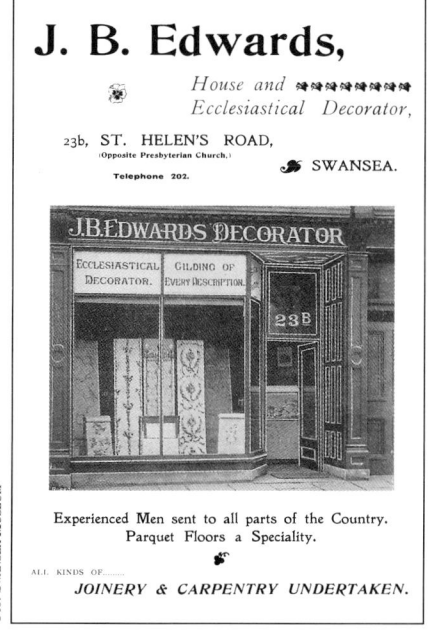

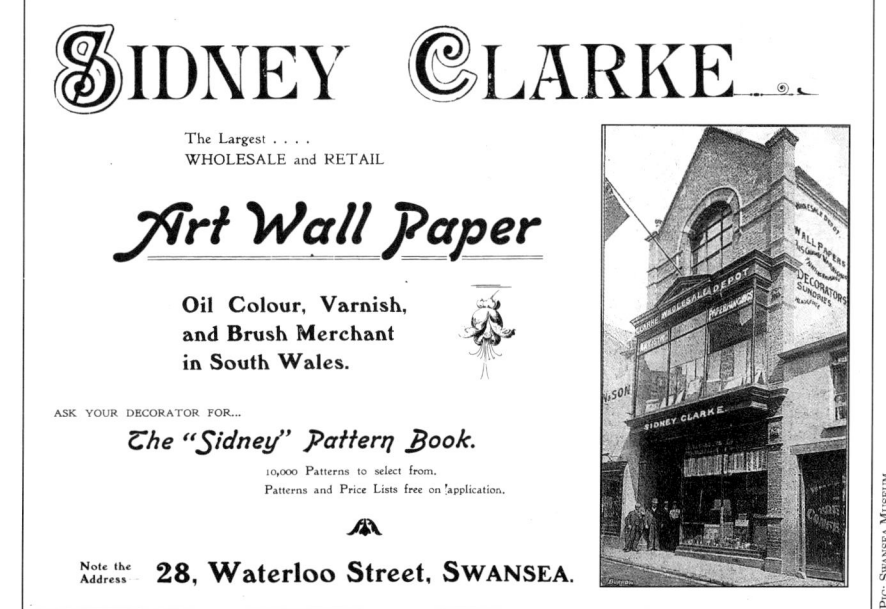

family of six lived above (or behind?) Clarke's — but **Pugsley & Son** at nearby 24, Waterloo Street had a lock-up shop. The firm dated back to 1855, but 40 years later the actual owner was William Gwynne, a prominent Swansea Oddfellow. They advertised as *"the oldest established Paperhanging and Painting business in Wales"*. They supplied materials like wallpapers, but were also contractors. In 1891 Tayleure's Circus set up on the large triangle of wasteland next to the library in Alexandra Road, which even then was under consideration as a police station site. It was a long and successful visit, but instead of a tent they had a temporary building, 100' x 80' x 90', decorated by *"Mr. Pugsley of Waterloo Street"*. The firm dealt a great deal in glass, claiming to be the first importers of foreign glass into Swansea. In December 1896, for example, the schooner "Lucy R. Wilce" of Falmouth put into the North Dock with 300 tons of glass for Pugsley's. (Imagine that quantity stowed in a sailing ship at sea, and then the

William Gwynne of Pugsleys.

job of moving it by horse transport to the company warehouse in Park Street!) In 1892 they put more than 3,500 feet of glass into the Goat Street Arcade mentioned above — a nicely convenient job.

A. Rubenstein of 24 Gower Street was a member of the Jewish synagogue in Goat Street. His shop around the corner in Gower Street sold paint and paperhangings.

George Marquiss went into the decorating business in 1869 at 46, Oxford Street. In 1881, *"his health gave way"* and he took his brother on as a partner. This firm of G. & S. Marquiss was dissolved in 1889, Samuel continuing at the original shop, and George moving to bigger premises at 6, Walter Road, where he also lived...

"thanking the Clergy, Gentry and Inhabitants...for their very liberal patronage.."

Samuel was left with a shop, with office and workshop behind and *"an efficient staff of regular hands regularly employed.."* He kept:

"plain sheet and stained glass, paints, varnishes...Mr. Marquis takes a special pride in his display of paperhangings, and it is impossible to look on the many exquisitely beautiful and varied designs, with their wonderfully blended and thoroughly subdued yet rich colourings, without acknowledging them to be works of art of the highest order.."

In the same publication in 1893, George describes some of his stock

"wallpapers of every class and grade, from the cheapest and plainest to the most costly and recherche designs, including fine flock papers, Japanese paper, Lincrusta Walton decorations, Anaglypta and the like..

and a business expanding with great rapidity. It is interesting that Samuel seems to date the original partnership as 1873, and it may not be too imaginative to detect some family rivalry at the very least!

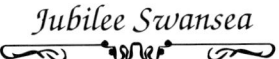
The building workers

From "the Firm" down all these concerns employed men. It is hard to discover the details, but we do know some names.

Bricklayers

Brickworks grew up around the fringes of the town, very often on redundant colliery sites, using the fire-clay found in the coal measures. In August, 1896, the Tunnel Brickworks in Fforestfach was firing three of its four kilns. In 1893 Graig Brickworks in Morriston produced an average of 15,000 bricks a day, ordinary, facing and ornamental. (Walters & Johns, surveyors, were the owners, with offices in Dillwyn Street, Morriston. They prided themselves on mechanisation, especially Scholefield's patent brick press, powered by steam. 25 men were employed.)

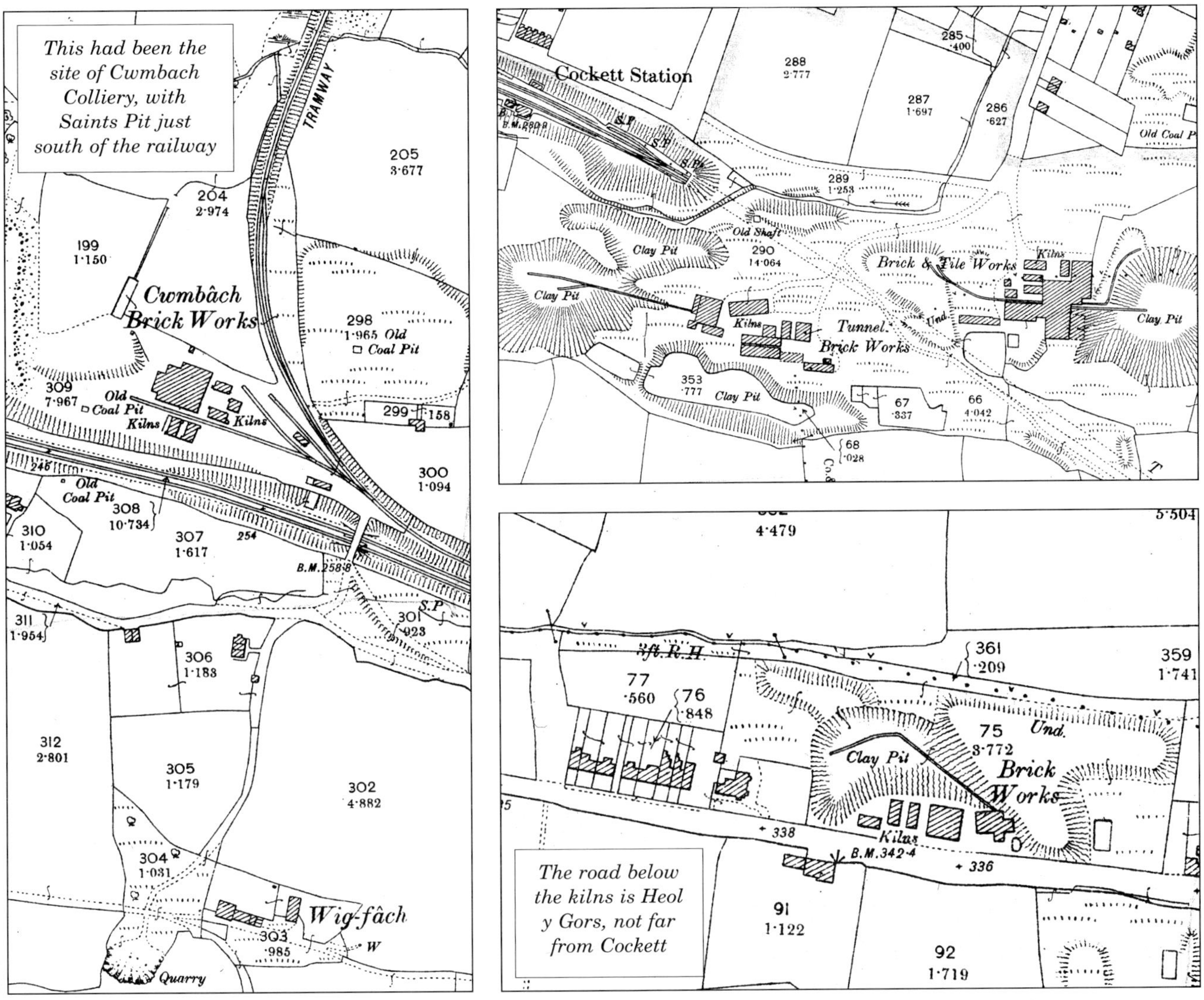

Brickworks around Fforestfach, Cockett and Gors in the 1890s. The area was riddled with mine workings — Weig Fawr and Weig Fach collieries were two of those still busy

Brick construction had become the norm by the nineties, and a number of bricklayers are listed in town in 1891 —

Thomas Shirrup from Truro, lodging in Ebenezer Street near High Street Station

David Jones of Carmarthen, living in Garden Street, a 71 year old widower, but not retired.

William Poles from Staffordshire (Brettall lane) living in nearby Wellington Street, behind the gasworks.

Edward Conolly had come from Cork to Princess Street, where the Grand Theatre was built.

And Joseph Beynon of Langdon place, Oystermouth Road, was a brickie's labourer.

The men who rebuilt St. Mary's Church in the 1890s. Wooden scaffolding, a superb array of headgear and moustaches, and notice a few of the bosses who have sidled in for the photograph.

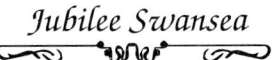
Stonemasons

For centuries before the nineteenth, all substantial Swansea buildings were of stone, and even with the coming of brick, the new houses of Mount Pleasant, for example, had stone facades. And for a long spell, carved stone in decorative combination with brick was the fashionable style for a status building. The Working Men's Club, the Public Library and the offices of the Poor Law Guardians, all from the eighties, set the tone in Alexandra Road. In Oxford Street were the striking premises of J.S. Brown (1893) and nearby the Empire Theatre (1899).

Some of the stonemasons in town were older men — Benjamin Williams of Garden Street was 73, John Austin of Singleton Street 63 and Benjamin Fowler of New Street 70.............but a few doors along lived James Fowler 36 years old, perhaps his son, and down the road again was Joseph Evans, mason's labourer, 18. Thomas Mainwaring was yet another mason in New Street, not too far from the old quarries further up the hill. John Jones in Williams Place had passed the skills on to his 17 year old son David. And there were plenty of other younger men in the trade — in Henrietta Street, Ebenezer Street and nearby Mariner Street (this was George Penhall, Cornish born), Princess Street, Langdon Place and Wellington Street (John Tittle).

Painters & decorators

Lewis Atkins house decorator 1 George Street
William Atkins 45 painter 2 Dillwyn Street
Joseph William Atkins (his son) 19 house decorator
Eli Sladen 42 painter 12 Singleton Street born in Rochdale
Richard Wellington 53 painter 3 Nelson Terrace born in Cornwall
Samuel Radford 36 painter 18 Kynaston Place born in Weston-super-Mare
George A.Cana 30 painter & decorator 18 Garden Street born in Nottingham

There are many more in this line — John and George Tyrrell, Henry Knill and his son William, Henry Tittle, the James Westwoods father and son, John Carter, James Curtis, Henry Morgan Mills, William Evans, Sam Macmillan and Edward Burn. These last three were lodgers, haling from Shrewsbury, Brierly Hill and Crewe, while the Tyrrells were from Liverpool.

Some other trades

Louis Harris 32 glazier 125 Rodney Street, Sandfields born in Russian Poland
Hoyman Harris 40 glazier 22 Garden Street born in Poland
Richard Crocker 18 plasterer 15 Singleton Street
George Fender 25 house plasterer 5 York Street
Samuel Fender 29 plasterer 15 Clifton Row
Phillip Jones 14 plasterer's apprentice Princess Street
James Read 36 lath cutter 71 Fleet Street, Sandfields born in Ilfracombe
Henry Thomas 61 house joiner 1 Clifton Row

We don't know what led Edwin Cleaver of Greenhill to steal a pot of paint and a brush while decorating the chapel house at Hermon, Plasmarl in 1896. But it is probably safe to assume that spells of being driven hard over long hours for little pay were followed by spells of idleness and poverty. Plasterers, for example, in 1899 worked 54 hours a week in summer, 48 in winter. Carpenters and masons in Swansea in 1888 worked from 6 a.m. to 5 p.m., Monday to Friday, finishing at 1.00 on Saturdays.

Safety was not a high priority. In 1899 William Jones of Jersey Street in the Hafod, assisted by George Jones of Mansel Terrace, was plastering the outside of Weaver and Co.'s vast new flour silo, just seaward of their ultra modern ferro-concrete mill on Victoria Quay, by the North Dock basin. By November 2nd the job was almost over, and William had done it all! That day, William Bennet the scaffolder had fixed four planks on their platform, and then hurried away, leaving them to find a fifth. They picked up one which was flawed and knotted. It broke. Both men fell from a great height and suffered grievous injuries. Though Dr. E.B. Evans of St.Thomas arrived promptly, both died. William at 63 was *"the oldest plasterer in town....a most capable workman"* — and George was 66! The inquest, held at the hospital, was fiery. The jurymen asked pointed questions throughout, and the coroner, Councillor Viner Leeder, was irritated into calling them *"corner men"* (biassed?). They angrily replied that this was *"groundless, baseless and insulting"* and that *"they neglected their business to oblige the officer"*. Two solicitors were present, as well as a factory inspector and Mr. Commings of the National Association of Operative Plasterers.

By the nineties, men were combining; there was an amalgamated society of Carpenters and Joiners, Secretary W. Cole, and the Operative Stone Masons, J. Collins, 5 Norfolk Street. The changing attitude of the Council is shown by its invitation for tenders for the Strand Power Station in 1899 —

> *"The Contractor will be required to pay not less than the minimum rate of wages for the time being in each branch of the trade.."*

The Poor Law Guardians had decided in 1897 to use only printers

> *"...recognised by the trade as paying the standard rate of wages"*

Sometimes trade rates were the same. For example when in 1896 Samuel and Henry Williams, masons, and John Jones, joiner, claimed a total of £7/4/8 from Jenkin Williams (a collier) of Sketty for work done, all three were on 8d an hour. That same year, the joiners claimed an extra halfpenny, but failed. In July 1898, the masons went for 9d, but had to settle for eightpence halfpenny. That November, the joiners and plasterers gave six months notice of a claim for the same rate, and on 1st May, 1899, 300 joiners and 57 plasterers went on strike over the issue. The two trades were differently placed. No joiner was long out of work at this time, almost all were union members, and almost all went on strike. Among the plasterers, though, nearly 150 held aloof. An unnamed local builder described the dispute as —

> *"more than the trade could stand...It is a fight for the mastery...unless we hold the reins, we do not know where these advances will stop."*

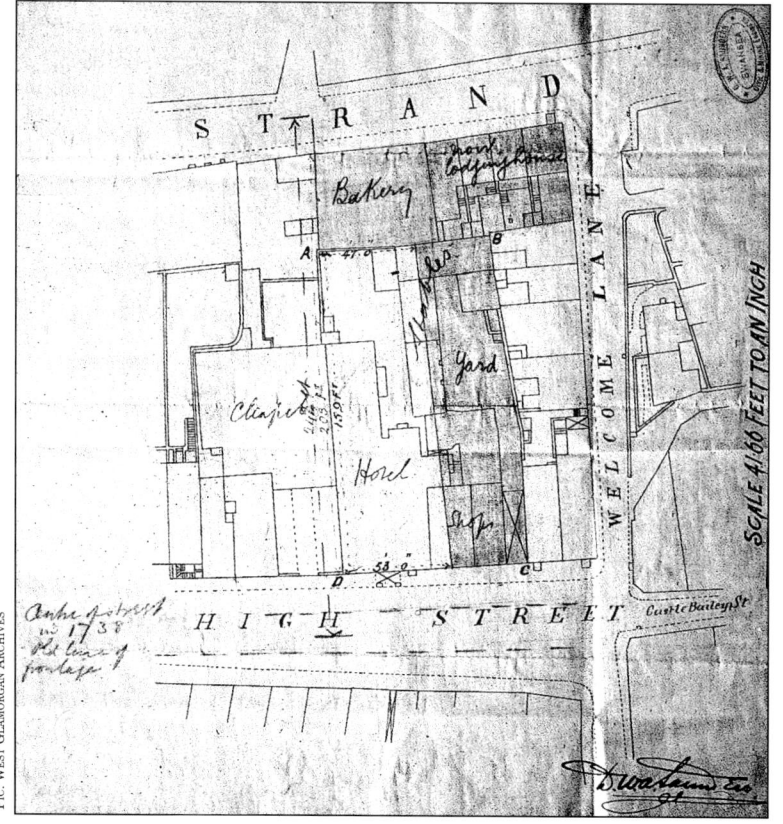

A plan from the church records — notice Paul Smith's bakery near the top.

The bigger men, the Firm and Gustavus of Waun Wen, were ready to give way — trade was not very good. But, in a meeting at the Working Men's Club in Alexandra Road, the men refused any solution not accepted by the whole Builders Association. Perhaps persuasion was used by the bigger bosses, for by 12th May it was all over, and the men had their rate. So work on two big hotels, the Metropole in Wind Street and the Cameron in High Street, was only briefly delayed.

The second of these was described as a

> *"thoroughly up to date hotel with 80 bedrooms....from the present High Street front right back into the Strand."*

The stables then on High Street were to be reconstructed at the rear, leaving space to rebuild the frontage. (Half the

This early postcard shows the new name "Hotel Cameron", but the old name is still visible too!

land was church property, and the old Cameron Arms had been built there under a lease from the churchwardens to Colonel Nathaniel Cameron in 1823.) Paul Smith's ships biscuit bakery at 43 the Strand was one business destined to perish. In fact the massive rebuilding does not seem to have been completed until 1908 — perhaps it was the death of Albert Mason, one of the two promoters, which caused the check. The main change seems to have been the name at this stage — "Hotel Cameron" for "Cameron Arms", — far grander — with the "Arms" only partly covered by the white paint! Anyway, the biscuit bakery on the Strand was still going in 1901 because Captain Paul Smith the owner was supervising production there on 28th October, the day before he died. He was 84 and had lived at Morant Villa in Eaton Crescent. Ships biscuits had been his livliehood for 20 years, but before that he worked on Richardson & Company's barques sailing to Cuba. He had been a friend of Thomas Ford, the great ship chandler of Pier Street. The bakery was still listed in a directory of 1902-3. The ovens were heated by truckloads of coal and biscuits delivered in large sacks and barrels by means of a horse and four wheeled wagon.

The other promoter of the hotel was William Pike. Thomas, Watkins & Co got the contract on a tender of £24,000, oddly the exact cost of the most dramatic redevelopment project of the decade.

Here is the rebuilt hotel, grand, lofty and substantial, in about 1910.

Demolishing St. Mary's

Between 1895 and 1899, the parish church of the town, St. Mary's, was very largely taken down and a new church built on the site — the last services in the ancient edifice, packed out, with hundreds left outside, were on 1st December, 1895. The last peal of bells rang from the old tower after the evening service on November 14th 1897. (By a macabre coincidence, on that same day the body of Richard Brown, sexton for 20 years, was found in the stoke hole, where he had been suffocated by fumes.) The new tower, the last main component of the rebuilding, was completed in August 1899.

Why had all this happened? The Vicar, J. Alan Smith, had faced the problem of population growth by a vigorous programme of church and mission building around the town, at Waun Wen, St.Thomas, Port Tennant, Brynmill and Mount Pleasant. Even so, he considered St. Mary's itself too small for evening congregations and special events. Also, he and many others, thought it too paltry and dated a building for the Swansea of the nineties. Sir John Talbot Dillwyn Llewelyn of Penllergaer, who gave the first £1,000 for the project, and, with his wife, leant full personal backing throughout, put it like this:

> "A great building movement is going on in Swansea. Edifices of beauty and importance are being erected...the present structure is quite unworthy of the town."

The vicar had no doubts —

> "when I first came to Swansea (in 1884) , I certainly was impressed with the extreme poverty and meanness of the Parish Church...(and thought)...any small restoration of the old building would be money thrown away",

and when criticised for spending so much money, he referred to the £30,000 the extension of Ben Evans store had cost. The old church was ridiculed:

> "I was passing the old building the other day when two sailors, — one white and the other coloured Americans — were leisurely surveying the fabric. 'What is that?'...

Old St. Mary's looking east.

Old St. Mary's looking west.

'Guess it's a hay store; and it looks like Seth Jefferson's old donkey — it is old, neglected and has lost its skin!'"

"The present church is so hideous and incongruous a structure that its removal altogether, even if nothing new took its place, would be a relief to the artistic eye....

"The man who designed the larger portion...we hope afterwards emigrated to build kraals for the Hottentots."

"The existing disconnected conglomeration of buildings is an unsightly disgrace.."

John Aeron Thomas, the mayor who greeted the Archbishop of Canterbury in 1898, was a chapel-goer, but he wished the project a fair wind, and even a fierce nonconformist like Dr. John Adams Rawlings gave a donation. It was an enterprise of the whole town, not just of the Established Church.

Things got under way when Canon Smith returned from Portsea with a snap of the newly rebuilt church there. Its architect, Sir Arthur Blomfield, was approached in 1891. A meeting at the old Mackworth Arms in Wind Street on November 23rd, 1893, was full of enthusiasm — *"no half measures!"* (William Pike, the mayor), *"the larger scheme!"* (William Walters of Penlan House), *"the very best!"* (Sir John T.D. Llewelyn). A.P. Steeds, manager of the Central Dry Dock, (on the riverside behind Weavers), said that to keep any of the old church, in which there was no architectural merit, would just spoil the proportions of the new one. And he was one of the very few avowed Conservatives in Swansea! Among the other enthusiasts were doctors like T.D. Griffiths of Druslyn House, solicitors like Hugh Bellingham, tinplate owners like Edward Rice Daniel and David Mansel Glasbrook, John Legg the plumber and electrician of Nelson Street, P.G. Iles the High Street grocer, John Coke Fowler the stipendiary magistrate, John Dyer the corn merchant, Frederick Bradford from the licensed trade, Sir Robert Armine Morris landowner, Ben Evans and Lewis Lewis drapers, Henry Chalk chandlery owner, J.M. Leeder the auctioneer, E.H.

Old St. Mary's from the south, east and north respectively. The proud new town did not want to be associated with such a plain, low building, "like one of the Pharaoh's barns" (Western Mail) with its untidy cluster of side chapels — "the existing disconnected conglomeration of buildings is an unsightly disgrace". The lower pictures show rebuilding well under way.

The foundation stone is lowered into place, May 1896.

Oakden the postmaster, and sellers of fish (A.J. Chappell), books (A.R. Way), music (Gwynne Brader), and high class groceries (John Taylor).When it was all over, in May 1899, the vicar was presented with an illuminated address, naming all these, and many more again. The spirit of the town was with him.

Lord Windsor.

Demolition began on 2nd December, 1895. The contractors were Cornish and Gaymer of North Walsham in Norfolk. A memorial stone was laid by Lord Windsor, Lord Lieutenant of Glamorgan on 19th May, 1896 — after the stone was manoeuvred gingerly into position, he performed his function *"by gently tapping it with his trowel"!* (made and engraved by W. Williams, the Wind Street jeweller). It was a bright but windy day, and the Council thoughtfully had the streets around the churchyard well watered to keep the dust down. (The need to water the dusty streets was a regular expense; over that year it cost the public £672/5/11, mainly for hiring contractors — £10 was paid for water out of the Swansea Canal.) Two years later when Archbishop Temple came for the consecration (on 20th October, 1898), we are told that *"unfortunately the weather was somewhat unpropitious"*, as all the umbrellas in the photographs might have made plain! At the luncheon in the Albert Hall afterwards (catering by Mr. Fitt of the Grand Hotel, Alexandra Road), the primate sat surrounded by the leaders of the town, many of them nonconformists, and was full of good will. The £24,000 needed was raised by all manner of means, but the limelight events were three huge bazaars on 25th-27th October, 1893, 28th-30th October, 1896 and 26th-28th April, 1898.

Archbishop Temple.

The twin steeple (1893) which was cut out as an economy measure.

A page from the 1899 Bazaar Handbook, beautifully printed, and substantial.

There had been hopes that the new church would quickly become a cathedral for a new diocese cut out of the huge see of St. David's. In the event, the split took twenty years, and when it happened Brecon had the cathedral. Nor did the fine building in Swansea ever seem much more than *"a good Parish Church..(for)..this grand and growing old town.."* as the vicar described it in one of his more human and moderate moods. One parishioner lamented that it was was merely *"a big cheap church"*, once Blomfield's earlier idea of a sort of double steeple had been rejected. The architect defended his unsteepled tower as *"pleasing, massive and dignified...by the use of extremely simple means"*, and the vicar explained he aimed at something plain, undecorated and economical. This was some reflection on the character of J. Alan Smith, who was very much a doer, *"a man late and early energetically engaged in well doing"*. (John Aeron Thomas). Even a sympathetic observer commented that on the ceremonial day in 1896, when the foundation stone was laid

> *"We know the progressive Vicar will forgive us when we say that he looked the proudest of the proud...his delight was hard to suppress on more than one occasion, whilst ever and anon it bubbled over in the shape of nervous excitement...(all this)...great strain and worry...(must mean)...complete rest for a few months.."*

He poured himself into large, uncomplicated projects. Before his time, the plan had been to just restore the original building — quite an attractive drawing of the intended result was made in 1881. Canon Smith did not entertain that idea. His achievements were solid and indisputable, his sensitivity to the views and feelings of others perhaps more questionable. The last sermon he preached in the old church included these words

> *"Majorities must rule...we must distinguish between feeling and judgement. I notice that business-men, perforce, make the distinction."*

This narrative has not been too sympathetic to J. Alan Smith, a line that might be continued by recounting that when he left town to become Vicar of Hay in May 1902, *"he was quite unable to call on his old parishioners before leaving"*. In fact the poor man had had troubles which gave him every excuse to drift

These three pictures show the old church being demolished. Notice the dome of Ben Evans, just visible on the left. All three views are from the west.

The top picture is dated April 1896.

The stonemasons and their work. Notice the beard and bare head of the vicar in the lower picture.
The upper photos were taken in August and May 1896.

away without ceremony. In February 1900, he lost his wife, Charlotte Isabella. Though a little unwell she went to Matins at St. James's on Sunday, but the next day just swooned and died *"due to failure of the heart's action"*. She had a reputation as a very active church worker, being *"untiring in her efforts on behalf of the deserving poor"*. Over the new St. Mary's she had been *"as enthusiastic as the Vicar"* and *"there was certainly no one prouder present at the opening of the church"*. Her loss decided him to find a new living. Then in late August, 1901, he was in residence at the bishop's palace at St. David's — he had to do this as Chancellor of the diocese. His youngest son Duncan, with a sister and cousin, went too. Duncan, who was 23, was on vacation from Hertford College, Oxford. One evening he was taking photographs on the rocks at St. David's Head, when a huge wave swept him into the sea. A good swimmer, he battled hard against the fast moving tide for ten minutes, but *"gradually borne on towards Ramsay Sound...he was seen to throw his arms up in despair, and waving a sad farewell disappeared..."* The following day the bells of St. Mary's were tolled in *"deep sympathy for the beloved Vicar..."* The inscription on the tomb said *"suddenly called home...Thy Will is in the sea"*. J. Alan Smith was at Hay until 1906, but his grave — and also that of his wife, of James, and another son Henry Faithful who died in 1950 — is in Oystermouth cemetery. It is a large but plain tomb, anything but prominent on a bank under the high trees. The vicar who built things died on 29th November, 1918.

In happier times, in 1891, he lived in the vicarage on Walters Road, almost opposite St. James's Church. He was 49 then, and his eldest son, Marcus Linton Smith, was already proudly described as an *"Oxford University Student"*. Also in the house on census night were a student friend of Marcus, the vicar's wife, his children Charlotte Priscilla (13) and the ill-fated James Duncan (11), Charles Sidney Linton, carpenter's assistant (a nephew), Smyrna- born Lydia Greaves, a missionary's secretary, a nurse, a cook and three maids. Just five minutes walk away, in a house called Mirador, lived the vicar's chief adversary.

The Opposition

Colonel William Edwin Llewelyn Morgan was a strong churchman. He was 44 in 1891, and on census night only he and four servants were at home. In 1892, he seems to have moved from Mirador to Brynbriallu, another large house, which was next door! He had been brought up, though, at St. Helens House, and from the family estate in that area gave sites for St. Gabriel's Church, Brynmill, opened on July 18th, 1889, and its vicarage, land worth £1,610 in all, — and then made a £2,200 donation to the building funds. He was soon a churchwarden. It seems likely, though, that at this same time he was making money from the house building which was surging over the hill between his old family home and Singleton Abbey, and when John Richardson Francis urged that the south side of Bryn Road be left clear of housing, perhaps as market gardens, in order to preserve a view of the new church from the Mumbles Road, he was not impressed. He felt the new walkway from the recreation ground was quite enough. (See the picture overleaf).

Colonel Morgan.

He had retired from the Royal Engineers in 1887, till then possibly being involved in Ordnance Survey work. After that he gave active support to many local groups — instances are Swansea Chess Club based at the Tenby Hotel in Walter Road, the Amateur Athletic Club founded in 1897, the Church Lads Brigade and the Swansea Gardening Association. He put a huge amount of time into the management of Swansea Hospital.

In the matter of St. Mary's though, he stood out against the tide. As early as November, 1891, he was *"prepared to fight the matter to the very end"*. To take down the tower and chancel would be *"an act of barbarism"*, and if in the passing spirit of the age *"they must destroy something"* let it be the nave, though

The gap in the tall houses of Bryn Road was left to give a view of St.Gabriel's Church, and to give access to the Recreation Ground.

that too held the affections of many Swansea people. For a brief while this compromise was accepted, but using the inferior fabric of the chancel as a reason (or excuse?) all but the Herbert Chapel was eventually demolished —

"bad construction...reckless alterations and mutilations, and clumsy and injudicious repairs... roughly built rubble stonework plastered over..."

were all said to have been uncovered as work proceeded. In December, the Colonel put an advert in "The Cambrian" opposing the *"alteration"* and attracted 632 supporters, though the newspaper, which was hardly radical, listed the names and called them men of an older generation, — Vivians, Webbers, Edens, Lindsays, Rossers, Beors and Pocketts. The big issue at this stage was the fate of churchyard graves which lay in the way of the enlargement of the building. Graham Vivian of Clyne Castle, one of the least popular men in the area, remembered how when the St. John's Church in High Street had been rebuilt as St. Matthews in 1884

"half-decayed coffins were broken into by navvies' pick axes".

This was exactly the sort of emotive line the Colonel avoided, and it was this restraint coupled with his obvious sincerity which gave him the ear of the public through to the very end. In 1899 he was to publish a fine book on the archaeology of the area which devoted a thoroughly proportionate 14 pages to St. Mary's (the castle, for example, gets 24). It is apparent that during the demolition he clambered about the site, making notes of what was revealed, accepting that masonry in the tower, for example, really was *"inferior"*, and taking photographs of features as they vanished. After pages of most efficient and useful recording, though, he could not help ending:

"St. Mary's Church has now been pulled down and destroyed. The only relics in the present structure to remind us of the old church are the tombs of Sir Matthew Cradock and John Hoby, the brass of Sir Hugh Johns, the recessed tomb and effigy, and the door of the rood loft, built into a wall — every-

Ceremonial beginnings, May 1896 (photograph by Gulliver). The day was "beautifully fine". The awnings were rigged up using the scaffolding already in place.

PIC: WEST GLAMORGAN ARCHIVES

PIC: SWANSEA MUSEUM

The platform guests — Mayor Frederick Bradford in the centre, with J.T.D. Llewelyn (head bowed) on his left and Alan Smith (long beard) on his right. They stood on a crimson carpet.

The event is witnessed by Swansea folk in their finery.

PIC: SWANSEA MUSEUM

thing else has perished, including the affections and sympathies of many of the old inhabitants. No effort was spared to save at least the chancel windows and the Herbert Chapel, but all to no purpose, friendship and money were alike sacrificed in vain."

In August, 1895, the Colonel, with his brother Thomas and sister Ann, attended the Consistory Court at Carmarthen, and argued through a series of amendments to the scheme, but by that time the climax of the controversy had passed. Amid the welter of letters, private and public, quiet talks with the vicar and his supporters, hearings and meetings, nothing surpasses the drama of a meeting in the Drill Hall (a building soon to be knocked down to make way for the Grand Theatre). It was 28th January, 1894. The Mayor, William Pike, reckoned that almost 1,500 were present. He and the Vicar, Albert Mason the previous mayor, and Sir John, spoke strongly in favour. "The Cambrian", which had an awful tendency to use six long words where two shorts ones would do as well, reports beautifully what happened next:

PIC: SWANSEA MUSEUM

Ann Morgan, the Colonel's sister.

"The Mayor asked if anyone wished to speak to the resolution, and receiving no answer was about to put it when Colonel Morgan rose from his seat immediately in front of the platform..ascended.. and was widely applauded. He said he rose that evening as a Swansea boy, as a member of a very old Swansea family, to say a few words in defence of the old Parish Church and the Churchyard. He did so in the interests of the Church and the town (applause). The chancel was the work of one of our best and greatest Welsh medieval architects...Bishop Gower...It was a most interesting building and yet they proposed to destroy it. Why? (How often is the present church filled?) The only reasons he knew of...were that it was too long or too narrow, or that it did not agree with the architecture of this Victorian age. If the chancel was destroyed, he could assure them it would create a sensation in the antiquarian world and bring disgrace upon the people of Swansea. It was the greatest representative of the decorative ages in South Wales, and yet they wanted to sweep it away. He did not want to speak harshly but...they did not have the knowledge to appreciate such work. The Chancel was a gem of art and he implored them not to destroy it. Then with regard to the Nave. It was ugly but very dear to many. (...the history of the town has been written on the walls and the floor...the graves are of men who have served the town as Portreeves, Mayors, Aldermen, soldiers and sailors..a generation has sprung up who know not or care not for the past...) He could see by the faces before him it was useless to appeal to old Swansea...He asked the newcomers...they could not have the same appreciation for the spot as those whose families had been christened and married and buried within these walls. But what about old Swansea? How did they view the matter? He appealed to the Christian charity old Swansea cried out for, and asked them to refrain from destroying the graves...[Sir John interrupted: "destroying?" , Col. Morgan:"well, disturbing".]...He held that the town was the trustee and guardian of the unknown graves. If they wanted a new church, let them go to another site. Let old Swansea retain what belongs to her, and new Swansea build up new places.

If the Church subscribed £20,000...it would show that there was a genuine feeling for rebuilding, and he and his friends to be in a hopeless minority. In that case he appealed to his brother sentimentalists to accept the decision (loud applause) and not thwart Canon Smith in his work (renewed applause). He had done his best for the Old Parish Church. He had fought for her, and now he left the decision in the hands of the town. (Loud applause during which Colonel Morgan resumed his seat).

It was a lot more than formality when Rev. A.A.Matthews

"...spoke in praise of Colonel Morgan's manliness, conscientiousness and self sacrifice, and said the town owed him a deep debt of gratitude".

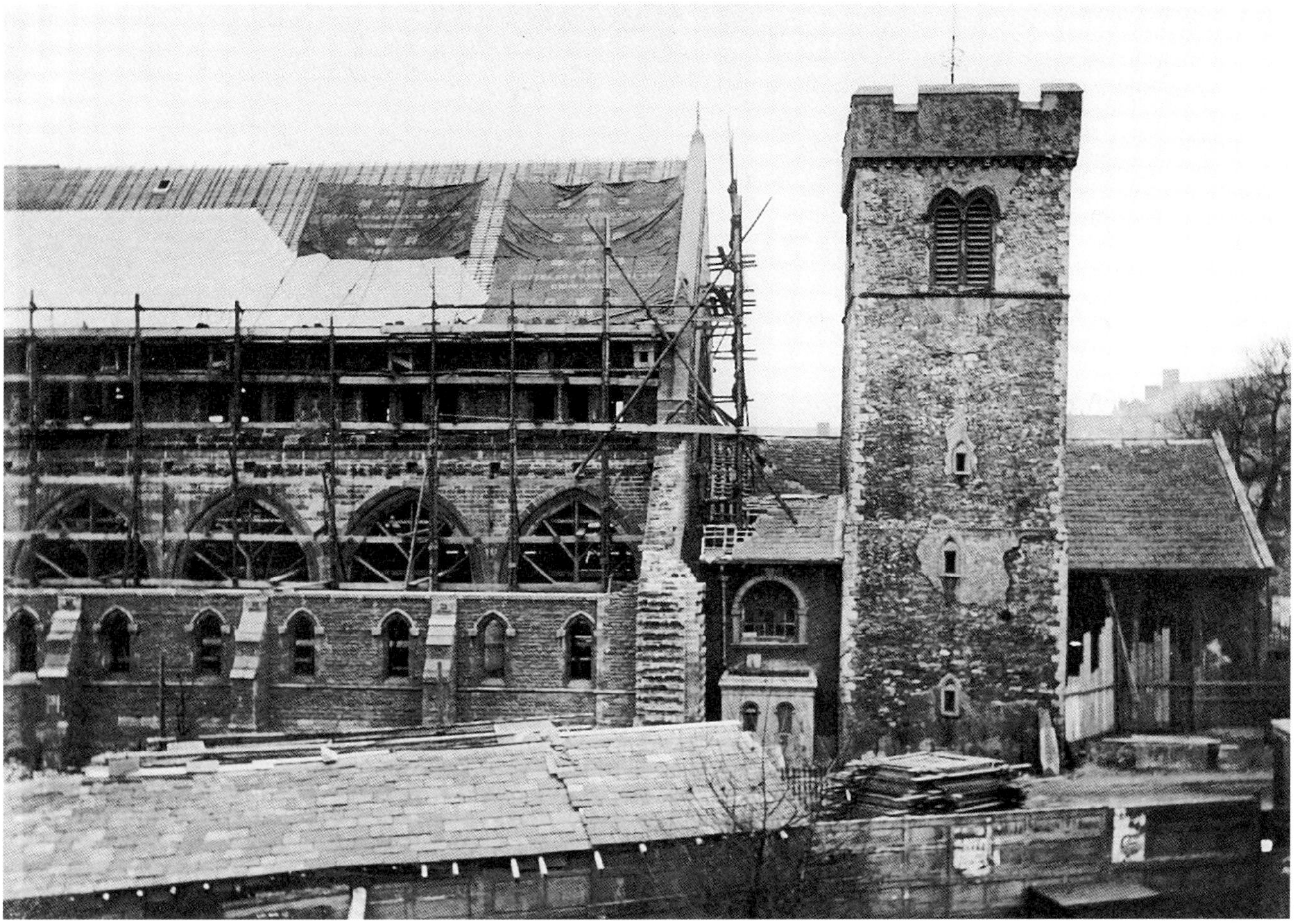

Pic: Swansea Museum

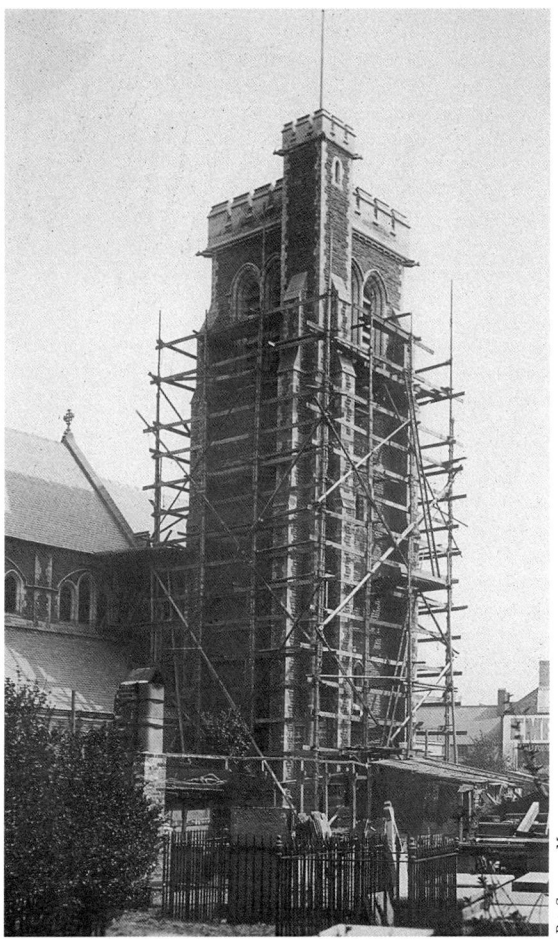

The new church was built beside the old tower. The new tower (called the Victoria Tower) was the final stage of the rebuilding.

The last picture was taken on 30th May, 1899.

Pic: Swansea Museum

Pic: Swansea Museum

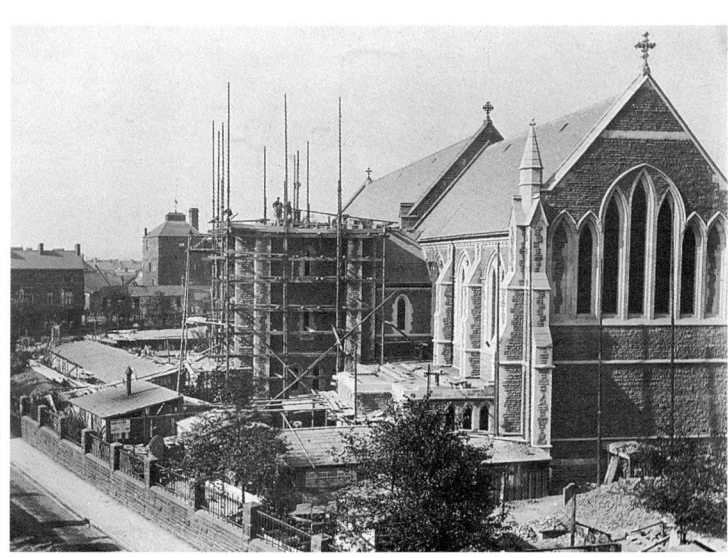

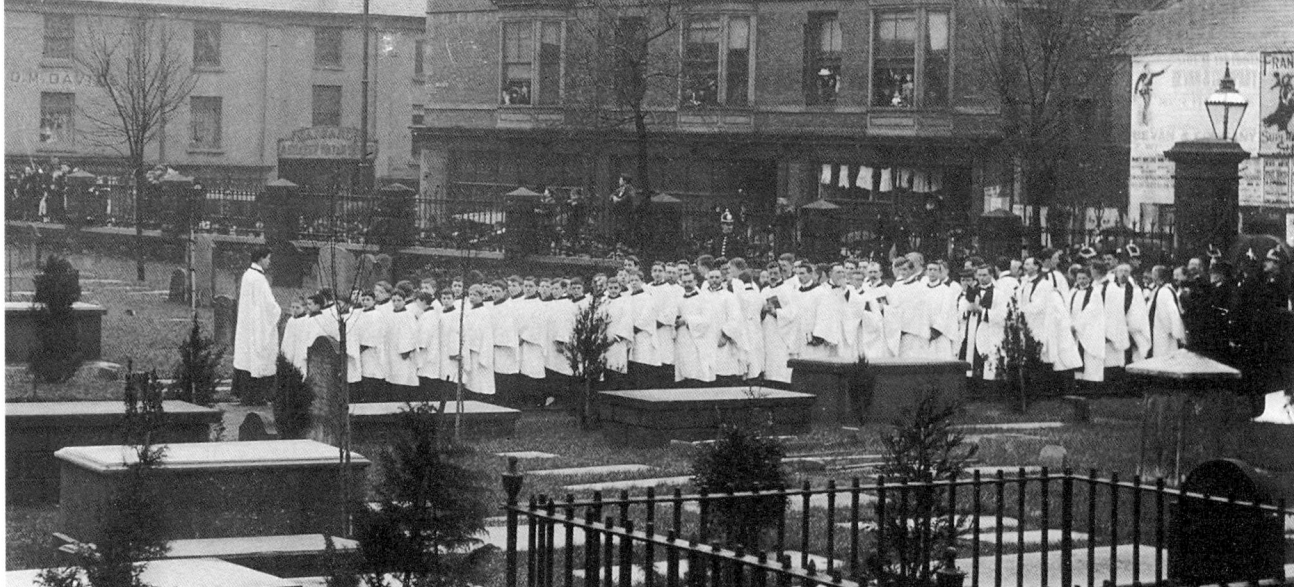

The new church was consecrated on a very wet day, October 20th, 1898. There was a procession from the Guildhall in Somerset Place. The clergy had to come only from the nearby new market where they "robed".

As these words fell from the lips of his close colleague they must have galled Alan Smith a little. (Matthews was Vicar of Holy Trinity, succeeding Rev. Gauntlett in November 1892, and succeeded by Rev. J.A. Harriss in 1897. The parish had been set up in 1856, its church close to the later library in Alexandra Road.) But when the vote was taken, the Colonel was found to be in a minority of just 6.

The idea of building elsewhere was not new. Extending St. James's Church in Ffynone was the most popular suggestion. One letter dealt with this rather effectively:

> *"The present site is more in touch with the class that Christ mixed with. He came to the poor and weary worker, not to the elite of suburban wealth."*

To the west and south of St. Mary's especially were areas of ordinary housing, though outside and set back from the graveyard wall. Until an "improvement" or slum clearance of 1876-9, the houses of Frog Street and Cross Street, on the south and east, had backed directly on to the churchyard. By the nineties, only in Calvert Street, to the north, was St. Mary's close hemmed in. In 1899, numbers 9 to 12 were surveyed by J.M. Leeder. They were rented by Messrs. Harries, Hurley, Tithecott and Williams, at 7/-, 5/-, 7/- and 10/- respectively. He considered them

> *"old and in extremely bad repair...[they]...must shortly be identified by the Local Authorities as unfit for habitation..."*

In fact, a look at the census just eight years before, suggests an area which was hardly the poorest. James Tithecott was a shoemaker from Buckland in Devon, while numbers 9, 10 and 12 had different occupants — David Holt, a coal trimmer, and his young family, William Jackson, a mason, and William and Ann Yeo who ran a grocery and bakers shop at number twelve. Otherwise there was a pub, where six foreign sailors were lodging, William Challacombe the hairdresser, a bargeman (Peter Smith), a laundress, a labourer, a straw hat maker (Eliza Ann Soozee), a builder, a tailor and a collector for a friendly society (George Brown from Putney). Quite a mixture.

Probably taken from the roof of Ben Evans looking seawards. Cross Street is nearest, with Frog Street running across from centre left and the Rutland Street Schools to the left of the church tower.

The fund raising bazaars at the Albert Hall were very elaborate. The top picture looks like the first of these, 25th-27th October, 1893. The fine ladies of the town are disguised as servants, and the seated gentleman may well be Lord Swansea, just a month before he died. The decoration was by Ben Evans store — "beautifully coloured hangings, Japanese and Chinese lanterns, swung across the hall.." The bearded vicar is in the middle of the second picture.

The Colonel and the Scientific Society

From 1890 to 1892, and again from 1894 to 1896, Colonel Morgan was president of the Royal Institution of South Wales, which owned the building which is now Swansea Museum. He loved to be there. He donated a great deal. In 1895 he gave pottery from Cyprus, shells from Ceylon and *"nine pieces of Swansea china"*. Apart from the specimens of Dillwyn's Etruscan Ware given by Ben Evans in 1892, these were the only products of the Cambrian Pottery the museum then owned. A man who knew the Colonel well later wrote of him that his was:

> *"...one of the most real and intimate friendships which the Institution has ever enjoyed. 'The Colonel' when not unwell or out of town, rarely allowed a day to pass without paying a visit before the lunch-eon hour...He delighted to study in our library; to secure some object of artistic or antiquarian interest for the Museum; to organise with his own hands to greater advantage the exhibits...to meet and gossip with members...the identity of a coin, the authenticity of a piece of china, some reminiscence of a Swansea family, anything about a Gower cave....to do something to help somebody else in his studies or enquiries was to him a great delight...The Institution received many gifts from him, their number is without limit, and they were modestly, almost furtively given. ...he asked and saw that his name, which had been written large on the cabinets that were his gifts, was removed from them all — he intensely disliked to parade his generosity...."*

Colonel Morgan was also a leading member of the Swansea Scientific Society, which held its lectures and meetings in the Royal Institution — the R.I. as a society and a building were, for the scientists, *"the nucleus around which we rally"*. In the Scientific Society report for 1894, he did hark back to the medieval buildings of the town

> *"...whilst excursions are made to distant places to see and admire old castles, yet a better and more interesting castle is allowed to remain in the centre of our town, blocked up by houses, unseen and unnoticed by any. We go long distances to adore the remains of a window of an old church....and return home to be passive observers of the destruction of the beautiful work of the greatest architect South Wales ever possessed."*

The Scientific Society — at Oxwich Castle.

But this was an untypical turn of thought, for the spirit of the society was *"not so scientific as to be sadly serious, or as light as to be tinged with levity."* On June 7th 1890, a large party went by horse-drawn brake to *"Rhossilly"*, leaving town at 9.30. After a long and crowded day,

> *"The return journey was begun at 7.30, and the ride home was as pleasant as the ride out. The sun-shine lasted all day long, and the twilight and evening were as genial as the day. Walter Road was reached at 10.30, and the party were unanimous in the expression of their enjoyment. Here, 'vowing oft to meet again', they parted with many a hearty 'Good Night!'"*

Arrangements were not always thought through, though. In May that same year, faced with the treck from *"the rising seaside resort of Porthcawl"* to Kenfig

> *"It having been decided by vote that the walk around the shore might prove too exhausting for some of the ladies, an emissary was despatched to the town to hire a brake..."*

Porthcawl in 1902.

In July 1888, over 100 went to see work under way at the Upper Lliw Reservoir near Velindre. Though one of the horse drawn carriages arrived at Lliw House only slightly late, its passengers missed the contractor's train provided for everyone else, and had to walk the last two miles. Halfway through the guided tour there was a dramatic downpour, which led to a stampede to the navvys' mission room. There they sat down to a *"knife and fork tea"* provided by the mayor, Lawrence Tulloch, not himself present because his young nephew Alfred had recently died in an accident at the East Dock.

After the trip to Paviland and Port Eynon in June 1892, the usual meticulous account in the report ended with the comment:

> *"The programme for the excursion was a capital one, containing a map of the district which had been kindly sketched by Mr. John Thomas, A.M.I.C.E.."*

The printed programmes were often very attractive.

One society activity was archaeology, with the Colonel in charge. In 1893, he led a team which excavated a prehistoric tomb on Penmaen Burrows, *"watched the operations carefully day by day...and noted down minutely the results."* In 1895, they sifted through the remains of St. Peter's Well in Caswell Valley. On the cliffs above Paviland in 1892 and at Oystermouth Castle in 1893, he read lengthy "papers", and at the Institution he gave lectures, for example on the name "Swansea" in 1896, on the prehistoric finds from the cave under the Osborne Hotel in Rotherslade in 1893. Norman earthwork castles were a favourite theme; on these he reckoned

> *"..the guide books, as a rule, were utterly and hopelessly wrong. One writer made a guess, and the other writers followed it by merely repeating it in different forms..."*

Most of what he said and wrote was clear, orderly and careful, and full of this sort of common sense.

Some of the programmes.

There were other outdoor talks. In August 1893, a party visiting the home farm at Dynevor Castle, Llandeilo, listened to Arthur Lloyd Jones, the Mumbles Medical Officer of Health, on *"the white cattle of Wales"*. This may seem an odd topic for a G.P., until you realise that before he trained as a teacher, and afterwards a doctor, the speaker actually haled from Llandeilo and was the son of a horse dealer. (Hopefully they were sitting comfortably, for the printed version of the talk runs to eleven pages of small type.) In 1888, Rev. J.D. Davies gave an on-site description of the (highly debatable) Roman road on Rhosili Down, an exposed spot even in Summer! He more than made up for this in June 1893 when a visit to Cheriton and Llanmadoc included a look around his own wood carving workshop.

One thing that saved the society from being too pompous, from getting over-intense, was the presence of plenty of women. At Paviland, in 1892

Rev. J.D. Davies.

> *"The scramble over the rocks was rather a rough one, but it was undertaken with the greatest good nature...several ladies being amongst the foremost of the explorers...*

> *The return from Paviland was more risky than the approach...The kindly services of one of the more stalwart of the members were all the more appreciated when he stood bare-legged in the sea-washed gap, and carried the ladies over the gulf."*

As early as a trip to Llanrhidian and Weobley in 1889 there were 18 females, and even in 1886, when

Sir John Llewelyn presented bouquets to all the lady members, it must have added up to quite a few flowers. In the membership lists can be seen mothers, sisters, wives and daughters of men involved, like Mrs. Dyer (John Dyer the corn merchant), Miss Bishop of Eaton Crescent (F.S. Bishop, works manager), Mrs. A. Bradford of Gwydr Terrace (Frederick Bradford, councillor and pub owner) and the daughters of Joseph Hall of Grosvenor House — in 1890 when she was 27, Adelaide Hall was also secretary of the St.Mary's branch of the Girls' Friendly Society. Miss Waters of Page Street and Miss Kneath of St. Helens Road seem to have joined independently. So does Miss Thornton, a member from 1892 to 1896, who gives her address as *"fever hospital"*.

PIC: SWANSEA MUSEUM.

An excursion under way — probably Oxwich.

By the way — the Fever Hospital

This was the isolation hospital, what was called *"a removable building...a temporary wooden expedient"* near the West Pier, on land allocated by the Duke of Beaufort at a nominal rent (£9/13/4 a year). The site was chosen as being convenient for any ships bringing in disease, and away from areas of housing. Even so, it was only considered the least unsuitable site available, and a temporary solution. The building had been bought as "Humphreys Portable Iron Hospital", initially disinfected by two men in canvas suits. A special covered handcart to move infected clothes and bedding was kept there. It generally dealt with outbreaks of smallpox and scarlet fever.

Most of the beach was dirty. This was partly to do with the fact that the foreshore belonged to the Duke as lord of the manor and he permitted waste disposal there. In July 1893, a deputation appeared before the Welsh Land Commission in London to protest — the mayor, H.A. Chapman showed his own photographs of the mess, and Sir John Llewelyn, when close questioned, replied *"at the present hour...carts are going there tipping..."* When winter gardens and a

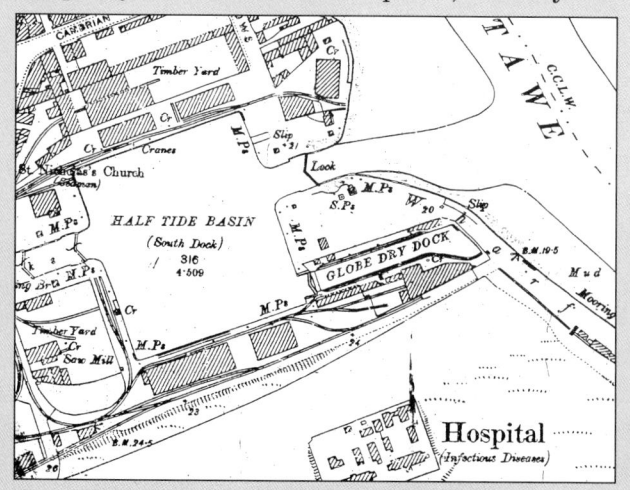

MAP: WEST GLAMORGAN ARCHIVES

The hospital stood on the site of the now closed Spontex factory.

pleasure pier opposite Victoria Park were discussed in 1897, Councillor Viner Leeder spoke of children playing among

"broken bottles...[and]...the noxious odour of dead carcasses".

But the hospital was in a specially appalling spot — the town scavengers had dumped *"mountainous masses of the filthy and nauseous refuse and offal of the community"* until it was surrounded.

Perhaps Miss Thornton was matron — Sarah Johns had that job in 1891, Miss Land at least from 1896 to 1899 — she was paid £48 a year, and the hospital ran for £423/11/11 in all.

Ladies organised teas, of course, but a number did more. In 1890, Miss Aubrey donated a woodpecker shot on her farm at Blaen Cadle. In 1895, Mrs. J.T. Davies of Eaton Crescent put on a display of Swansea China. In 1896, Mrs. Fisher presented a large number of plant specimens *"collected, arranged and named by herself."* Miss Sergeant was joint leader of an expedition to Caswell in 1891. And there was Miss Minnie C. Vinter who lodged at 25 Walters Road.

By the way — Minnie Vinter

She joined the society in 1888, was a committee member by 1891, and actually gave lectures on music, swimming & flying, and fungi. She spoke to the Royal Institution too, for example on "Naples Aquarium" in 1890. Though she was only 26 when she joined, she had the head start of being head-

Lord Aberdare.

mistress of the High School at Llwynybryn. Born in Bayswater, she had a Cambridge maths degree and was *"a certificated student of Girton"*, before teaching at Kensington High School as head of maths and science, from 1884 to 1888. Then she came straight to the new school at Swansea, also run by the Girls Public Day School Trust. She is remembered as wearing *"a black and white figured gown with well-boned bodice"*. The school opened on 18th September, 1888, 49 girls being taught in a house to which some modifications had been made. In 1890, Lord Aberdare, the Trust's president was 75. He had to apologise at the prize-giving that neither the mayor, nor any leading nonconformist, had been invited, and put it down to Miss Vinter's non-Welsh background. He also excused her absence, *"enjoying a well earned holiday abroad"*! By 1892 there were 128 pupils, paying fees ranging from 3 to 5 guineas a term. When the High School was taken over as the Girls Intermediate School in 1895, she went on to run Langland College in Eastbourne, still advertising in "the Cambrian" in 1899. (Miss Benger took over at Llwynybryn from 1895 to 1918, in 1897 there were 230 pupils, — she died in December 1951, aged 87, and was buried at Oystermouth.)

As early as 1886, Sir John Llewelyn had wanted to link the Scientific Society to the drive for a technical college, and for more and better science teaching in the elementary schools. Teachers joined. The Grammar School on Mount Pleasant became the Boys Intermediate School, and by 1896 five of the staff were members, and Dr. George Sherbrook Turpin, Head of the Technical School, was on the committee. More important really were teachers from the ordinary schools — Thomas Roberts (Brynhyfryd), the Misses Thomas (Waun Wen), Miss Bielski (British Schools, Morriston) and Mary Davies, who seems to have taught at Danygraig and afterwards the infants at Rutland Street. Mary Shepherd, a member, was a 33 year old schoolmistress from Much Wenlock in Shropshire, lodging at 7, Picton Place near the Blind

PIC: SWANSEA MUSEUM

The Society on an unidentified excursion.

Home. Another teacher-member was John Cadwalladr who, in April 1897, was assigned the lease of 26 Dillwyn Street — house, yard and garden — by the trustees of the National School. (He died in September 1910, after 39 years as head of the National Schools in Oxford Street, where his wife taught the infants, and the Parochial Schools on Oystermouth Road. He was 66. By then he lived at 50 Mansel Street. He was buried in Oystermouth Cemetery.) On the visit to Mewslade in 1890, Idris Lewis of Terrace Road School explained the raised beach there by means of large coloured drawings he had prepared. On occasions like this, ordinary teachers might rub shoulders with people of note like Sir John, or John Roberts and J. Lovat Owen, chairman and vice chairman of the Swansea School Board.

Other less exalted folk were also members. Edmund Amos of Rhondda Street, Mount Pleasant and James Jenkins of Gore Terrace were members who also have the look of quite ordinary people. Ezra Bunney made his living through a series of rather eccentric small shops, but in 1894 he gave a lecture on bee-keeping. John Legg was church warden at St. Mary's, the town's leading plumber and electrician, and by 1899 he had moved his residence from the business in Nelson Terrace to Bryn Road — but he still had a "hands on" knowledge of his craft. So, in August 1893, on a visit to the medieval castle at Penrice, he was able to give a knowledgeable description of the water supply, and

> "...exhibited a piece of the old conduit pipe...made by casting strips of lead 12 feet in length, 6 inches in width, and a quarter inch thick, and then bending round and soldering the seam, and soldering length to length. Evidence of the age of this conduit was given by the fact that several fine old trees had grown completely over it, the pipe being embedded in the centre of the trees. This supply pipe...was not intended to stand any pressure, but merely to conduct the water from a spring on Cefn Bryn to a huge vaulted underground tank near the castle..."

He went on to say that this conduit continued to supply the mansion at Penrice until a Cardiff firm mistakenly fitted a ball cock, causing pressure which led to massive leaks...and then described with some pride the new system his own firm had just put in place!

The society also had the best of social connections, and used them. It began life as the Swansea Geological Society in 1877, under the leadership of Councillor Philip Rogers of Henrietta Street. The new name came in 1879, but two years later there were still only 50 members. Things looked bleak until a relaunch at the Royal Institution on 25th April, 1885. In Cardiff a Field Naturalists group was thriving, and it was thought that

"Swansea People ought to bestir themselves in favour of local scientific culture"..

C.R.M. Talbot, H.H. Vivian and Lewis Llewelyn Dillwyn put their names forward; John Talbot Dillwyn Llewelyn did more. In July he welcomed a party of 120 to Penllergaer where they were shown around the conservatories and *"collections"*. Their train took them from Victoria Station to Gorseinon. The society visited again in 1891 —

"...the Hon. Baronet, looking all the better for his recent trip to Egypt, delivered a brief address."

Guests massed at Penllergaer.

They came again in July 1895, and this time met the gardeners, Warmington and Stafford, the family, and eventually Sir John, who returned in time to speak to them on "The Progress of the Garden". The description of the estate by the society secretary has very much the feel of one of Sir John's father's photographs as shown here.

"The foliage was thick, luxurious and variegated, and many a charming peep was obtained of the valley, through which meanders a pretty stream.."

In 1887 *"Graham Vivian himself"* showed a huge group (and many more were left behind ticketless) around the whole of Clyne Castle, and they were vastly impressed —

"...our national museum at South Kensington..can hardly compare in many respects."

In 1889, Morgan Stuart Williams invited them to Aberpergwm House, Glyn Neath. In 1893, Emily Talbot allowed them *"with pleasure"* on to her Gower lands —

> *"I should much liked to have joined the party".*

In 1887 they went to Cat Hole cave in Parc le Breos, Parkmill,

> *"...with tapers to light the dark....one of the wheels of the dog cart got twisted and some male passengers had to walk."*

Averil Vivian, widow of Henry Hussey, with her stepson Aubrey, greeted them there again in 1895, seventy strong, and

> *"Colonel Morgan called the scientists together by means of a whistle, which played an important part in the afternoon's proceedings, especially during a ramble through the thick woods."*

At times the privileged atmosphere is strong. In June 1892, 60 visited Culver Hole, near Port Eynon:

> *"The Rev Mellard, the Rector...had been good enough to have the lower entrance ...cleared of the large mass of pebbles and sea wrack which is washed there...and had also been thoughtful enough to see a ladder should be put on the spot..."*

During the Penmaen trip of May, 1893, tea was taken in a building the very name of which was terrible to many of the ordinary population; did any of the servants maybe overhear the archly humorous comments passed....and shudder?

> *"tea was partaken of about five o'clock in the commodious and comfortable Boardroom of the finely placed Gower Poor House, by kind permission of the Guardians, and with the assistance of Mr. Dunn, the master. Some servants were kindly sent up from the Rectory. Some ladies of the party took the arrangements into their own hands an hour or so beforehand, and, when the general body came*

up to the Workhouse, they had the pleasure of finding the capital meat-tea well laid...The 'test of destitution' was not too rigorously applied at entry...the visitors...pretty generally declared that 'going to the Workhouse' was not always so serious or sad a thing..."

There were enough engineers and works managers among the society to make industrial sites attractive, and again contacts were easily made. As early as 1880 John Glasbrook took them to his Garngoch Colliery, near Penllergaer. In 1886, the dock superintendent Robert Capper, with his wife, entertained 250 ladies and gentlemen to watch Number 1 Dredge at work, laying on *"tea, coffee, cider, cakes and biscuits"* on the riverside. (Dredging the river was an expensive job — in September 1891 so much cinder was washed down from the works at Morriston that £758/12/2 had to be spent.)

In July, 1896, F.G. Southern conducted them around his quarries at Llandybie and in 1897 the quarry manager at Penwyllt near Craig y nos received a party.

PIC: SWANSEA MUSEUM

The ornate Cilrychen limekilns near Llandybie.

PIC: SWANSEA MUSEUM

A bucket dredger at work between the piers.

By the way — Sir John Jones Jenkins & the Society

In 1897, Sir John Jones Jenkins, chairman of the Mumbles Railway and Pier Company, showed the members the beginnings of the new pier at Mumbles. In February the pillars for the pier were being made in Widnes. By June, 375 feet of trellis work above sand level was in place, and Lady Jenkins ceremonially started a steam winch to set the first screw pile into the rocks. In March 1898 Sir John decided he could not continue as chairman of the Swansea Harbour Trust. He had been its confident, energetic and acknowledged leader and inspiration since 1891. Now he felt his Mumbles plans might be thought to conflict with the interests of the town. His new vision was for industry to spread all around the bay, with *"everything that was beautiful"* starting to the west of Mumbles Head.

"...in Cardiff at the present time they were making very large docks to accommodate the largest ships afloat. Newport was doing the same thing...while at Liverpool...they were constructing docks which could accommodate ships 1,000 feet long. He could remember when the largest ships which visited Swansea were about 200 tons register, and when Jenkins, the butcher, brought ships to the port of 800 tons, people from the valleys walked down to see them. [William"Butcher Jenkins" was a cattle dealer from St. Mary Street, who briefly owned Sketty Hall, and was noted for his fleet of Bideford-built, Swansea-coppered vessels like "Agnes Blakey" and "Catherine Jenkins". He died in 1850.

PIC: SWANSEA MUSEUM

Sir John was born at Clydach in 1835.] *He himself went to see them several times. He saw the yards and measured the ropes...a very wonderful sight. Instead of ships of 800 tons today, they had steamers carrying 6,000 to 10,000 tons, and he was informed a ship was on the stocks at Belfast 720 feet long...They had at present at Swansea no accommodation for ships 720 feet long...they must always look forward...he thought they should turn their attention to the Mumbles and get a deep water dock there...Mumbles had very large commercial capacities...it would be no detriment to Swansea...*"

Lady Jenkins opened the completed pier on May 10th 1898, but on June 29th 1900 she died, it was thought poisoned by oysters she had eaten. Lady Katherine Jenkins was sister to Edward Daniel the elder, (father of Edward Rice Daniel) and had been married 36 years. It was a bad period for Sir John, for his mother Sarah died in April 1902 at Bath Villa in Morriston.

PIC: SWANSEA MUSEUM

Of course, all this was in the future when as chairman of the Rhondda & Swansea Bay Railway, he greeted a 130 strong group of members at Briton Ferry on 5th May, 1895; their excursion train was cheered as the first passenger service over the company's line into Swansea. They inspected the Neath river bridge, which was far from finished, and the daring of some of even the more august members, as they inspected the site, led the Colonel to speak of Blondin.

In 1896, the Society looked over the Port Talbot Dock, and its railway, led by the engineer, Mr. Havelock Case, with a special train to Taibach, then another up to Bryn to see a cutting and tunnel under construction. On December 2nd, 1895, Henry MacDonnell, manager of Weavers flour mill, gave a very detailed talk on modern flour making. He ended with *"pictures thrown on the wall"* — of which more below.

There was also a lot of interest in purer science. Sub-sections had their own talks, discussions and site visits, collecting scientific books and geological and botanical specimens. Boating expeditions as far as Oxwich dredged up marine flora and fauna.

By the way — *C.W.Slater*

Charles Slater

C.H. Quick

Brunswick Chapel, newly built and alone.

The leading marine biology enthusiast was Charles William Slater, a Methodist lawyer. He was a member of Brunswick Chapel in St. Helens Road in the nineties — with C.H. Quick the Sunday School Superintendent, he installed electric lights in the schoolroom there. In later years he moved to Mumbles, joined the Wesleyan Chapel on the seafront, and wrote a book called "The Corner Pew, a series of sketches of Mumbles Methodism". The real names of people and places are often left out. This is how it opens —

"Our chapel faces due East...Until a few years ago the sea rolled right up to the road whenever the tide was in; and when the easterly gales were on, the waves raced across the shelving beach and broke madly over the low sea wall in clouds of spray, which rendered the road impassible and the chapel itself unapproachable from the front. Then the front door of the chapel had to be kept closed, and those who lived on the main road used to go out at their back doors, and, with others who had arrived by devious courses, creep round to the back of the chapel, and get in by means of the little side door through which the preacher and the singers usually entered. These are now called "the minister" and "the members of the choir", but the change in the name has not been accompanied by any change of habit or ability. They still go in through the little side door, but I am not quite sure that other people take as much trouble to get to chapel in bad weather as the old folk used to do...

Some years ago, somebody decided that the steam tramway from the market town five miles away must be carried right on past the village to the rocks by the Lighthouse. So they built a sea wall parallel with the road, but about a hundred yards further out, reclaiming the intervening area from the sea, and with the assistance of local "tippers", converted it into what is euphemistically termed "made ground". It has almost ceased to smell now. The exiled waves now roar at a safe distance, but the unbaffled east wind, in the day of its power, still tears across the bay...and through the front door of our chapel. Despite the new interior swing doors with patent climax hinges, it still finds its uncomfortable way into every pew but one. And that is the Corner Pew..."

He goes on to explain the pew's other advantages, and describe its various occupants, like the bearded Swansea Postmaster who refused to change to the Anglican Church in order to get into *"Sassiety"* —

"His faithfulness to Methodism cost him many opportunities of playing bridge until the small hours of the morning, and of Sunday golf and whist drives amid the elect."

In his chapter *"In Quires and places where they sing"*, there is a paragraph on

"...the Solicitor man who from time to time endeavours to circulate a legend that, once upon a time, he too, sang tenor in a choir somewhere else, but who, at any rate, now rumbles along on a sort of senile bass, sometimes putting in the old fashioned "grace notes", so dear to bygone Methodists, and which are like nothing else in the world that I know of, except a pig's tail, or the little twiddle at the top of Arnaud Massey's back swing in golf..."

This may be the same solicitor who

"...having lived here about sixteen years and being hopeful of securing admission to the village in about fourteen years more...is now quite subservient"

and he may well be mischievous enough to be writing of himself! His beliefs were strong, and his respect for simple piety tremendous, but his writing is leagues away from the superheated intensity of some of the evangelicals and temporance men of the time. His friendly pastiches of chapel notables read like Quiller Couch, and his lovely quiet humour sparked by the oddities of mankind is quite in the mould of Mrs. Gaskell. He wrote beautifully.

Born in Burslem, Staffordshire in 1856, Charles Slater came to Swansea to work for John Aeron Thomas at his offices at 18 York Street in 1880. In 1890 he lived in St. Helens Road, the next year Gwydr Terrace, Uplands, and by 1906 his Mumbles home was "Hazelwood" in Newton Road. His wife died in 1908, but he lived on until 1941. He became an active member of Oystermouth Urban District Council. In these later years, with his white hair, beak-like nose and grey suit, at least one person tells how he reminded her of a cockerel!

He was secretary of the Scientific Society from 1886 to 1892, and his enthusiasm for science can readily be picked up from "An Hour by the Shore", a printed version of his talk to the Society of November, 1887. It is full of detailed information, but put over with remarkable liveliness —

"...This small bundle which I have just picked up...What do you say? You don't care what it is, and you wish I'd be quiet? Very well, sir. You don't want to vex me, but really you can't stand my everlasting jaw; and you don't see what good there is in all these blessed shells and things? Now, sir. I could pass by your disgust at my verbosity, but you have insulted Nature in hinting that some of her products are useless. It will talk to you until you recant, or else your strength fails..."

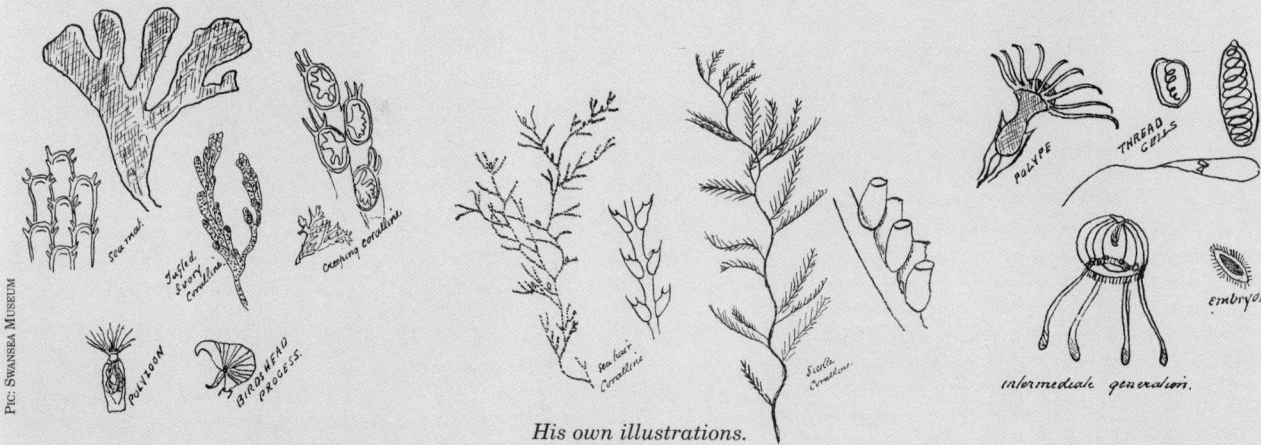

His own illustrations.

In 1880 he lectured to an estimated audience of 850 in the Albert Hall on "Local Water Wonders". He was also a keen photographer and poet, and as a nonconformist lawyer, he must have seen the ironic side of appearing for the landlord of the Dublin Arms of Bridge Street near Dyfatty in 1892, when he was accused of allowing Sunday drinking!

The society organised many, many specialist lectures — a series on astronomy in 1895, another on electricity in 1896, including a talk by E.M. Manville, the London based engineer who had advised the council on building the Strand power station. As we have seen, the visual aids at lectures were up to the minute, and the technical expert was Bernard H. Morgan of "Penybryn" 35, Walter Road — though by 1899 he had followed the westward drift as far as Sketty Road. He was 43 in 1890 and worked as manager of the Vivians' silver refinery, very likely at White Rock. He became president of the Swansea Amateur Photographic Association. At their fourth "Annual Lantern Exhibition" in 1894 the members contributed views of the Lake District, the West Country and Wales, all *"snap shots taken with hand held cameras"*. At the annual soiree of the Scientific Society at the Albert Hall in November 1892, Mr. Morgan showed *"beautiful slides"* of Ancient Egypt *"thrown upon a screen"*. These are sometimes called *"limelight views"* and in 1890, at the Royal Institution, he gave what was actually called *"a slideshow"*. His projector was *"a rigid biunial lantern"* which cost £41/7/-, and was powered by cylinders of hydrogen. He was even able to project photographs of minute organisms taken through the society's microscopes. As early as 1889, H.H. Parlby's photographic store (established 1865) at 99, Mansel Street, near the Albert Hall, was hiring out

Mr. Parlby took part in the church bazaar in 1899.

magic lanterns. This was an interesting shop, combining a dispensing chemist with perfumes, soaps and toiletries and photographic supplies. His "Jubilee set" comprised —

> *"...a good mahogany polished dovetail sliding bellows camera, a quarter photo size, perfectly light proof, with dark slide and instantaneous shutters, powerful French lens in brass tube, developing and fixing solution , etc..."*

In November 1892 Mary Grenfell of Maesteg House gave a talk about her recent visit to the Holy Land to *"a large and mixed audience"* at the Albert Hall, showing *"sixty beautiful tinted slides"*. A Mr. Root and his daughter had laboured for 6 months to convert Miss Grenfell's glass negatives into something which could be projected — it looks as if they hand coloured each one.

In the late eighties, the R.I. had planned to build on an observatory behind the museum, where they would install a telescope; this fell through, and members made do with visits to Sir John's observatory at Penllergaer. The most energetic botanist was Rev. R. Jackett, who ministered at St.Stephens, Port Tennant until 1893, and then St. John's, Gowerton. He gave guided botanical walks — to Glais, Caswell, Clyne Valley, Crymlyn bog and many other places, gave talks, and contributed a list of 419 local plants to the 1891 report.

Side by side with this analytical approach went a more sentimental regard for landscape.

> *"Three Cliffs looked lovely in the distance, and we sighed as we passed Crawley Woods to think that the ill behaviour of a few should have resulted in the closing off of that beautiful spot...It is to be hoped the embargo will soon be removed."* (This is not explained)

> *"...it was impossible to avoid exclamations of admiration as we saw extended before and beneath us the blue summer sea, with Worm's Head in the distance.."*

And yet, look at the use of the word "improvement" in this comment on the long journey down to Rhosili in 1890 —

> *"There is little in the way of new building or improvement in the line of route, save the new stone villa which Mr. John Hopkins is building on the slope of Cefn Bryn.."*

A few interesting members

The core of the membership is like a "Who's Who" of Swansea's upper middle classes. Here are just a very few of them.

C.H. (Christian Henry) Perkins J.P. was a strong Liberal, a founder member of the club in Wind Street. He was a committee member of the Scientific Society as early as 1880, and in September, 1888, for example, gave sixty or seventy people, seated among the ruins, a lively talk on Penard Castle. He lived in Eversley Road, Sketty and was long chairman of Cockett Parish Council — it was he in March 1897 who led strong local support for a Gower Light Railway running from the Clyne Valley, all the way to Port Eynon. He loved exercise and used to walk into his office in town, *"at a brisk pace...with a cheery face.."*. This fits in with his long term support of Swansea Cricket and Football Club, where he was a committee man and helped select teams. When Sir John Llewelyn's son William came of age in 1890, Perkins presented him with an album of pictures of leading cricketers he had put together himself. A staunch Unitarian, perhaps he also walked in to the High Street Chapel on the Sabbath. He had shares in anthracite collieries in the valley. His wife was a charity worker and Poor Law Guardian in her own right. In a meeting in 1899, she gave her (very conventional) opinion on workhouses —

Bertie Perkins.

> *"The Guardians tried to make it as nice as they could for the old people and children; but they should like to make it very hard for the able bodied. They did not want them there."*

Their sons were Arthur, Harold, Travers, Richard, Bertie and Donald. In April 1900, Bertie, who was a lieutenant in the Cyclists Corps in the Boer War, married Alys Sandbrook of Rhydygors, Cockett, at St. Paul's Church, Sketty. C.H.Perkins died in May 1913, aged 86.

Dr. James Kynaston Couch was a Society member. He came from a medical family. His great grandmother worked at Swansea Infirmary from at least 1836, but Mrs. Couch's bad temper and other things led to her sacking in 1840. One complaint was that her grandson, James, was living on the premises — he grew up to be a doctor, being present at revolutionary experiments in anaesthetics at University College Hospital, in 1846. His son, James Kynaston Couch, joined the Scientific Society in 1892 and spoke to them on "Sleep" in 1893. James (the father) was born in a large house near St. Mary's, later had a surgery at Camden Cottage on Oystermouth Road, and for 34 years practised at Mansel House, on the junction of Mansel Street and Christina Street. His son lived there too, quite near the Albert Hall, and so very convenient for society soirees!

Thomas Henry (Tom) Couch, born 1865, had shown an early interest in his uncle's sail making business in the Strand. By 1886 he was manager for Williams, Torrey & Field, a leading Swansea shipping firm. His job was to supervise the regular sailings to Baltimore, Philadelphia, New York and New Orleans, Shanghai, Singapore and Yokohama, Lisbon, Oporto, etc. He was James Kynaston Couch's brother. Once the U.S. tinplate trade slumped, he diversified his shipping interests, and he launched his own travel agency in later years.

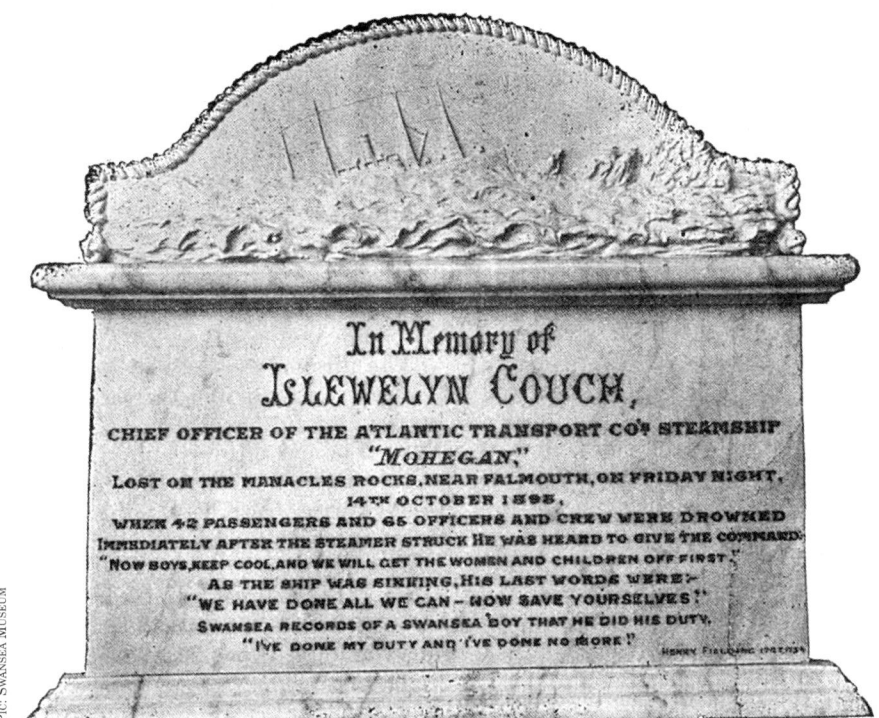

Tom Couch in 1897 and Jimmy Couch (below), a friend of my grandfather, from the next generation.

The memorial, (destroyed in the 1941 blitz).

In 1892, Doctors A.K. (perhaps a mistake for "J.K."?) and J. Couch were listed at 6, Christina Street. By 1902, Dr. J.K. was at Mansel House, Christina Street, possibly the same place.

In November 1890, a John Couch was put in charge of the newly created Dock police force, a post he held through the nineties, being described as "inspector" in 1899. The only established link here is the surname, and it ought to be said that while the relationships of all these Couches, except John, have been outlined, but there is plenty of possibility of error!

James Kynaston had a brother, Llewelyn, chief officer of the S.S. "Mohegan". He was drowned when she hit the Manacles Rocks, between Falmouth and the Lizard in heavy seas on 14th October 1898, en route from Gravesend to New York. The Porthoustock lifeboat saved 44, but more than 100 drowned. Llewelyn was buried at Danygraig, his aged father James, then living at the Grove in Uplands, being too ill to attend. A fund was set up in his memory to aid his widow and daughter, and to put up a memorial tablet in St. Mary's, which Ivor Thomas carved at a very reasonable cost. Roger Beck spoke at the unveiling, on 26th March, 1900. At a time when many Swansea men were facing danger in the Boer War, he painted a picture of disaster at sea. Were you to

"lean over the rail of a steamer in mid ocean in the dead of night, when the lights were out. The only sounds heard in the black darkness were the dashing of waters against the side of the ship: below, the muffled throb of the engines; and at regular intervals the sounding of the bell and the cry of the lookout man that all was well. ...imagine the quiet scene changed in a moment by a crash and a shock into one of direst extremity and excitement. The crowding on the deck of the helpless, and their anxious appeal to those in authority — 'What shall we do?' It was then that the spirit of a man was tried to the extremity..."

Roger Beck, Quaker industrialist, 1841-1923.

By the way — *Llewelyn Couch and the Cornish shipwreck*

Llewelyn Couch had a record of bravery. In 1897, probably when mate of the "Mississippi", the Norwegian Government had commended him over the rescue of the crew of the barque "Persia". George Maule, a Texan horse shipper, said to be "horse foreman" on the "Mohegan", survived by clinging to a plank for seven hours until the Falmouth lifeboat found him, and he recounted how Mr. Couch coolly supervised the women and children into the boats, putting on lifebelts for them. Others remembered him ordering all lifeboats to be cut free as the ship sank, and then diving from the stern as the vessel disappeared. On the plaque were what were thought to be his commands on deck — *"Now boys, keep cool and we'll get the women and children off first"* — and his last words — *"We've done all we can, now save yourselves"*. How far legend has taken hold here is hard to gauge, but the story that, once in the water, he made himself a sort of human raft for up to 17 people, does invite doubts.

The "Mohegan" had sailed a totally wrong course ever since passing the Eddystone light off Plymouth at 4.17, and was much nearer the shore than intended. She passed close to Falmouth, racing along at 12 or 13 knots. The passengers, many of them Americans on their way home, were dining. James Hill, coxswain of the Porthoustock lifeboat, was standing at his stable door, and saw her just half a mile out, lights blazing — he ran off to raise the alarm. About the same time the captain must have ordered a change of course, and then the stopping of the engines, but the impetous was too great, the rocks made a huge hole, and, within fifteen minutes she was gone. The "Mohegan" was less than 3 months old, and was on only her second voyage. Recent surveys had found her to be in good condition. The whole tragedy was so strange that there were strongly held beliefs that the Captain, Richard Griffiths, had quarrelled with his employers, the Atlantic Transport Company, engineered the whole thing, then made good a secret escape! He was a Merionethshire man, and most bizarrely, his body, headless, was washed up three months later in Caernarfon Bay. Others held that magnetic properties of the Manacles reef had affected the compasses. These were afterwards found to be in good working order, and witnesses recounted how the work of the helmsmen was checked and supervised by Griffiths and Llewelyn Couch, both experienced seamen. The exact cause remains a mystery.

Dr. Lancaster.

Dr. E. Le Cronier Lancaster lived in Winchester House, Christina Street. With Northampton Place and St. Helens Road, this was Swansea's Harley Street, with the hospital at the further end. Born in Clapton near London in 1862, he was educated at Merchant Taylor's and St. John's Oxford. By 1887 he was obstetric officer at St. George's Hospital. He was associated with Swansea Hospital from the 1890s to the 1920s, treatment of tuberculosis being one of his specialisms. He became secretary of the Scientific Society, as well as curator of conchology and zoology at the Royal Institution.

Dr. William Morgan, F.C.S., was born at Abercrave in 1853, educated at Llandovery, and trained at St. Thomas's Hospital. He became surgeon to tinplate works around Clydach and

Pontardawe, before moving to Swansea in 1882. There he became surgeon to the Nancarrow's Morfa Works, to the G.W.R. and to a number of insurance companies. His address is just given as Swansea Laboratory. He ran the South Wales Chemistry School in Orange Street, afterwards moving to Nelson Street, and he had 60 students by 1887. A move in the nineties towards forming a technical college, by encompassing engineering also, failed. He was also Public Analyst for Glamorgan, Carmarthen and Pembroke and when he died suddenly, in December 1896, this role was taken by **Clarence Arthur Seyler**, (a leading member of the Society by the mid 1890s), working in partnership with the old man's son. Like Dr. Lancaster, he was from Clapton, born in 1866. He graduated in sciences from University College and worked in London as an assistant officer of health and analyst, before coming to Swansea.

In 1893, some councillors made a strong move to reduce Dr. Morgan's rate of payment. He was contracted make 24 water samples in a year at one guinea each, paid £150 a year for 350 samples of all sorts, and 6 shillings and eight pence per sample after that. It was said this amounted to twice what other towns paid, and that the doctor's attitude towards his employers verged on the arrogant. On the other hand, the field was huge — water, drugs, spirits and food were all mentioned, and there were 250 milk vendors alone. Discussion was lively. James Jones

> *"...warmly remarked that the police would do well to confine their attentions to the big grocers such as Taylor & Co., Alderman W. Richards* [His main shop was by the Palace Theatre — see "Jubilee Swansea", I, p.33-4] *and himself. It was not honest nor honourable to prosecute the poor widow..."*

Others defended the doctor as a *"Swansea boy...risen from the ranks"*. Gwillym Morgan suggested some members had been *"seen"* (lobbied) by the analyst, but the mayor made him withdraw his allegation.

Captain Adolphus Naerup of 5, Pier Street, joined in 1892. He was a Norwegian, born in 1843. His wife Maria (37) was Irish, and the birthplaces of their three children, aged 10 to 16, are Ireland, Norway, Ireland. He ran his own shipbroking firm, and when the wooden barque "Eliesar" of Liverpool brought what was said to be the first foreign cargo of wheat for Swansea into the Beaufort basin, he was the agent for Weavers. By 1899 he had moved to Norton, where he called his house "Solheim".

Dr. William Morgan, 1897

Clarence Seyler, 1897.

Captain Naerup.

SWANSEA FLOUR MILLS, SWANSEA.

Pic: Swansea Maritime and Industrial Museum

William Weaver was born at Spaxton in Somerset, son of Charles Weaver,

> *"being a miller there...the family for generations had carried on the same business.."*

Schooled at Bridgewater, he was the first man in Britain to win the Gold Medal of the National Association of British and Irish Millers for scientific milling. He opened a successful mill at Worcester, and in 1892 was invited to come to Swansea as managing director of the mill by the North Dock which took his name. In 1900, he was living at Rosehill, Western Lane, Mumbles, the old residence of the Bath family.

Charles Pollyblank, A.I.E.E., was a mechanical and electrical engineer for the Harbour Trust from 1885 to 1892. He organised electric lighting for the whole dock area by June 1890, using the engine of the disused dredger "Abertawe" in an engine house by the Cuba Inn to provide power. He left to set up on his own account at 47, Wind Street, over a shop between the George Hotel and the New Theatre. On 8th

William Weaver.

January 1892 he took out a whole page advert for his new business in "The Industrial World", newspaper of the tinplate industry. His main product was "Norton's Patent Tinplate Sawing Machine" which he claimed trimmed tinplates, up to 70 a minute, to an *"absolutely true...perfectly smooth edge"*, far better than any guillotine shears. This meant that customers making tin cans or roofing from terneplate could work from the edge provided, and further wasteful trimming was avoided. Like others he was making a living by supplying Swansea's staple industry — in the same building was Thomas Price's Payne Furnace Company. By 1895 he had moved as far as 10 York Street, near the Royal Institution, and advertised phosphor bearings, fuel economisers, steam engine governors and gas engines. How had he coped with the tinplate depression? He lived at Trafalgar Terrace, Oystermouth Road in 1893, and was an officer of the Swansea Regatta. By 1899 he was dead, and his widow was living at the Grove in the Uplands.

J.C. Vye Parminter up to his death in November 1896 lived at Broadway Villa, 1 Walters Road, Uplands. He was 61, *"but carried his age remarkably well"*. Originally from Bristol, where he was a J.P. as early as 1856, he was described as *"a genial and worthy citizen"*, and had worked as a company secretary. As a magistrate since 1878, he attended the bench unfailingly on Thursdays. He was an artist, curator of art for the Royal Institution, of which he was a member for 30 years, and Conservative agent for West Glamorgan. As early as 1892, his wife Agnes, also an artist, gave a very large portrait of Rev. E.B. Squire, the former vicar, to the Royal Institution. She had been running art classes from their home at least from 1890 —

> *"...painting from the Costume Model, Miniature, Tapestry, Art Pottery, screen and fan painting, drawing..."*

She was still teaching in 1898, but now at Exeter Villa, Uplands. They had two sons, Arthur an architect in Paris, and Henry, born 1875, in the Swansea coal trade.

By the way — *Frederick Sillery Bishop, George Nancarrow, and the new spirit in the copper works.*

It can appear that the leaders of society in the later years of the century hadn't the stature of the generation or two which came before. Peel, Palmerston, Disraeli and Gladstone — though the last overlapped a bit! — seem on a higher plane than Roseberry and Joe Chamberlain. Locally, John Henry Vivian, Lewis Weston Dillwyn and his sons seem greater men than what came after. Perhaps they just were. Or, perhaps the media, the newspapers and their staff, started to treat the "great" with less deference. Or again, perhaps it was harder for the new men to act with impressive and untroubled authority in a world where social norms were under question, and economic prosperity less assured.

Whatever the truth, some of Swansea's industrial leaders of the 90s appear worthy rather than imposing.

Frederic Sillery Bishop M.A., J.P. was born in Stoke in 1848 and educated at Cheltenham, Oxford and Cambridge. He managed the Grenfell family's copper works on the Eastside, from 1876 to 1892 and then just the Upper Bank Spelter Works. He was chairman of the Rural Sanitary Authority, on the committee of the Metal Exchange, and involved with the Blind Institute, and the R.S.P.C.A.. He and Mrs. Bishop were the leading Anglicans in the temperance movement in Swansea.

F.S. Bishop.

In October 1894, "The Cambrian" described him as *"a gentleman noted for his piety and philanthropy"* — it had reported fully his lecture at the Y.M.C.A. in March entitled "The Inspiration of the Bible". He was the president — the Y.M.C.A. had been founded in 1868 and then stood in Dynevor Place, near Mount Pleasant chapel.

Appointed by another pious man, Pascoe St. Leger Grenfell, who died in 1879, he managed the works from then on. But when the younger generation of Grenfells pulled out of the business with appalling suddenness in October 1892, and a reporter went to see him in his office at Upper Bank, *"commodious and comfortable without being showy"*, it was fairly obvious it had all come as a great surprise to him too. Some suggested he owed his job to his worthiness rather than to any ability or energy. Claud Grenfell, who was not a charitable man, said

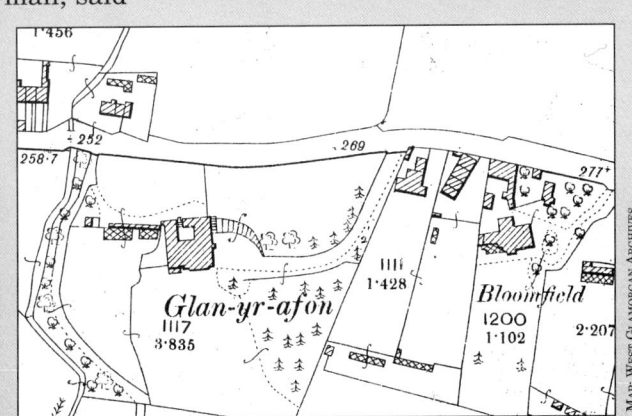

The mansion of Glanyrafon on Gower Road has been replaced by the houses of Glanyrafon Gardens.

"We want a Grenfell there...I feel sure that a child could do as well as Bishop"

It might be answered that Bishop dealt with labour relations effectively at a difficult time, twice carrying through 5% wage cuts without alienating the men. He lived at Glanyrafon in Sketty, and in 1891 is listed as 43, and living there with wife Ann, children Edith (13), Alice (10), Cyril (7) and Sylvia (5). There was a governess (Mary Nicholls from Callington in Cornwall), a housemaid, cook, assistant cook and schoolroom maid. By 1899 he seems to have had a house in London as well. He was a magistrate.

George Nancarrow was probably descended from Cornishmen. It is a distinctive name, and for example, William Nancarrow, of 10 Rutland Street, a boatman with seven children, was from Falmouth. George, though, lived at "Trefula", in Mackworth Villas or Mackworth Villa, Mackworth Street, St. Thomas, and afterwards at Llwynhelig, a huge stone house in Ffynone. That was a vast change, because the street in St. Thomas included shunters, dressmakers, fuel workers and plumbers, with George and Ann Nancarrow, their cook and housemaid, at number 19 on the end. He was treasurer of the Royal Institution from 1887 to 1896, when he resigned *"owing to pressure of business"*. He worked for the Grenfells at their Eastside copperworks, like his father and grandfather before him, and then became manager of the Morfa Copper Works at Landore — they were part of the same company from 1894. The old easy acceptance of social class and power was going. George Nancarrow found this in local politics. He had been a councillor for St. Thomas, but was beaten by Councillor Lee. Later, in 1898, J.H. Williams became the sole Labour man on the council, and represented this ward. Even so when Nancarrow died in October, 1910, (aged 61), five hundred coppermen followed the coffin to St. James's Church.

Messrs.Bishop and Nancarrow were both involved with the Morfa Copper Works. Neither had to do with the strike there in 1890, but it is an illustration of a new and harsher spirit in this old industry. This was a time when the profitability of copper was almost gone, and, at the same time, unionism was growing stronger. A dispute began with four men being sacked who refused overtime on the terms offerred. Union leaders Harry Orbell and Tom Mann interceded, and the men were reinstat-

Mackworth Terrace, home of George Nancarrow, and also Dr. E.B. Evans — see page 161.

ed. The company said they had apologised. They denied this and were dismissed again. Then two more men were sacked, in theory for disobeying orders, but they just happened to be the local union chairman, John Williams, and the check secretary, Mr. Lewis. Both these men were cautious officials employed at Morfa for 27 years, and had been trying to play down the dispute. Secretary Lewis died before the settlement; his widow blamed the management. At the end of July, with a strike imminent, the works manager, W.S. Carlton, called in a deputation of the men, and offered a pay rise and a consideration of reinstatement, if the whole workforce would give up the union.

> *"The men stood around in groups near the gates...the deputation soon appeared...[on hearing the proposal]...a sarcastic smile overspread the faces of the men..."*

There was no suggestion of abandoning the union. It was a Saturday and work finished at 1.00. They hung around the works, and on the adjacent roadside, but not until 6.30 were they all paid for the preceding week.

> *"The girls engaged at the works ...poked fun at everybody as they walked up the road..."*

The strike was now on, involving about 400, and the following Monday they marched through the main streets of Swansea with a banner proclaiming "Morfa Copper Men in Defence of the Union". They were well received, and there was little bitterness at this stage. But the dispute dragged on until October. The union had to disburse £75 a week in strike pay, some to men who, it was said, had only joined days before the dispute. Funds dwindled, hunger grew. Some families had only 5 shillings a week to live on. Men from other works subscribed to support them (Atlantic Fuel workers £1/2/6, Hafod Isha £8/14/5, Glasbrooks' Timber Yard — by the South Dock basin — 11/6) One newspaper used a headline *"Hard policy of capitalists...the starvation weapon is being...tried..."* Clerks were eventually told to stop work and go home. The furnaces deteriorated, and it may have been this that led the London directors to accept arbitration at a plant where there had recently been much investment. Colonel Roper Wright and John Hopkin John were chosen by the two sides as arbitrators. The workers gave a limited apology and the management reinstated those dismissed.

Mr. Evan Lewis and his Family

Evan Lewis was sub curator of the Royal Institution from from 1867 to 1906, and by the time he retired very few of the members he had first known were still around; in his retirement speech he commented on the lack of ladies in those days, suggesting that

> *"..when he joined the ladies joined.."*

He had had other ambitions, applying in 1880, when he was 40, for the post of Swansea's Chief Librarian. He could claim to have acquired an understanding of *"the intellectual tastes and requirements of the town"*. His testimonials were impressive, from, for example, Doctors J.A. Rawlings and George Padley, J.T.D. Llewelyn and J.C. Fowler, the stipendiary magistrate. George Grant Francis, recently retired as Honorary Librarian at the R.I., never one to pass over inadequacies, and with a memory to match, reckoned that he had

> *"..on no single occasion...to complain of any point of your conduct or duty.."*

But Evan was not successful; the job went to a Leeds man, S.B. Thompson, who was not quick to move on. Thereafter Evan Lewis

Evan Lewis.

PIC: SWANSEA MUSEUM

The second Mrs. Lewis.

The minister and deacons of Walter Road Congregational, with Evan seated, second from the left.

seems to have been content with a dutiful and assiduous role on the fringes of the great and the good. Dr. Salmon, Principle of the Technical College, commented in 1906

> *"..there was no need of a catalogue* [at the R.I.] *when Mr. Lewis was with us.."*

He was Honorary Curator of the Scientific Society, 1877-81, then joint secretary with Slater, 1881-92, and John Thomas the engineer, 1892-3. Then his son Llewelyn Collwyn Lewis took over, first with Dr. Lancaster, then with G. Arbour Stephens.

Evan Lewis was a family man, married first to Margaret Jones of Merthyr, and when she died to Selina Bowen, widow of Jenkin Bowen of 86 Walters Road. The Bowens would have been neighbours, for the

Lewis family home had become, since at least 1880, "Llwyncelyn", 4 Walters Terrace, — but it was not always so. In 1867, Evan moved into the basement rooms in the Royal Institution which his predecessors had used since 1841. It was not salubrious, and in 1874, the death of his 4 year old son John Henry was thought to have a lot to do with the conditions. The R.I. dithered, but Evan acted, moving out into Henrietta Street. Walter Road was another step up the social ladder.

His eldest son, Idris Evan, became what was called a sub-inspector of elementary schools in 1900, but died in 1904, aged just 36. The youngest son, Llewelyn Collwyn, was made secretary to the Technical and Intermediate Schools in Swansea in 1896, and was based at Mount Pleasant. He loved his work, at a time when this area of education was becoming accepted as a priority in society. He was described as *"bright, sociable, amiable"*. One Sunday, July 29th 1900, he went to chapel, and, in the afternoon, to Mumbles with friends. They ended up at Langland Bay, sunbathed and then went in the water. Collwyn was a strong swimmer, and when he cried for help in just four feet of water

Husband seated, wife standing. The quite amazing piece of furniture was in Chapman's studio in High Street. (See page 134)

Idris Lewis.

Collwyn Lewis.

Collwyn (standing right) with friends Mr. Treharne, Richard and Sidney Harris.

everyone thought he was joking. The inquest at the Osborne Hotel was told by his friend Stanley Mansel Jones that Collwyn was only in the tide for 4 minutes in all. By the time William Howells, who ran the refreshment hut on the beach, and Mr. Hemmings, a coal merchant who lived nearby, rushed into the sea, all they could drag out was a body. Dr. Arthur Lloyd Jones came down from his house at Rotherslade to examine the remains of a man he had known well. It must have been an awful blow to Evan, this loss of a much-loved son, who seemed to be rising to achievements he had been denied, but all we know is that he entered the occurrence, with all the other births, marriages and deaths, in his own "Family Register". Collwyn was buried at Danygraig.

The tragedy caused a great fuss. There were letters and even maps of the bay in the press, with Frank Tunbridge, the Swansea auctioneer who lived at Gorse Cottage, Caswell, and Roger Beck, who lived at "The Rhyddings", high above Langland, taking a leading part. A series of public meetings followed. It transpired that the Oystermouth Council was only bound to ensure "decency" on the beach; it seems they were actually prohibited from organising safety measures. There had been previous incidents. In August 1897 a lad was drowned, his death put down to a rotten lifebouy. Since then Roger Beck had provided a decent one, and a lifesaving boat manned by Henry Smith of Chapel Street in Mumbles. The boatman was not paid, just allowed to display a collection box, which had yielded 4 shillings when last opened. To boost this he used to give rides in the boat, which some said took him away from his real job! However, on the day in question, he was quite rightly enjoying his sole half holiday of the week — he went off duty at 12.00 and Collwyn drowned at 4.30. Interviewed, Henry Smith confessed himself puzzled by the tragedy, as the waves were high, but there were no currents. Roger Beck's recommendations for the future were that Henry be given "distinctive dress", the lifebelt be better placed, and that

"those who bathe should listen to him or Mr. Kift, and not be too wise in their own conceit".

Evan himself died in April 1928.

The superior residents of Ffynone

Opposite the Vicarage stood St. James's Church, and around it and behind it lived a lot of Swansea's richer citizens. This is an attempt to link some of them to their very desirable residences. St. James's Crescent is an even semi-circle behind the church, and we will start on the town side. It begins with a very substantial three storey block, built as semi-detatched houses, with ornamented ground floor bays and decorative plasterwork above **(1)**, (Edward Plant, Wolverhampton born solicitor.) Next is another pair of semis, big enough but plainer, faced with rather dull red brick, windows and quoins of stone **(2)**,

2·519

Spring

Old Quarry

244 + A

B.M.247·2

Rheanva

PENMAEN TERRACE

FAIRFIEL

M.268·7

265

17

248

L.B

ROSEHILL TERRACE

B.M.266·6

Ffynnonau

16

MONTPELLIER TERRACE

Lodge

Fn

270

Brooklands

18

BROOKLANDS TER

WOODLANDS T

Springfield

Hillside

15

14

13

6

19

20

21

ST. GEO

Devon Terrace

12

5

HANOVER STREET

11

9

L.B

Richmond Villas

4

3

BURMAN STREET

10

SQUARE

8

ST. JAMES'S

2

1

Chap. B.M.66

64

7

Belgrave Terrace

ST. JAMES'S CRESCENT

St. James's Church

R O A D 71

80·9

82

101

F.P.

BRUNSWICK ST.

CAW

120

111

B.M.110·4

W A L T E R'S

M.S

Swansea 1

P.

Vicarage

BURY STREET

E STREET

B.M.116·3

B.R.Y

Llwyn-y-bryn

97

L.B

The numbers on the map can be followed in the text.

St. James's Church before the trees had grown.

D.W. Johns.

probably **Barclay** or **Berkeley Villa** (John R. Johns, timber merchant, 1891.) Next comes a very large red brick house of notable eccentricity — the acute gables have ridiculously narrow slit windows, the balconets are of carved stone, and the chimneys are steepling **(3)**, probably **Charlton House** (Henry Hood, managing director, printing works). Mr. Plant came to Swansea in 1880 as partner to Richard White Beor. In 1899, Beor, Fry & Plant had offices at 11, Temple Street, between the Theatre Royal and the Glamorganshire Bank. In later years he is described as thickset with a pince nez and handlebar moustache. Mr. Johns was the son of David White Johns, a Quaker, who lived close by at 69 Walter Road. Father (58) and son (35) had become partners in a timber yard at Bathurst Street, by the South Dock, and a builders yard alongside the railway arches of Broadquay at the southern end of the Strand, where you could get tiles, bricks, cement, sewage pipes, *"chimney pieces"* and Welsh slate. They had a branch in Combe Martin.

Next is St. Winifred's Convent School, (Principle Margaret Corballis), — three gables, three lofty storeys — a very large brick building with ground at the side and back, stone walls and railings. At the lower end is the attractive entrance porch, set to the side of the frontage, a feature of every house in this run **(4)**.

Following the school wall takes you into the roadway called St. James's Gardens, straight and rising. The rectangular gardens themselves are opposite — they were formally transferred to the corporation by William Walters of Penlan House in February, 1897, and opened as a park in the June, after the council had spent £525 on laying them out. The first house is the charming **"Ty'r Nant"**, much smaller than many, its name carved unobtrusively halfway up the gatepost, its main feature a lovely curved bay, and unusual but restrained decorative brickwork **(5)**. In 1891, this was he home of Crawford Fulton (59), a Scottish wine and spirit dealer, (he died in 1905 and was buried at Oystermouth). The firm was Fulton

& Co., and in Cardiff, Fulton & Dunlop, the second a Bristol man, and it had existed since 1864. Their premises were at 59-60 Wind Street, nearly opposite Green Dragon Lane. They imported wines and spirits, dealt in Bass, Worthington and Allsop beers, Pilséner lager, Schweppes "aerated waters", Guiness stout, and much else, delivering all over the area. The business was still going in 1951. Mr. Fulton was one of nine brothers from Ayr; his brother Andrew had been mayor of Cardiff.

In melodramatic contrast to Ty'r Nant is the exceedingly tall, gaunt stone mansion which

Ty'r Nant (5).

PIC: NIGEL CLATWORTHY

Westbrook (6).

PIC: NIGEL CLATWORTHY

Northill (7).

follows, starkly impressive when approached uphill like this. The name is clear, again on the gatepost, **"Westbrook"**, home of Robert Leyshon, 45, a Neath born solicitor, with grounds and outbuildings right along to Bullin's Lane. **(6)**

Now back to the crescent at the Uplands end, and leaving aside the houses which front on to Walter Road, stroll up, past their walled yards to **"Northill"**, its name on a dingy metal plaque over the front door **(7)**. This is in the centre of an imposing frontage facing the road, but on the lower end of the house is a fine stone canopy, under which the family might sit at ease, facing down the long garden. In 1891, this meant Albert Mason (57), his daughter Florence and son Frederick.

By the way — Albert Mason

Albert Mason was born in Holm Lacy, Herefordshire. As a young man he was goods and shipping agent for the Great Western Railway in Cardiff, then Swansea. In 1875 he became the business partner of R.B. Powlesland, in a firm established in 1863......and though Powlesland died about 1885, it was the name "Powlesland and Mason" which remained familiar well into the twentieth century. The core of their work was a standing contract with the G.W.R. as sole agent in moving goods to and from the stations and freight depots in Swansea, Landore and Morriston, a huge responsibility in a thriving town. Beyond this, though, the firm advertised their readiness to "ware-house" and ship almost anything by road or rail, with furniture a big part of the trade. Their telephone numbers were 7 and 11! While they owned some railway locomotives used on the harbour lines, in these days before motor lorries, nearly everything was down to horses. The offices were in Great Western Chambers, Wind Street, (a very apt address, to go with their telegraph address, "Western"), but practical operations centred on premises in Clarence Terrace, described like this in 1895:

TELEGRAMS: "WESTERN."

POWLESLAND & MASON
GREAT WESTERN RAILWAY
FURNITURE REMOVED BY ROAD OR RAIL
POWLESLAND & MASON
RAILWAY & SHIPPING AGENTS CONTRACTORS
SWANSEA

TELEPHONIC Nos.

EXCHANGE. 7 and 11.

GREAT WESTERN CHAMBERS, SWANSEA.

PIC: SWANSEA REFERENCE LIBRARY

"...There is ample warehouse accommodation....and large sheds are provided for the shelter of enormous furniture vans, and carts of every size and description...Amongst the many appliances in the warehouses and yard for the safe and rapid handling of goods...may be noticed a weigh-bridge by Pooley...The stabling, which is contained in a roomy two storey building, comprises thirty-six stalls and a loose box; the haylofts, corn room and chopping room...being situated in

the storey above, whence the fodder is lowered by shafts. The chopping machine is driven by a powerful modern gas engine, and every appliance is at hand for the economising of labour. The firm has thirty five horses always employed, and the staff regularly engaged numbers from a hundred to a hundred and fifty, with the frequent temporary addition of extra hands when there is any great press of work...”

It looks as if Albert Mason kept the organisation of all this in his own hands, but he did more. He was chairman of Swansea United Breweries, formed in 1890 to amalgamate the Orange Street Brewery and the Glamorgan Brewery in Wassail Street. He was a councillor from 1882, alderman from 1889, and mayor in 1891-2. His mayoral year was described as *“the kindest heart-ed tyranny”*, centring in his mind on the Bath & West Show coming to town — there are things about him which suggest that in a world of religious earnestness and social climbing, he was easy going, at ease with life. John Aeron Thomas descibed him as *“amiable, kind, courteous...”* In a postal poll in 1894, readers of the South Wales Daily Post voted him “the most distinguished councillor” by quite some way — perhaps it was the beard! He became a Harbour Trustee, and vice chairman of the Trust on the retirement of George Burden Strick in 1893. At the town chamber of commerce in January 1890, he spoke out against

Albert Mason.

“the old and antiquated Town Dues [which] *had driven a large amount of the coasting trade...to Newport..”*

He was a Poor Law Guardian. A churchwarden at St. James's across the road, he was treasurer of the fund which presented the Vicar with his illuminated address in 1899, also passing over what was called “a purse of gold”. In 1893 he was vice president of the Swansea Regatta. He died on 30th April, 1900, of *“an acute internal malady”*, and was buried in sloping ground at the Norton end of Oystermouth Cemetery.

From Northill runs a terrace of 15 houses, **(8)** three more or less on the crescent, — these are older — the rest looking across the gardens. The corner house is double fronted, the next is a single, but all the rest are arranged in pairs. All are brickbuilt, with a plain top storey, an ornamental bay on the first floor, and highly decorative stonework at ground level. The front doors are panelled, some with attractive glass in the sidepanels of the doorway. The pathways are of a variety of tiles, and all the gateposts are fancy.

It is not hard to imagine the uniformed maids trundling betasselled perambulators to the park across the road, then sitting gossiping among the ornamental shrubs. Edward Plant, at the other end of the terrace, employed a resident governess, Hilda Mathews, to look after his children Mabel (11), Arthur (9) and Edmund Hubert (5). Here are some examples of the families at this end —

James Madge, 44, Ship Store Dealer and family. Madge, Symons & Company were ships provision merchants of 5/6 Broadquay, a large four storey warehouse with loading doors and hoists at the

lower end of the Strand. James Madge was commander of the Royal Naval Artillery Volunteers who latterly met in Cambrian Place, and disbanded in 1891. They were very active in the eighties, with Alexander Moffat as secretary. The business was in the hands of H.A. James by 1897 and Mr. Madge is afterwards described as a share broker, with offices above an ironmongery at 62 Wind Street.

Alfred Charles Jonas, 51, Colliery Owner and Merchant. In 1898 he wrote a long series of articles for "the Cambrian" on Gower history.

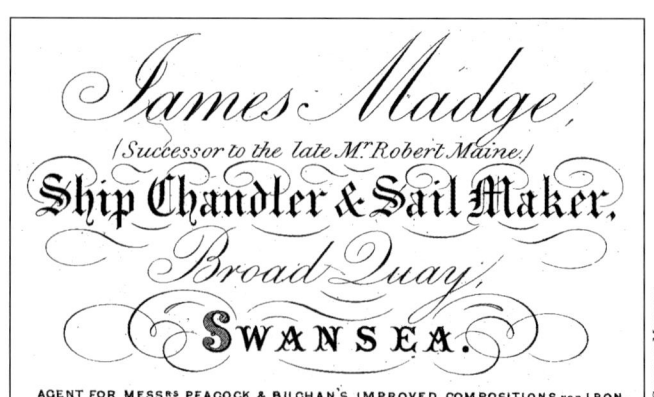

James Livingstone.

James Livingstone, 59, J.P. and Colliery Inspector (1831-1912) — this was numbered 5, and called "Eastville". A man of this name had been mayor in 1875-6. He then lived in Brynycoed, Mount Pleasant, and was a leading coal shipper, managing Livingstone, Richards and Beaumont, offices in Coleridge House. (Henry Beaumont lived at Rheanva in 1892.) James Livingstone's son Frank was master of Messrs. Simpson's barque "Janet Cowan", carrying coal and bricks, wrecked off Cape Horn in May 1890. She was a fine ship, but a gale took her rudder. The crew were lucky to reach the Falklands.

George Graham Sutherland, 57, Teacher of languages. This was number 6, St.Andrews College in 1889.

(These four houses, all leasehold, were auctioned at the Royal Hotel, High Street in May, 1892.)

Standing alone at the top of the terrace, on the corner of Ffynone Road, is **"The Hawthorns" (9)**. One look at the stained glass, the balustrading and particularly the purely stone frontage, tells you this is the most finely and lavishly decorated house of the lot. And the man of the house, William Usher is full of interest.

By the way — William Usher

A 36 year old widower in 1891, he had lived in "the Hawthorns" for at least two years with his 11 year old daughter, Ellen Mary, who was born in London. In 1890, he was one of the new men on the County Borough Council; the electorate was larger, the council had expanded to 40 members, and change was in the air. Councillor Usher from the Victoria Ward wanted to make sure it happened. In January he carried a proposal that rich men in rates arrears should have their names published, but failed over having evening council meetings which working men might attend and over awarding no contracts to firms who paid their men less than 3 shillings a day. He responded:

> *"I beg to move that the names may be taken...It may be useful at the next election...it is right for the working men to know how their representatives vote."*

He had to be restrained by his friends from fighting on this to the death. In February, he accused J.R. Davies, *"one of the oldest tradesmen in the town"* of overcharging the council for printing work. After an enquiry, he was proved largely right, though *"a cosy previously unquestioned arrangement"* would seem a better description than corruption.

In November he was at a union meeting at the Albert Hall convened to combat an employers' scheme for a "free labour union", and agreed specifically with the charge of

"shipowners praying for ships they had overinsured to founder"

Yet this angry radical lived in a large and exquisite house, and his profession.....? In an 1899 Directory he is listed quite simply as a money lender. His own front page advert in the "Cambria Daily Leader" 9th May, 1899 runs —

"William Usher and Co., 14 Picton Place
The Oldest Established Financiers and Bill
Discounters, £3 to £3,000 leant daily.
No Fees"

Probably interest though! (Picton Place was on the south side of Heathfield, just before it ran into St. Helens Road — the Blind Institute in South Hill Place

The Hawthorns (8).

PIC: NIGEL CLATWORTHY

was nearby.) It was a business which might lead to legal cases like that brought against him by David John Tribe of the Smithfield Arms, Dyfatty Street — near the slaughterhouse — in October, 1892. He claimed Mr. Usher had entered into a partnership with him in the hay and corn trade...Usher dismissed it as just a loan, but the court went against him.

MONEY. | | MONEY.

MONEY LENT

ON

PLATE, WATCHES, JEWELLERY,

Or any other available security,

At the rate of Fourpence in the £ per month. Ticket or Contract, One Penny, good for twelve months ; no other charges.

HENRY BARNETT.

6, HEATHFIELD STREET,

MONEY. | SWANSEA. | MONEY.

There were other money lenders. M.L. Marks *"the popular financier"* had preceeded him in the same premises — *"£3 to £500 advanced daily at very low rate...private back entrance..."* in Picton Lane. I.Seline was at 5 Grove Place, and the Swansea Advance Company was over William Challacombe the hairdresser's, at 13 Calvert Street, behind St. Mary's. And there were more unpleasantly modern concerns like the Swansea Assets Recovery Company at 16 Goat Street, opposite the police station, — *"...purchases debts from Tradesmen...who have not time to look after the collection of their troublesome debts..."*

Perhaps Mr. Usher's approach just moderated, but his radicalism could be wonderfully bold. At the Guildhall in August 1891 he spoke in favour of using the council's

"...159 acres of land at Town Hill...ripe for building purposes...[for]...artisans' dwellings...[each with]...a little bit of ground...In order to make the hill get-at-able, they could erect a tramline up Constitution Hill, a line running up from High Street near Waun Wen. The slums which abounded in the town would soon be forsaken when better houses were offered...Why not better the working man and make him a good and loyal citizen, by giving him a comfortable house, in which he could take an interest? ...they could erect houses with 6 rooms, a scullery, bath, with hot and cold water for £160...The interest on the £160, at 5 per cent, would be £8 and the ground rent £2/8/-..."

It was brave talk, to which, to be fair, most councillors responded favourably

Brynbriallu (11).

Devon Terrace (12).

Now turn left along the attractive cottage-style houses of Richmond Villas **(10)**, most with side-porches linking them to their neighbour. Inside were —

William Henry Mill, 49, retired Cornish jeweller

Thomas Randles, 64, bootmaker

Herbert Rake, 50, stockbroker

James Merry, 52, analytical chemist/assayer from Birmingham.

Edward Thomas Brooke, 52, from Bristol, "living on his own means"

Richard Eynon, brewer's manager from Pembrokeshire

Joseph Gregor, 53, timber importer, Cornwall

John Dyer, 59, from Braunton near Ilfracombe, with his wife Anne Marie. They gave a lot of money to Swansea Hospital, including £2,000 in 1904-6 for the Devon and Dorset Ward.

Set back, across the road, are Colonel Morgan's successive houses, Mirador and Brynbriallu. **(11)** Then, on the bank, is a little three storey row, approached from the road by a single, rather grand flight of steps between stone pillars inscribed "Devon" and "Terrace". **(12)** The residents?

Elizabeth Fry, 48, "own means", and her two sisters

George E. Bowen, 27, accountant

Richard Garnet Cawker, 59. chartered accountant, offices in Temple Street. In 1897 he was president of the Swansea Devonian Society. Other presiding Devonians mentioned in this book are R.D. Burnie, M.P. (1895), Henry Billings, builder (1898) and Charles Reed, Ben Evans's horse manager (1900). Their regalia is in the Glynn Vivian Art Gallery.

Edgar James Pritchard, 24, Bristol born, manager of oxalic acid works

...and Miss Vinter lived at number 3, from at least 1889, convenient as it was to the High School.

On this upper side of Ffynone Road, there follow three large stone houses, set in their own gardens — **Hillside (13)**, **Bryncerrig (14)** and **Springfield (15)**.

Hillside (13).

At **Hillside**, in 1891, lived William Stone, J.P., 64, and *"own means"* here probably means retired. He was a Somerset man, from Huish Champflower, coming to Swansea in 1868. He made his money as a timber merchant, with wharfage by the South Dock — in 1893 he held this in partnership with W.H. Forester, the iron merchant. In 1897 he was offering firewood *"cut into short lengths, at 7 shillings per load, delivered free"*.

He also became a director of John Taylor & Co., the high class grocers, of the Swansea Gas Company

and the Swansea Bath and Laundry Company. Mr. Stone is recorded at Hillside in, for example, 1889, 1892 and 1897.

At **Bryncerrig** was Morgan Tutton, shipowner and councillor (see
"Jubilee Swansea" I, page 44.) **Springfield** was the home of John
Thomas, solicitor, and Swansea's Town Clerk — he was a bachelor,
40 in 1891, living with his spinster sisters Ruth and Charlotte. In
1898, Dr. T.D. Griffiths of Druslyn House at the bottom of Mount
Pleasant called for *"better men in authority....a new Town Clerk, who
was the real manager of Corporation affairs"*, but this was a
renowned critic, who was anyway attacking the system, not the man.
The accounts of council meetings suggest he wielded considerable
influence, and earned respect from the members. H.A. Chapman
paid tribute to his *"ability and energy"* at the end of his mayoral year
in 1893. The mayor's fire was nicely balanced by the official's regard
for legality and orderly conduct of business. In 1893 he had nearly
all the councillors on his side in an open quarrel with Viner Leeder
over the "taxing" (formal checking) of a legal bill. He seems to have
had little sympathy with the representatives of labour. When asked
about a reported letter from the Trades Council, he replied, amid
laughter —

"I have not seen one. I will look in the basket"

(Marcus Moxham, the timber merchant, had been at Springfield in
1865.)

In far wider grounds beyond these were **Ffynone** (or Ffynnonau),
Rheanva (or Rhianfa) and **Brooklands. (16, 17 and 18)**. In
Ffynone was the Lindley family, only the children being listed on the
census — Frances, Eugene and Emma, 6, 4 and 2, all German born.
There was an R.S. Lindley lodge of Oddfellows at St. Jude's schoolroom, Terrace Road. Robert Searles Lindley, C.E., F.R.G.S., was the
engineer who ran the Morfa Works for Williams Foster and
Company until 1897, and it may well be significant that the firm had
a German parent company, Frankfurt Metalgessellschaft from 1888.
"The Cambrian" for October 1892 describes how a deputation *"waited upon him"* at his house, and prevailed upon him to stand for the
Ffynone ward. He was elected. In a council meeting in October 1893
he spoke strongly in favour of technical education —

> *"...when a young man he was greatly struck by England's posi-
> tion in the world. But as he grew older things changed. England
> sat down, satisfied with what she had attained...Zurich had one
> of the finest technical schools, and there were excellent metal-
> lurgical schools in Germany...*[he spoke of being in Warsaw and
> Russia]*...The Germans were coming up very rapidly...would
> soon leave them behind in the race. Why were there so many
> Germans in Swansea and district, holding responsible positions
> at the various works? It was because they were scientifically
> superior..."*

By 1899, he was still a local J.P., but his address was Godstone,
Surrey.

W.H. Stone.

John Thomas.

J.C. Woods of Rhianfa (see overleaf).

PIC: WEST GLAMORGAN ARCHIVES

(Ffynone had been built in the early 19th Century by the Jeffreys family, passed to the Walters from about 1840, from whom Lindley bought it in about 1888. In 1897, William Walters of Walters & Nash, provision merchants, bought it back, and lived there until his death in 1911.)

In 1889, Miss Davies lived at **Rheanva**, and later it was J.C.Woods. James Chapman Woods, solicitor and poet is listed there in 1899, and his tree-shaded, overgrown grave at Oystermouth (1933, aged 73) is engraved *"of Rhianfa"*. His first wife was Jessie Louisa, 1/8/1855-26/12/1895, and his second, Mary, was a novelist.

At **Brooklands** lived James Jones.

By the way — James Jones, grocer

Brooklands was built between 1859 and 1863 on a plot of more than two acres between Rhianfa Lane — originally the driveway of the house of that name, — and what became Rosehill Road. It belonged to Evan Matthew Richards and his family, until it was bought by James Jones in 1880. He was born at Cefn Llwyd farm, Llanbadarn Fawr, near Aberystwyth in 1837, and after a very basic education was apprenticed to a local grocer. He came to Swansea in 1856. His firm employed a traveller in Carmarthenshire, and James made a great success of this over 13 years, with his knowledge of farming, the country and especially of the Welsh language. In 1867, he opened James Jones & Co. in Goat Street, and by daring speculation in large scale buying, of flour for example, made *"a pile of money"*. He was a wholesaler, and in 1893 held stocks of:

> *"...tea and provisions, spices, arrowroot, almonds, farinaceous foods, rice, oatmeal, peas, barley, hominy, beans, various kinds of seeds, patent goods of every description, biscuits, liquorice paste, confectioery, canned meats and fruits, dessert fruits, oils, extract of meat, sauces, pickles, cocoa, isinglas, and gelatine, all kinds of paper for wrapping purposes, twines, and an extensive variety of household sundries.."*

He invested in tinplate works, becoming chairman of Glanamman Tinplate, joint owner of Dynevor Tinplate at Pantyffynon and a big shareholder in the Clayton works at Pontardulais. He was a pioneer of the idea of shipping tinplate out to the States and food products back. He put money into the Rhondda & Swansea Bay Railway in the eighties, and into Weavers Flour Mill in the nineties. These later interests were partly to do with pride in his adopted town, where he was a J.P., councillor (from 1880), alderman, mayor (1888-9) and harbour trustee. At a meeting in September 1890 he made the comment that

> *"...though he liked Englishmen well enough, he thought it would be well for the commerce of the country* [Wales] *if they stayed at home..."*

This was a West Walian talking in a town which, in all classes of society, was a melting pot of incomers, very many of them English. Good humoured fun was made of these words for many a long day!

He was an enthusiastic leader of the Oddfellow Movement, raising the very successful James Jones lodge. One man remembered being a member of the Manchester Unity Lodge invited to Brooklands on 16th June, 1898, and being lucky enough to be one of the 15 invited quietly into the house from the throng on the lawn —

> *"James Jones was in his best story telling form, rich and rare..."*

A lodge meeting outside Brooklands, (18), about 1893.

He put a lot of time and energy into friendly societies, acting as secretary of lodge after lodge. When the Annual Moveable Committee of the Manchester Unity visited town in 1895, he chaired the organising committee, and used the occasion to open the Friendly Society Hall he had funded in Cwmbwrla. His last big interest was getting a university college for Swansea, promising to donate £1,000. The college went to Cardiff, but he was elected a member of the university council, and it was fitting in a way that he should have to travel to Aberystwyth, whence he came, to take his place. He was high sheriff of Cardiganshire, and, as such, attended the Queen on her visit to Bristol on 15th November, 1899. He died on the train between Cardiff and Swansea on his way home the following day. He was 62. In May 1896, his friends had presented him with a portrait in memory of his 40 years services to the town — he afterwards gave it to the council.

As mayor, 1888-9.

Across the road from his front wall stood **Cilwendig, Llwynhelig** and **Ashleigh (19, 20 & 21)** the homes of William Thomas, David Jenkins and William Watkins and respectively. Like massive triplets, these vast stone houses were more imposing than stylish, symbols of the success of "the Firm", Thomas, Watkins and Jenkins. They were all Swansea men, all 58 in 1891. (For a great deal more on "the Firm", see page 44-45.) Ashleigh was bombed during World War II, and is now the site of the synagogue.

The subtle class differences in this part of Swansea show up in the ratable values of the houses. For what one ratepayer called *"his baronial property"*, Brooklands, James Jones was rated at £170. Walter Road houses were in the £35-£60 bracket, Henrietta Street, still considered middle class was £15 to £22, Hanover Street on the slightly less favoured side of Walter Road down to £16 to £20.

Pic: Nigel Clatworthy

Llwynhelig (20).

Pic: Nigel Clatworthy

Cilwendig (19).

Pic: West Glamorgan Archives

Like many Victorian suburban views, this area has been transformed by the trees they planted.
Today many of the houses have a gaunt, damp aspect as a result.
From left to right, you could then see Bryncerrig, Springfield, Westbrook and Ty'r Nant across the gardens.

The quite superior folk of Walter Road

The Scientific Society's trips seem to have terminated in Walter Road, which made plenty of sense, as so many of the members lived there. When Mansel Street and Walter Road were laid out in the 1850s, they ran through open fields, backed by a fairly empty hillside. At the town end was an unplanned, untidy set of buildings which already existed, but much of Mansel Street beyond this was developed in a much more deliberate way. On the lower side were mainly two storey houses, with some nice features, but not pretentious. Opposite, though, began the much taller three storey cellared town houses, front doors at the top of a flight of steps, railings, stone nameplates set in the walls, like "Parnham" (78) and "Elmsleigh" (79), still to be seen, opposite the top of Christina Street. Either side of Verandah Street, were homogeneous terraces of residences like these. So where Walter Road began (and Mansel Street ended) at the junctions with Page Street and Calvert Terrace, it was just a case of the building style continuing to change gradually, though undoubtedly becoming grander the further west you went.

This is especially true of the Mount Pleasant side, where the fine terraces were broken only by two chapels — Walter Road Congregational and the Baptist Memorial Chapel — and by two adjoining licenced premises, the Tenby Hotel and the White Rose. Numbers 137 to 143 were three storey, some

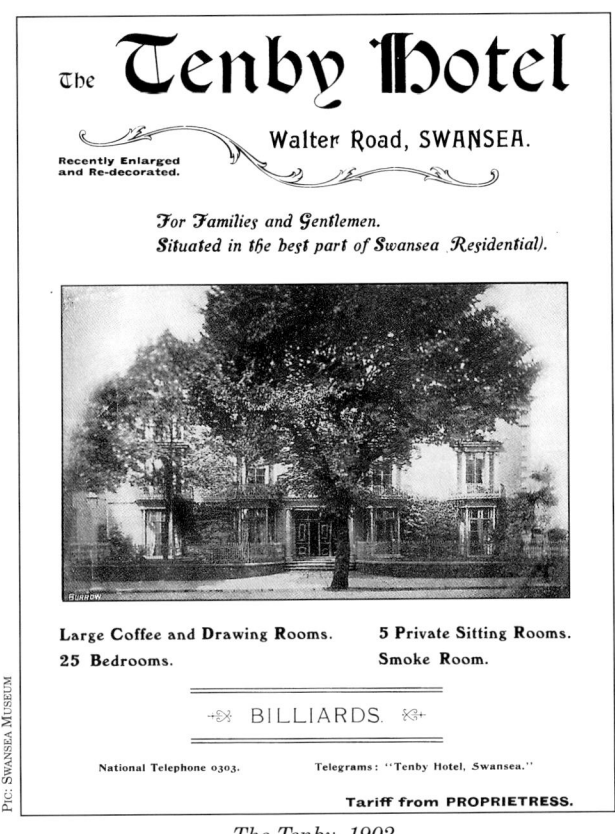

PIC: SWANSEA MUSEUM

The Tenby, 1902.

PIC: NIGEL CLATWORTHY

Imagine the proud householders, and the maids,
a hundred years ago.

with arched windows. Between Burman Street and Humphrey Street was a run (106 to 126), evidently built as a single terrace. There is uniformity in the wooden ground floor bays and doorways, in the decorative plasterwork of the top two floors and in the slate roofs....but planned variety in the styles of the little top floor windows. 106 on the corner was the only double-fronted house. Another similar row followed, — with the Frickers at 100 notable for their contribution to Swansea's musical life — but between Bullins Lane and St. James's the extravagance of the stonework and plasterwork decoration goes up several gears — numbers 92 to 96 were basically the same sort of house, but with a facade which could hardly be more elaborate. 96 to 94 are sometimes described as Granville Villas, 93 to 90 as Southville Villas. This second name is a little puzzling, as the terrace running from the Uplands side of St. James's Crescent also has a claim to the name "Southville" — on the corner today is Southville Garage, and Alexander Moffat is said to have lived in this row, even though his address was 92 Walter Road. Has the numbering changed, or was Southville both sides of St. James's? Lewis Lewis the draper lived at "Southville", possibly the house on the corner of the upper junction with the crescent, with yard and outbuildings all the way up to Northill. The residents around here were a distinguished lot in 1891 —

The tower of 77-78 Walter Road is between the trees (1902).

PIC: NIGEL CLATWORTHY

Granville Villas / Southville Villas — the crescent
starts on the left.

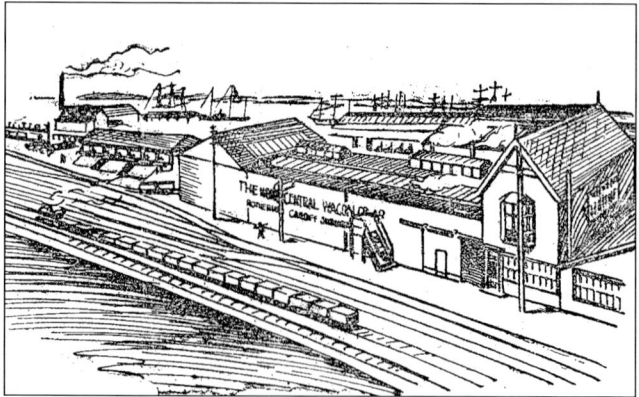

Mr. Burnie's waggon works, 10 years later, with a rival concern near the Prince of Wales Dock.

R.J.D. Burnie.

H.W. Crowhurst, joint managing director with F. d'Oyley Mears of the Swansea United Breweries (89 — he called it Buckton Villa), H.S. Ludlow, secretary of the Rhondda & Swansea Bay Railway (90) and Edward Oakden, postmaster (91) — he retired in October 1892, having worked 25 years in Swansea.

The lower side of the street was more broken up by junctions with streets of smaller houses, middle class still, but less well to do. Let's move back towards town. From the Girls High School (Llwynybryn), there was first a row of five very large semis, the last (68/9) with that very conscious decoration of the late nineteenth century, notably very fancy tiles hung on the gable and frontage. 78/77 has a tower in imitation of Mirador and Hillside, a style copied from the Queen's house Osborne on the Isle of Wight — "Mirador" is Spanish for lookout. David Mansel Glasbrook, the coal and tinplate owner, lived for a while at 80 or 81 (he called it "Pendre") and Richard Letcher, secretary of the Glamorganshire Bank in Temple Street, was at 74. Robert John Dixon Burnie, his wife Georgina Thirlestone, 4 sons and a daughter lived at 71. Born in Dawlish, of Scottish descent, he was managing director of the Swansea Wagon Works on Crymlyn Burrows, and M.P. for Swansea Town, 1892-5. He was quite radical, addressing striking dockers at the Vetch Field in 1892, and calling the Boer War, 7 years later, *"imperialist claptrap"*. Next door was James Owen, minister of the Baptist chapel on the opposite side. David White Johns and his family were at 69 — he was the timber merchant. From there, a terrace ran to Westbury Street, house names carved on the gate pillars — 66 was Blairmont House. Stephen Sanders Mock, who worked for Richardson & Co., ore merchants, was at 64. A very large semi on the opposite corner was probably Westbury House, like others here set on quite a sloping

A Williams gatepost at number 46.

J.Moy Evans, see next page, as artist.

plot, the land slipping away at the rear. Between this and Russell Street were two terraces, 58 to 52, and 49 to 32, with a pair of semis wedged in between these two rows. The second run have acute pointed gables, some with finials. Number 48 (only) has a superbly enlarged and decorated top storey. Metal gateposts were the norm along here, some stamped "T.W. Williams, Wellington Foundry, 1871", a concern still active in the nineties. (Thomas Williams himself was a Calvinistic Methodist, for years superintendent of the Sunday school at Bethany in the Strand. He died in August 1900. The foundry was in Greenfield Street, later moving out to Dunvant. The company name can be seen on drain covers and the doors to coal cellars, with dates from the 1870s to the 1920s). Thomas Charles, a cycle shop manager for J.S. Brown was at 47, Robert Nash of wholesale grocers Walters & Nash at 40, J. Moy Evans, solicitor, lived at 38, Bernard Morgan, projectionist to the Scientific Society, his wife Charlotte, 2 daughters, an aunt and a servant at 35 — all in 1891.

31 on the Russell Street corner was probably built as a shop, and the St. George across the road, as a public house, too. As far as Henrietta Street there was first another terrace (29-25), — very solid, rather grand, big red and yellow brick chimney stacks — then a single building (24-22), attractive with metal balconets. After that Walter Road lost its grandeur. The next two terraces were still of three storeys, but much plainer, and beyond Nicholl Street the houses had two floors. Even so, at number 18 in 1891 lived William Harris, 68, and his son, also William, 37. In nearby Russell Street was John T. Harris. They are all described as *"marine engine builders"* and *"shipbuilders"*. The old man died in December, 1895, the last of the original Harris Brothers who opened the Cambrian Dry Docks in about 1865. Their two docks and gridiron were on the river, between the South Dock and the Guildhall. John T. was the son of William senior's brother, John. He was chairman of the Swansea Ship Repairers in 1897, and we have already met his brother, William Edwin, as secretary to the Constitution Hill Tramway.

Two others you might have met in this area were Alex Moffat and William Terrill.

Alexander Moffat came to the fore in the Scientific Society and the Royal Institution in the mid-nineties. At that time, he worked for T.P. Richards & Co., as office manager. The firm owned 21 vessels, sail and steam, in 1895. (Thomas Picton Richards lived at "Maes Yr Haf" between Uplands and Sketty.) With W.H. Towers, Charles Watson of the Albion Dry Dock, F.C.T. Naylor, R.L. Sails, John Dixon and George Lennard, Moffat sponsored North Country Reunions at the old Mackworth Arms in Wind Street — the actual term "Geordie" was used. Moffat must have worked up north because his birthplace was Meath in Northern Ireland. His hobbies were yachting — in

Moffat in 1919.

The young Moffat (1895).

His boss, T.P. Richards.

He became a very keen motorist.
His first (?) car, about 1905.

September 1890 he took delivery of "Trixie-wee" a 32 foot boat, built to his own design — and a passion for all things Viking. He was very wholehearted in his enthusiasms. In his opinion the Norsemen had a huge influence on South Wales. At the end of the museum copy of the Scientific Society's Journal for 1895-6 which has an article by E.M. Roberts claiming Swansea was of Celtic origin is a characteristically diffident comment in pencil by Moffat — *"Nonsense. A.G.M."* He was 35 in 1890, living at 38 Walter Road, just down from Westbury Street, with his wife, Jessie Florence, who was 11 years his junior. By 1899, they had moved across to 92, on the corner of St. James's Crescent, probably the finest house in the most decorative terrace on the north side of the street.

William Terrill F.C.S., was a Cornishman who came to Swansea in about 1869 when he was 24. He had studied under Thomas Huxley. He lived in Hanover Street, then 42, St.George's Terrace, Walter Road. A founder member of the Geological Society, he gave four papers in the first two years, and became secretary. From 1886 he put more energy into the Swansea Sketching Club, of which he was chairman or secretary for about 15 years — a photo of one of their excursions, to Oxwich in July 1890, shows a heavily moustached and bowler hatted man, clutching a pipe in one hand and a camera tripod with the other. In the 1894 exhibition he showed *"Snap shots taken with hand camera"*. He was an assayer of metals, and his paintings included views of works at Landore and Red Jacket. He ran classes for 11 to 21 year olds in inorganic and practical chemistry at the Royal Institution (in which he was also most active) in 1890, and again at Martin Street Schools in Morriston in 1891 — he worked with Bertie Terrill (1889, 16, Westbury Street) and Cosmo Johns. He died in 1901, when only in his early fifties, after a long illness, perhaps cancer. Serious, knowledgeable and energetic, he was said to be

"...a humble man...too sincere to be popular, too intellectual to be appreciated, except by a few..."

Walter Road in winter, looking west, with both chapels in view, and the clutch of shops near its eastern end — George Marquis, house decorator (6), William Abraham, butcher (8), Seymour Arthurs, grocer (9), J.T. Davies, chemist (13).

Horses, carriages, carts

When a cycle factory was set up in the Strand in 1897, it was predicted that:

"A special feature will be the construction of motor cars for which there is believed to be a bright future".

In March 1899, the Swansea Motor Company began a service between Wind Street and Sketty, via St.Helens, Brynmill and Uplands. It owned three *"motor cars"*. Before the end of that year, they also ran east to St. Thomas and Port Tennant. When in July building land was advertised on the hill above Parcwern and Singleton by the Coedsaeson Estate Company, Eversley Road, they could say *"Motor Cars pass the corner of the estate".*

But road transport in the nineties was really to do with horses. The street trams were horse-drawn until 1899 and competed for space with all sorts of carts and carriages. A great deal of shunting in marshalling yards at Paxton Street or Hafod, or in the sidings which served every large works, was by horses. Industrial tramways, generally just meaning a horse and cart on rails, were still very much in use — Phillip Richard had permission to lay a new one at his Worcester Pit, Fforestfach in 1893. Two or three horses used to pull the carts piled with tinplates from the Cwmfelin Works down Cwm Road,

The banner reads *"Success to our Carnival".*

between the cottages and the Bwrlais Brook, towards the docks. The police were often on horseback, and a horsedrawn van went round all the police stations each morning to collect prisoners.

Horses were celebrated by the annual Tradesmen's May Show and Parade. In 1892, the vice presidents were Col. Morgan, Ben Evans and Captain Isaac Colquhoun, Inspector of the Swansea police. The 300 *"turn outs"* were judged in Eaton and St. James's Crescents, before processing down Walter Road, Mansel Street, Delabeche and Alexandra Road to High Street, Wind Street and Oxford Street. The creak and rumble of wagons, superbly painted, and the stamp and whinny of the great horses, each groomed to perfection, must have been quite a sight in the tree-lined Uplands or clattering through town, even in an age more familiar with such things. The horse drawn fire engine took part, the brigade in uniforms supplied by Phillip Jenkins of Castle Square. (The men were police constables, specially trained. The horses were always hired from Bullins, whose business is described below.) They all dispersed in Phillips Parade, behind the hospital. There were 14 classes, and winners that year included H.W. Leaker the milkman driving his own cart, (Woodland Dairy, Sketty — *"New milk and cream delivered to all parts*

This is post 1912, because the brigade is clattering out of the police station in Alexandra Road, which was built in that year. The first steampowered fire engine locally was tried out in the Guildhall yard in 1892.

of the Town Twice Daily. A Special cow for Infants and Invalids"), T.A. Turtle of Pugsleys, and S. Eaton of John Taylor & Co., grocers. In the first two classes, the full results were as follows, names of the drivers being given first:

Class 1 —Brewers, contractors and merchants
1. Tom Arnold, Powlesland & Mason
2. W. Wedlake, Allsop & Son
3. D. Ladd, Vivian & Son

Class 2 — Corn, flour & potato merchants
1. Frank Joslin, C. Allen & Co.
2. J. Newcombe, John Dyer
3. T. Mullings, John Dyer

By the way — *Corn, flour and produce merchants...and the villagers of Braunton*

Michael John Michael, mayor in 1848, was a member of a family said to be the oldest flour merchants in town — there is a record of him taking a consignment from Leghorn in 1835. As late as the nineties, his son James had offices at 3/4 St. Mary Street and held the lease of two thirds of the warehouses around the Beaufort Basin, off the North Dock. In 1892, though, these premises were taken over by Weaver & Company, who quickly became the Ben Evans of milling. There were others. Straddling the railway at the end of Squire's Quay were the warehouses of E.J. Turner and Thomas Price, a single limited company by 1893. They also ran the North Dock Food Mills on the opposite side of the Strand, backing on to the Unitarian chapel in High Street. Their advertising copy would not suit modern sensibilities —

"...a beautifully prepared food for infants, which is equally adapted for invalids...various foods for horses, poultry, pigs, cows, etc...[and they boasted their]...process of rapid grinding...will probably replace the present antiquated system...dispensing with needless labour..."

John Dyer had the look of a jovial countryman. He was 59 in 1891 and had run a Swansea business since 1859. One Dyer mill and warehouse reached from Squire's Quay to Padley's Yard, and his second faced south, fronting on to Broadquay, a building later known as the Lion Stores, with its carved stone lion on the top. His birthplace was **Braunton** near Ilfracombe. A remarkable number of Swansea folk had been born in that same village, for example:

John Dyer.

Pascal Wedlake, coal merchant, 5 Dillwyn Street.
John Mock, haulier, 13, Singleton Street.
Benjamin Coopsey, labourer, 24 Singleton Street.
George Keift, police sergeant, 24 Wind Street
Elizabeth Coates, milk vendor's wife, 4 Wassail Street.
Richard Reed, master printer, 27 Orange Street.
John Harris, labourer, 21 Wellington Street.
Samuel Tucker, coal trimmer and Rosa Darracott, servant, both at 9 Cambrian Place.
Thomas Slee, labourer, 78 the Strand.
George Beer, coal haulier, the Strand.

It must have been the prosperity of the town across the channel, and the very long established trading links which were responsible. People and news travelled readily across this stretch of sea.

PIC: SWANSEA MUSEUM

Charles Allen.

Charles Allen lived in Courtenay Street, and later Montpellier Terrace, and had premises in Padley's Yard, off the Strand. His firm was started in about 1883, and boasted of stocking *"almost every variety of potato"*. In May, 1899, they advertised the arrival of the steamer "Viking" from Portaferry on Strangford Lough, County Down —

"Potatoes, potatoes, onions...now discharging..." Also in stock were Palermo lemons, Egyptian onions and *"milky cokernuts"*. In November 1899, the "Diadem" arrived with potatoes and onions from France.

Padley's Yard was Swansea's minature, but quite as intensive, version of Covent Garden. William Rew, potato merchant was at 130 the Strand, at its junction with the yard. Thomas Day (hay and corn) and Leys the potato merchants were there. The oldest business was probably Joseph Buller, dealing in *"bran, pollards, barley-meal, potatoes and...*(a very old trade indeed)*...salt"*. Thomas Harrison was also based in Padley's Yard. Born in Westmoreland, he set up in Swansea in about 1873, living also in Montpellier Terrace by 1891. He boasted potatoes from England, Ireland and France, parsnips and carrots, and fruit from the orchards of France — apples, pears, plums and cherries. All these concerns were produce importers, rushing unrefrigerated perishables out to the shops as fast as the horse drawn wagons could take them. There was some small scale trade. In 1891 the ketch "Heather Bell" arrived with a cargo of potatoes from Ramsey, Isle of Man. Other enterprises were more far reaching. In 1893, the steamer "Gypsy", 81 tons, of Aberdeen, started to bring in strawberries, eggs and butter from Lorient, Douarnenez and Brest in Brittany —

"...the steamer comes in [to the river, probably] *on any tide. Cargo is discharged on Mondays, goes straight into railway waggons, and is in London, Manchester, etc by 5 a.m..."*

PIC: SWANSEA MUSEUM

This warehouse was probably on the upper Strand. Notice the tiny figures to make it look bigger.

James Strick and Son were wholesale fruit and vegetable merchants. The family came from Cornwall. By about 1900 their old premises in Pont y Glasdwr Street, Greenhill, were rebuilt. (The small building with a chimney is in the older view at the bottom and the newer at the top.)

So there was pride in horses. They might have names. John Brader's black horse which presumably delivered wagonloads of pianos, organs, concertinas, violins, mandolines, melodeons and guitars from the Wind Street shop was "Bob". Charlie Allen's bey mare was "Tottie". But they were also a business asset which might be over-exploited. The West Glamorgan branch of the R.S.P.C.A. met in Swansea, the committee of 28, prominent citizens to a man. In 1886 the sole inspector, Mr. M. Hamar, obtained 31 convictions for *"working horses in an unfit state"*, and sent *"written monitions"* to another 21 owners for this. It was easily his

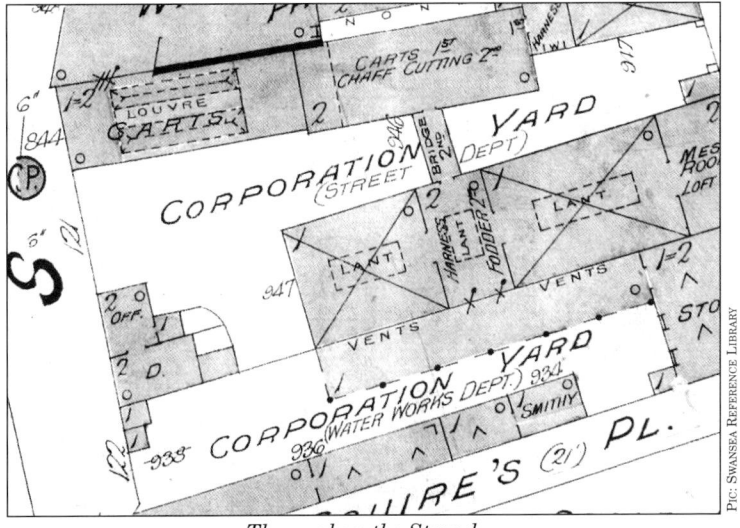

The yard on the Strand.

biggest problem. Even corporation horses, based in the yards on the Strand and on Cambrian Place, and used in road repair, *"scavenging"* and the removal of *"night soil"*, were said to be killed sometimes just by the excessive weights they were expected to pull. They drew waggons and *"tip carts"*, and on 9th May 1895 the Strand operation alone involved 38 drivers, 29 carriers, 13 sweepers, 2 tippers, 2 orderlies, 2 stablemen and 3 night soil men. 32 horses at the depot were supplemented by others hired in at need. They cost 12 shillings and tuppence per horse per week to feed. Huge stocks were held. In April consumption had included 402 bushels of oats, 60 of maize, 42 of beans as well as bran, peas, barley, linseed and much else. Horses cost £39 to £56 to buy, and they too were named —

"Tinker, Farmer, Virgin, Bowler, Judy, Champion, Punch, Traveller, Darby, Blossom, Drummer, Smiler, Merriman, Duke, Best and Dolly."

Census descriptions suggest pictures. John Holding of 117 the Strand (a shop on the corner of Baker Street) was a *"van boy"*, perhaps hanging perilously from the back between deliveries. The Clarence Street Laundry said *"vans collect daily"* — their *"carman"* David Gwynne lived on the premises, or very nearby. W.H. Palmer, baker of 34 New Oxford Street declared *"Best Home Made Bread delivered Daily by Van."* William Peters's Wellington Street Bakery, by the gasworks, made the same offer. Downs the furnishers of High Street/Morris Lane had a fleet of vans. There are van drivers, and John Rumbleton of Princes Street is another *"carman"*; a Rodney Street man is a *"carman (fish)"*. These must be horse vans too. (The word was about to change its meaning, but Caer Street was a name which may have derived from the cars delivering to the old market in Castle Square, and Simon Llewelyn's fine carriage on the Oystermouth Railway in 1817 was also a *"carr"*.) The census ennumerators favoured the word *"haulier"* and applied it to concerns big enough to get the haulage contract for the port, (Westlakes, Rowlands) and to single person businesses and employees — William Dodds of 21 Goat Street or David Lloyd, a Gower man living at 6, Anchor Court, behind the Cornish Mount in the Strand. At the rear of the houses which lined the east side of York Street were four courts — Bennet's, Dewsbury, York and Rosser's. These were terraces of tiny houses built behind the fair-sized dwellings facing the road, six being built back to back. York Court seems the poorest, with its sprinkling of washerwomen, dressmakers, laundresses and charwomen, though there are "respectable" occupations in each — a shipping clerk, an electrician and even William Burnett, pilot. In or near Rosser's Court, very well within range of the smells from Hancock's Brewery in Little Wind Street, were Jesse Sims, William Price, Francis Williams and Frederick Ford, all brewer's draymen. You could also drive a railway dray, like John Edwards of Picton Place, be a *"railway town porter"* like Alfred James of Ivey Place — just opposite his work at High Street Station — or a grocer's porter like William Shipland of Worcester Cottages, Welcome Street, — though perhaps these last two pushed hand carts, or just carried, for the well to do. George Taylor of 4, Gam Street and William Taylor of 9 Waterloo Street were both Gower born hauliers, and are likely from the family which owned Taylor's horse buses. These ran from Delvid Farm, Llangenith from 1896 on, the first being a converted farm wagon which carried people and produce. For the Taylors stabled their horses at the Oxford Inn (at 3/6 a week), then sold on produce on behalf of busy farmers, and bought babies' feeding bottles, stockings and much else for their families — all part of the service! By 1899 there were also services to Pilton, Port Eynon, Overton, Oxwich and Llanmadoc. An "omnibus" (meaning "for all") took any passenger. The Tramway Company ran buses from St. Helens to link with Midland and Rhondda & Swansea Bay trains at their stations in St. Thomas. The distinction seems to have been between this and a hired carriage. In 1899 'buses ran from Goat Street and Temple Street to Sketty and Port Tennant. (The raised comma — as in 'bus- was still often used, and Michael Gorman of 2 Wassail Square in 1891 is described as a *"buss driver"*.) Colonel Pike's conveyances met all trains at High Street, and omnibuses from the Castle Hotel in Wind Street met *"all trains"*. One of the colonel's drivers was remembered as a Mr. Gorman, licensee of the Crown and Anchor in the Strand — perhaps this is Michael again, and the suggestion must be that his wife ran the pub. In March 1897, Charles Ford, driver of the Sketty bus, was fined £1 for carrying 17 passengers in a bus designed for 13...which gives an idea how small a horse bus might be. Cabs were smaller. By 1900, the uniform rate for hire was 1/- up to a mile, and sixpence for each half mile beyond that, plus 2/- an hour and sixpence for each quarter of an hour longer. Rules were also laid down for extra passengers, and there were supplements for any journeys north of the Alexandra Road, Mansel Street, Walters Road line, — though much more carefully defined! No driver would relish Clifton or Constitution Hill or Rosehill. There was a permanent inspector of hackney carriages — James Gill in 1899. In 1892 there were 64 cabs in town, which, in May, were arrayed in front of the councillors in the Guildhall Yard. Edward Leaker, a Somerset man living at 6 Francis Street, near Victoria Park, was one of the cab proprietors. So was Thomas Pugsley, Barnstaple born, at 8 Caswell Street. Two new stands were established at Dillwyn Street and Portland Street in 1892. Mr. E. Jarrett of Gwydr Mews and Windsor Street, Uplands called himself a *"cab proprietor"*, but his *"wagonettes, landaus, etc, always in readiness"* make him sound like a smaller version of one of the larger firms described below.

There were traffic offences. William Palmer was fined ten shillings for *"furiously driving"* in Castle Street in 1890. Henry Thomas parted with 15/- for driving without lights at Sketty in 1896. And there were accidents. In January 1890, Councillor W.H. Davies was riding home to Morriston when his horse slipped near Bowen's siding, *"just above the Hafod"* — he was thrown and cut his head. That same month, a runaway horse pulled a hansom cab down College Street. P.C. Bennet tried to grab the reins, but ended up being dragged along. The driver was thrown through the window of the Welcome Coffee Tavern at the top of Welcome Lane, *"...on to the counter from which refreshments were served..."* and Frederick Thomas, 13 year old son of a paperhanger from nearby Gower Street was killed. In March 1890 *"a car"* belonging to Mr. Russell, confectioner, dashed out of control out of Henrietta Street and around the Tenby in Walter Road where it *"capsized completely"*. The horses had taken fright. The occupants were only shaken. In January 1895, John Beynon, a brewery drayman, hit a telegraph pole on Neath Road, was thrown out, and then crushed against the pole by another dray. He left a widow and six children. In April 1893, Thomas Glasbrook, the colliery owner, was killed when his horse threw him on to the track of the Mumbles Railway near the bottom of Sketty Lane — he was 47. He lived at Norton House with his sister Margaret and younger brothers John, Isaac and Sidney, making up Glasbrook Brothers, the leading mining firm in town. He had left his horse at Col. Pike's livery stables while in town. It was said to be *"rather restive"*, but on the other hand the eldest Glasbrook knew horses — he had been *"hunting all winter"*. The accident happened while he was *"fixing his gloves"*, and the horse ran off wildly, leaving him bleeding profusely. ...In November 1890, George Thurogood, manager of Col. Pike's Mews in George Street, gave his employer some very bad publicity. His horse shied, bolted, threw him out, and hurtled off down St. Helens Road and Northampton Place, with his trap, being eventually stopped in Gower Street, possibly by men from the nearby Bullin's stables. The Colonel ran what were called *"livery and posting stables"*, largely in Rutland Street, and his competitors were the Bullins and the Rossers. The Swansea Scientific Society favoured each firm at varying times. In June 1889 a party of 59 needed *"a four horse diligence, a three horse coach and a break"*. In 1894 their trip to Parc le Breos was in, to vary the spelling, *"four well-horsed brakes"*. In August 1895, Colonel Pike sent *"two well equipped brakes"* to Calvert Street at 8.30 for the St. Mary's choir outing (45 strong) to Crawley Woods and Port Eynon.

Bullins and more Rossers

In Bullins Mews behind St. James's Crescent lived the family whose name it had taken. Thomas (42) and Mary (35) Bullin had four children, all Swansea born. He called himself *"cabmaster and cab inspector"*. The firm was called Ll. & T. Bullin after the brothers Llewelyn and Thomas who founded it in about 1850, and a publication of 1893 sums up the business like this:

> *"The premises in Heathfield Street...comprise a long range of excellent stables and loose boxes, coach and carriage houses, a large covered yard, haylofts, , harness rooms, a well appointed office...The firm have a very fine stud of good, sound and reliable horses, suitable for riding and driving, ladies' hacks, hunters and ponies. The 'rolling stock' consists of a large number of open and close carriages, hansom and other cabs, phaetons, breaks, dog carts, wagonettes, wedding equipages and funeral carriages... Private carriages are kept and horses taken into livery at reasonable rates...horses and carriages...would do credit to the private establishent of any gentleman. The coachmen and drivers are men of reliable character and remarkable for their punctuality and unobtrusive attention. The firm have an excellent old-established connection, and number among their patrons professional gentlemen, the clergy, the leading merchants and manufacturers, and the elite of Swansea society..."*

Anyone with the cash could hire a cab at almost any time, or take a carriage to use with their own horses. They boasted flies, victorias, broughams, shilliberes, breaks and phaetons. In 1889 a fly to Penclawdd and back cost 16 shillings. Even the fire brigade hired horses from Bullins!

The carriages are outside Bullins Mews. Mount Pleasant Chapel and the Swan were either side of the Dynevor Place junction with Gower Street, which is the main road here.

The charabancs of the twenties were successors to the horse drawn carriages.

Throughout the decade they worked from Heathfield and Ffynone Mews off Hanover Street, though by 1897 they also had an office at 1, Russell Street, just off Walter Road — the phone numbers were 65, 65a and 65b repectively. By 1903, they also had premises at Picton Mews, at the top of Dillwyn Street. This had been the headquarters of their rivals, Rossers, and signals a merger or takeover.

In 1891, John Rosser of the Livery Stables in Mansel Terrace was interviewed on his 80th birthday. He

"...remembers Swansea in the days of the Portreeves...when it was a little bathing place, and the buildings in Cambrian Place were lodging houses..."

The reporter called him the founder of the business, but a James Rosser ran the stables at 35/36 Wind Street, at least for a time, — perhaps the father or brother of John? "J.H. Rosser" was the company name, and there are references to J.H. Rosser of Picton House. The premises in Picton Mews were a new enterprise of the early 1890s, and the census in 1891 lists John L. Rosser (40 years old) and his family at 17 Picton Place — perhaps this is the grandson.

When the Swansea Merchants & Shipbrokers ran their first excursion in June, 1890, Rossers supplied *"well-horsed equipages"* to take 40 of them to the King Arthur in Reynoldston. When Cwmgelly Cemetery opened in September 1895, the councillors hired a four horse break from Wind Street to take them there.

A description of the Wind Street head-quarters in 1888 emphasizes the firm also built coaches —

"...Carriages and business carts of all kinds are made...Mr. Rosser also carries on a large business as livery stable keeper...A four horse coach is always at the disposal of pleasure parties..."

The stables and coach sheds were immediately behind what became Hancocks Brewery, and probably opened on to York Street and Little Wind Street. Perhaps brewery expansion also pushed on the changes in 1903.

Coachbuilders

Many of the needs of the town in terms of vehicles, parts and accessories seem to have been met by local traders. There were very specialised craftsmen like William Fewings a *"coach smith"* of Hawarden Crescent. **John Jones's** carriage works in Fisher Street, were concerned to point out that they could match Bristol or London prices. They had showrooms fronting the street, offices and *"works"* at the rear. They boasted of experienced workmen, — smiths, wheelwrights, body-makers, painters and trimmers — and well-seasoned timber! They provided drawings and an estimate on each commission. They aimed at *"gracefulness of outline, lightness and finished workmanship"*, and it might be suggested that horse drawn carriages, just like sailing ships, reached what the makers might have called an acme of excellence

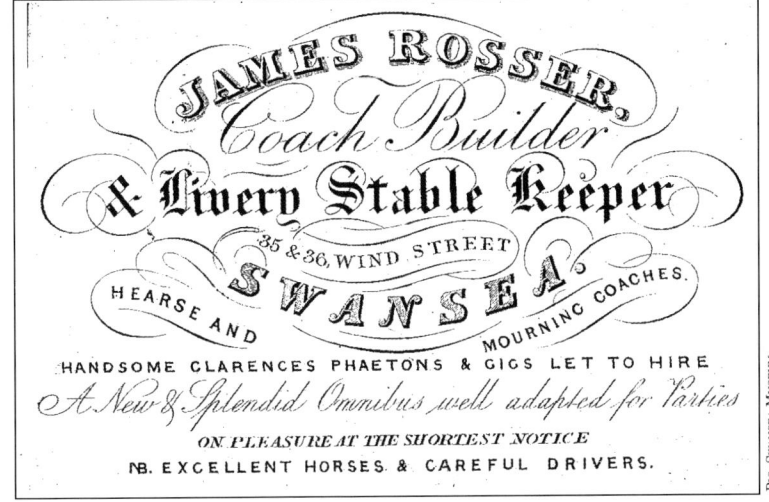

By the twenties, Bullins were motorised.

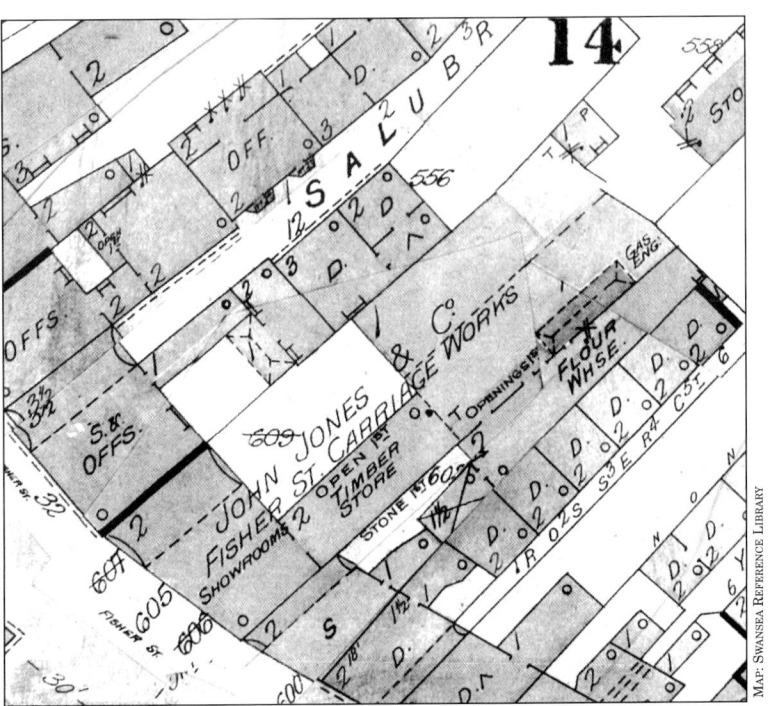

The carriage works fronted on to Fisher Street, with the tiny houses of Rosser's Court beside it.

just before becoming outmoded. A Fletchers ralli car of the 1890s which still exists is certainly light, elegant and beautifully finished. The "dished" wheels are evidence of great skill, and the painting and trimming must have taken weeks. (**E.E. Fletcher** was at 49 Oxford Street, and the firm is said to have started there in 1897.) John Jones's advertising has an old fashioned ring, but perhaps this was good business, in pandering to those well-off and those aspiring to distinction, or as they put it, *"the support of influential families in Swansea and for many miles around"* —

> *"We beg to thank our numerous customers for the support given us during the last 14 years, and hope by continued attention to all orders entrusted to us to merit a continuance of past favours..."*

(Written in 1889, this gives a foundation date of 1875, confirmed elsewhere.) They also did repairs and painting. John Jones was from Pitton in Devon — he was at the Devonian Society re-union at the Albert Hall in November, 1896. It may be relevant that the firm built and painted all the vehicles for Ben Evans Store, that Ben's depot was just around the corner in Frog Street, and that Charles Reed *"the old and experienced horse superintendent of the firm"* — picture him riding a very fine bay called Tenby in the 1892 procession — was another Devon man. In April, 1899, they completed *"one of the largest delivery vans in the country"*, — and it was for Ben Evans. Mr. Jones, who was 49 in 1891, lived around the corner at 12, Salubrious Place with his wife Mary, who was from Knelston in Gower, and four children.

Very nearby at 10-12 York Street was another *"carriage manufactory"*. It belonged to **Joseph William Birchall** until 1890, when he retired due to ill health, and sold off his stock. His home was still over the business when he died that March, aged 74. A bachelor, he was the last of a long line, the first Birchall to be a carriage builder having opened in Fisher Street in 1717. By 1891, the concern was probably **Morgan & Co**, who were unusual in being *"shoeing smiths"*. Perhaps they did business for Pike's and Rosser's stables nearby, or for all the horses used in the railway yards around Victoria Station. (See page 24).

M.Palmer's at 49 Oxford Street was a slightly older firm — about 1871. They had a showroom of 30 feet in frontage, with showrooms extending 300 feet back. Their products included —

> *"...light spring vans, wagons, market carts, dog-carts, trolleys, manure carts and agricultural vehicles..."*

It was Palmers who built the first motor bus body for Taylors of Llangennith in 1910...including curtains it cost £100. (There seem to have been several Palmers involved. A James Palmer, 40, from Parracomb, Devon, lived over the business in 1891, and later there were other Palmers in Gower Street, all of them in coach building.)

When Gower came to Swansea, it was to Oxford Street. The market was the magnet, but the pubs stabled farmers' horses and the coachbuilders did not specialise in fancy stuff. **Joseph Thomas**, carriage maker at Hoskins Place, was also a wheelwright and agricultural implement maker. **William Edwards** at 55 Oxford Street *"late Manager and Successor to E.Jones & Son"* kept the same range, though he was only an agent for the tools.

John W. Miles ran the **Swansea Carriage Factory** at the other end of town, 208 High Street, opposite the Mackworth. Established about 1890, the showroom was *"spacious and admirably lighted"*. The works included a smithy with two forges, *"tire bending machines"*, a large timber store, *"a well fitted upholstering department and a dust-proof shop for painting and varnishing"*. They built *"anything from the lightest dog cart to the most ponderous drag or four-in-hand"*. They were specially proud though of their *"medical car"* —

"...This car is certainly the most convenient ever offered to gentlemen of the medical profession. It is easy of ingress and egress, has a movable head which opens and closes at the pleasure of the occupant, is tastefully upholstered, and is fitted with an additional seat, which may be raised or set down as required, and is mounted on cee springs, with patent wheels and axles..."

Even so might Dr. T.D. Griffiths of Dryslyn House at the foot of Mount Pleasant have journeyed to visit moneyed patients in Ffynone. John and his wife Ellen lived over the premises. They were in their early forties. He was from Newbury. She described herself as *"assistant carriage builder"*.

Mount Pleasant and De La Beche Street, Swansea.

PIC: SWANSEA REFERENCE LIBRARY

Druslyn House is in the centre, with its carriage shed at the rear. Dr .T.D. Griffiths presided at the B.M.A. meeting in Swansea, 1903. (To the left is "the Willows", its high walls having been demolished as part of a greenhouse development by Messrs. Pearson in 1896.)

George Tucker was a wheelwright and coachbuilder in Wyndham Street and **John Westley Jackett's Central Coach Factory** was in Wassail Square. He lived at 7 Wassail Street, with his wife Sarah and seven children. He was Cornish.

With the vehicles themselves went a real array of accessories — John Jones offered brake blocks, rein rails, brake and door handles, carriage lamps, aprons, morocco leather trimmings, cushions, rugs and mats....and even *"circular glasses for broughams."* In 1890 they advertised Birds *"Patent Noiseless India Rubber Tyres...as used by the Prince of Wales..."* (It is fun to speculate why he needed to be so quiet!) **Rees**

& Jones of Landore, with branches at Morriston and Clydach, were saddlers and harness makers who also did leatherwork for colliery pumps, leather belting and the like. Set up in the heart of heavy industry they had diversified. **The Saddlery Company** in Alexandra Road combined snob appeal with low prices —

> *"...Cheapest House in Wales to buy Handsome Harness, Riding Saddles, Bridles, Whips, Spurs, Carriage Aprons, Lamps, Bandages, Knee Caps...*
>
> *...Don't pay fancy prices for Carriage Lamps. 500 pair best bevel edge British Plate Glass Red back lights, 8s.6d. per pair..."*

Ben Evans's Harness and Saddlery Department offered, among many other things, horse clothing and *"Clark's No.1 Clipping Machine, 8/6..."* **David Williams** set up at 152 High Street (well above the Station) in 1888 when he was 36, and his stock, largely made on the premises, has quite a distinctive sound —

> *"...single and double harness...riding and hunting saddles, ladies side-saddles, bits, bridles, stirrups, girths...hunting, riding and driving whips, brushes, sponges and all stable requisites..."*

He was from Newport, Pembrokeshire. **S. Pile** in Orange Street and Union Street near the market announced —

> *"Horses measured accurately for Hunting and Ordinary Saddles, and made to give ease to rider and horse, and fitted with the best patent bars, which are warranted to free the stirrup leather directly the rider is thrown...[he also sold]...Harness Compo's, Chamois Leathers..."*

All round town were men who drew a living from this world of horses and horse-drawn vehicles; here are just a few —

Alfred Bowles from Fairford, Glos at 14 George Street, wheelwright
Joseph Ancile from Overbury, Worcs at 39 Singleton Street, saddler
William Huxtable Bowen from Blackpill at 2 Burrows Place, ostler
Thomas Powell, Swansea born, at 38 Langdon Place, stableman
Thomas Evans (Swansea) at 3 Bond Street in the Sandfields, stableboy (15)
William Hudson from London at 27 Wellington Street, coach fitter
William Hodgson from London, same address, coach painter
Alexander Watchman from Scotland, same address, paint grinder
Alexander Campbell from Scotland, 19 Wellington Street, apprentice carriagesmith
David Davies (Swansea), 27 Wellington Street, coachsmith and his son Lewis (13) coach painter's assistant
Samuel Cawker (Swansea) at 108 Rodney Street in the Sandfields, coach blacksmith
Joseph Lowe from Birmingham at 52 Wellington Street, horse driver (His wife Martha *"sells sweets"*)
Henry Latty from South Petherton in Somerset and Henry Smith of Cobham, Surrey, both at 114 New Oxford Street, coachmen
(A Bridgewater man in York Street called himself a coachman too, but was his name really Thomas Obbs as recorded on the census?)

Frederick James Parker, son of a farmer and auctioneer in Alford, Lincolnshire, came to Swansea in 1892 *"as manager of a large horse, harness and carriage exchange"*.

He afterwards set up in his own right.

F.J. Parker.

Or go by bike...

In 1893 the tramway company applied for permission to put in more passing loops along St. Helens Road. Dr. Rawlings, who lived at "Preswylfa", a large house along that stretch, objected because of the roadspace being used up. He was criticised —

> *"...it was all very well for the Doctor, who had his carriage...those who were not so fortunate...had to get to their business and meals as speedily as possible ...by tram..."*

The critic was a fellow councillor, J. Viner Leeder — he was a lawyer, later thought of as one of the characters at the council table, but contemporary accounts of debates show him treated with intellectual and social disdain by his fellows. (The Swansea public had far more time for Viner Leeder, in 1894 voting him the wittiest man on the council, with a hundred vote lead over his nearest rival.) In April 1899, he married Emma Nicholas, a 33 year old widow of a baker from Waterloo Street. Their honeymoon was in Madeira. Emma arrived at the registry office *"on her bicycle"*. By the nineties, improved roads, better bikes, and practically no cars made cycling a wonderful means of transport and a popular pastime. The invention of the Safety Bicycle was a huge filip —

> *"Not many years ago cycling was looked upon ...as the most peculiar accomplishment of an athlete...its difficulties and dangers the same as beset the professional tightrope walker...it never reached the point of assured popularity until the Safety was invented and came into common use. In this year of 1897 all the world goes a-wheel or would like to..."*

J.C. Woods the solicitor would cycle from Ffynone to his office at Worcester House near the castle. The Llangyfelach Rural District Council, meeting at their offices in Fisher Street in July 1899, discussed

Pic: Swansea Museum.

buying cycles for their two Surveyors of Nuisances. The same month, the Y.M.C.A. sponsored a Bicycle Gymkhana at the cricket field in Mumbles — Maslen Brothers who built bikes at their West Cross Depot entered a team. An annual cyclists' carnival grew up, and in 1895 J.E. Williams of 10 Bay View Terrace was able to hand proceeds of £90 to Swansea Hospital. It usually raised £500 in all for charity, and in 1896 the patrons were J.S. Brown, Ben Evans, Mr. Eddershaw the furnisher and Sergeant O.A. Bird. By 1898, a cycle track had been laid out around the Recreation Ground at St. Helens —

Cycle racing at St.Helens.

> *"...one of the most popular resorts from early morn until late in the evening. On Thursdays [early closing?] the track is so crowded that the construction of an inner cycle track is under consideration...in consequence...permission has been given for youths to play cricket temporarily on the town end of the Victoria Park..."*

On the nextdoor St. Helens rugby and cricket field was a track for cycle races. A 1900 guidebook described *"pleasant runs"* for cyclists:

> *"The road to the Mumbles is level all the way, and the surface good. The Gower road is up and down but very pretty."*

Cycling became a great feature of Bank Holidays. Thomas & Sons, tailors of 9 Heathfield Street, *"Celebrated for Gentlemen's Breeches"*, also found it worthwhile to be *"Official Tailors to the Cyclists' Touring Club"*. By 1899 there were at least four cycling clubs in town —

The Swansea Harriers was a cycling and athletic club.
The Eastside Cycling Club, established 1886, chairman Major Arthur Richardson, Secretary William Merrell.
The Speedwell based at the Oxford Coffee Tavern, president Sir John Llewelyn
The Defiance in Temple Street, secretary Douglas Davies....undoubtedly linked with...

The Defiance Cycle Company at 15 Temple Street, nearly on the top corner, opposite Ben Evans. (There is a photograph showing the shop in "Jubilee Swansea", I, page 29)

Douglas Davies was a *"well known Llanelly champion cyclist"*. In 1897, the shop became part of a chain *"with branch depots"* at Llanelly, Neath, Port Talbot, Haverfordwest and Tenby. A Mr. John Williams had previously run the first of these, and he was installed as manager of a new cycle factory on the Strand, employing 50 men. The leading shareholders were C.E. & H.M. Peel, metal dealers, who lived at "Sunnyside" in Underhill, Mumbles.

William Parfrey opened a business in Orchard Street in 1879, moving to larger premises in Wassail Square in 1889, and on to 17 Oxford Street in about 1892. His forge, lathes, drills and planes there were steam powered. He built the Malvern cycle, light and strong, *"for road riding and path racing"*. These, it seems, were the machines for serious cyclists.

James Parfrey of 43 Oxford Street was a Bristol man who lived on the premises with his wife and children. His prominent plate glass showroom windows faced the National Schools across the road. Surely a relative of William, he had been in the business in Swansea since 1866, until 1887 in Fisher Street. He was a record holder on the tricycle having covered 25 miles in one hour 45 minutes, and in 1893 he was

The Malvern Cycle, ridden by Arthur Butt in the 100 mile road race at Swansea.

champion of Wales and Monmouthshire. By that date he had 15 gold or silver medals and three silver cups. The bikes were made in workshops in Picton Lane — they bore his own name, like the Parfrey Racer. He was also the Swansea agent for Rover cycles.

Again in Oxford Street, at 62, was **Cambria Cycles**. The company was established in 1897, managing director J.S. Brown, who will be met below. Thomas Charles, a Londoner living at 47 Walters Road was a director. In 1898 they were offering an aluminium bike, total weight 28 pounds. They had a Market Street, Llanelly branch, and their 1899 price was seven guineas for a ladies or gents cycle. That same year, the **Swansea Cycle Company** was just around the corner at 8 Dillwyn Street....having broken away from the Defiance Company (*"late leading hands"*). They built frames, but seemed to emphasize repairs and servicing (7/6 p.a. paid in advance). Their machines cost £8/10/-(Gents) and £9/5/- (Ladies).

Dan Morgan's Cycles was established in 1881. (Dan had been *"cycling manager"* for J.S. Brown, as late as 1895.) By 1900 they were in Swansea's cycling quarter, at 57 Oxford Street, a former grocer's shop, offering purchase, exchange, hire and repair. They boasted themselves *"Largest Retailers of Cycles in Wales"*. Their own make was the Druid, but they were agents for Royal Enfields, Raleighs, Premiers, Centaurs, Sunbeams and others.

Thomas Ford, the big chandlery in Pier Street, sold Rothwell Cycles and Lucas accessories by 1898.

The craze was not swallowed by all. John Coke Fowler, the stipendiary magistrate, praised cycling, but called for the introduction of the proficiency tests he had seen in Paris — *"the velocipede is fast and silent"*. In October 1898, Morgan Crombie, a Morriston blacksmith, was knocked over in Pleasant Street by Emmanuel Thomas on a bike *"with neither lamp nor bell"* — Crombie then did £5 worth of malicious damage to the bike! The same court which heard that case fined Henry Perkins, an engineer, and Captain Patrick O'Connor £1,

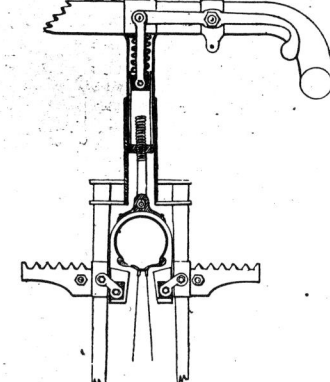

A peaceful outing near Lilliput, just beyond Blackpill. (The Mumbles Railway track was moved on to the seashore here during the nineties).

Pic: Swansea Museum.

because, outside the Mermaid in Mumbles, *"they were falling off their bikes, being too intoxicated to sit erect."* Dr. Daniel Evans, in health talks at the Y.M.C.A. in 1899, warned that 1 in 10 middle aged people might greatly injure their circulatory systems, their heart and arteries, by immoderate cycling. Pressing on up an incline or against a head wind, he said, was dangerous for the untrained cyclist, while the professional was developing for himself a *"tremendously enlarged heart and degenerate blood vessels."* Mrs. F.J. Erskine, writing at length in "the Cambrian" in 1896, considered *"cycling for ladies...good in moderation"*, and far cheaper than a pony and cart, but *"women ought not race!"*

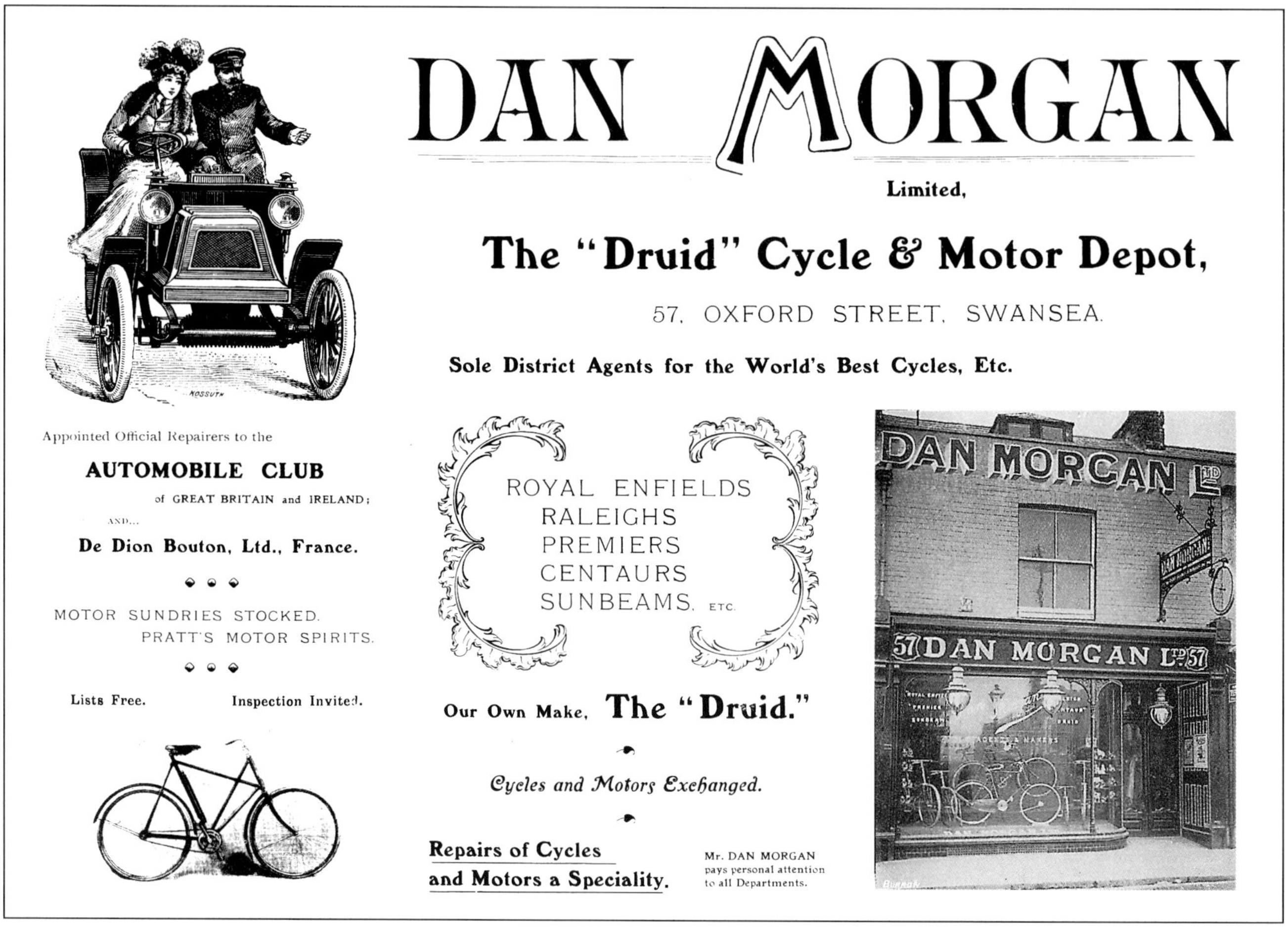

By the way — Mr. John S. Brown

J.S.Brown was born in Montgomery and gained business experience in Ironbridge, Northampton (Wilsons) and Dublin (Thomas Dockerel & Sons, Ironmongers). He came to Swansea in 1879, opening an ironmongers at 62 Oxford Street. He and two assistants ran the shop. He was a man of imaginative enterprise who rapidly built up a large business and workforce. He caught public attention — at the May Day parade through the streets in 1892, his employees came last, comically dressed and riding bikes. By 1893 he had premises at 21, 62 and 64 Oxford Street, as well as in Plymouth and Nelson Streets. He specialised in electro-plated cutlery. In his showrooms you might see —

"grates, stoves and ranges, gas cooking and heating stoves, fancy marble mantlepieces...agricultural implements,

PIC: SWANSEA MUSEUM.

fenders, fire irons, firedogs, ashpans, chandeliers, gas brackets, stair rods, locks and keys, masons' and carpenters' tools, ...kitchen utensils..." (1888)

"...paints, oils...rainwater goods...boilers, saucepans and all manner of household...utensils ...sanitary appliances...nails, cisterns, ovens, lead piping..." (1893)

He introduced the use of electric light to Swansea in his own premises in 1886. By 1893 he was Swansea agent for the Anglo-American Brush Electric Light Corporation of London and Elwell-Parker, Ltd of Wolverhampton. He was responsible for installing lighting in all sorts of large concerns, for example the Atlantic and the Graigola Fuel Works, copper works at Middle Bank and Black Vale, tinplate works at Gowerton and Gorseinon (Fairwood and W. Lewis's), the Elba Steelworks, Hancock's and the Swansea Old Breweries, and even the Montivideo goldfields in Uruguay. The Corporation and the Harbour Trust were his customers — in October 1893 he got the contract for maintaining all police and fire brigade telephones and alarms, and in 1899 he fitted three 2,000 candle-power arc lamps at Danygraig railway junction, charging £92/10/-. In March 1897 Wallace Jones, deputy engineer to the Triple Scheme, gave a lecture on the history of electricity at the Royal Institution. He explained that where once

"every wire had been pinned on to a porcelain insulator...[now]...wooden casing was generally used...unless buildings were new and damp.

Appropriately...the room was brilliantly lighted by arc lamps...the electricity very kindly supplied by Mr. John S. Brown from his electrical depot at the docks."

On the roof of the large premises he built in Oxford Street he fixed a

"...search light projecter [sic] similar to what is used in the Navy, and which is said to have a

The main premises in Oxford Street.

Today the tower has gone, but the lion still sits on the roof.

JOHN S. BROWN

OXFORD STREET, SWANSEA,

Sole District Agent for all the Leading Cycle
Makers in the Kingdom.

PRICE LISTS AND ALL PARTICULARS FREE.

New " Up-to-Date " Dunlop Pneumatic Tyred
Safeties from £10.

New Cushioned Tyred Safeties from £6 17s. 6d.

Any Machine sold on the Gradual Payment System.

Any make of Machine taken in Part Exchange.

Repairs quickly and cheaply executed by
experienced workmen.

Immense Stock of Cycle accessories at bottom prices.

——————

(ESTABLISHED 1879.)

lighting power equal to 13,000,000 candles. The light has on several occasions been made to serve most useful purposes, as its rays are dissembled [sic] for 20 miles around town..."

It was used as a celebration of the Cyclists Carnival, and later to broadcast Swansea election results. In the 1900 election, George Newnes the newspaper owner beat Sir John Llewelyn, a result signalled by the light shining steadily into the sky.

In 1885, representatives of the Premier cycle company called at his shop and *"begged him to accept their agency for Swansea"*. He was reluctant, finally agreed, and sold 30 bikes in his first year. In 1893, his cycle shop was called The Padlocks Cycle Depot and was at 10 Nelson Street, its showrooms 6,000 square feet, the largest in Wales. By 1896, he stocked all the leading *"Safety Bicycles"* — Singer, Premier, Swift, Humber, Rapid, Raleigh and Rover, keeping 400 new and second hand bikes in stock. (Just three years before, his brands had far more cumbersome names — Rudge Cycle Co., Coventry Machinists Co., Bayliss, Thomas & Co., Taylor, Cooper & Bednell and the St. George's Engineering company of Birmingham.) He offered reductions for cash sales and hire purchase. Demand was phenomenal, and he travelled to London and the Midlands to buy ladies' cycles. Then he hired the Drill Hall and ran lessons for ladies *"throughout the season"*. When that building was demolished to make way for the Grand Theatre, he laid out a new school, 117 by 42 feet, *"on the first floor of his ironmongery warehouse"*, electrically lit of course, and charged 2/- a lesson. This was next door to Cambria Cycles, a separate company he floated in 1897.

He involved himself in charities, but like Ben Evans and Lewis Lewis, did not enter public life. In 1891 the family — John (33), his wife Elizabeth (25), son Arthur (1) and one maid of 17 — lived at 15 Picton Place. Elizabeth was from Newport, Monmouthshire. By 1899 they lived in Blackpill at a house called Oakleigh. It was probably opposite Clynderwen (later the Bible College) on Webber's Hill, the short narrow rising section of Derwen Fawr.

The High Street of the Town

With its name as evidence, High Street had been the "principle thoroughfare" of the town for centuries. By the nineties, Oxford Street was contending that title, but three of Swansea's leading men of business fought hard against the trend.

Mr. R. E. Jones, Hotelier and Restaurateur

Richard Elwin Jones became known to the public as "R.E. Jones", but his Christian names suggest Welsh parents, even though his birthplace of 1853 was Liverpool. He worked on the "Liverpool Mercury" as a print compositor until 1878, when he was drawn to Cardiff, perhaps by family links. His wife was probably from Maesteg. He was always attracted to new ideas, like the concept of a cafe or restaurant, either

R.E. Jones, 1896.

existing in its own right, or attached to a hotel, where good cheap meals were always available — *"dinners from a shilling"*. He started business in one room in the Rotunda building in Cardiff, and by 1887 was owner of the 100 bed Washington Hotel in St. Mary Street, and had become a councillor. In that year, though, his wife's illness led him to retire, leasing out his premises.

In 1889 a restless temperament drove him into a small scale specula-tion in Swansea, which his natural insight and enterprise soon devel-oped mightily. In 1891 he was listed as *" restaurant proprietor"* living at 41-3 High Street with his three sons — David Parry, Richard Elwin L. and Stanley Bassett Jones, 15, 14 and 12 respectively. He is still listed as "married", but his wife is not present — perhaps she was in a nursing home? His place of residence was the Angel Hotel, and on census night there were just three guests, a Scottish tobacconist and his wife, a clerk to the new county council and the inevitable com-mercial traveller. There were five staff, including Annie Ace from Oxwich and Mary and Alice Seaborn from Bridgend, perhaps his own neck of the woods. By 1896 he was running the Angel described as *"near the Great Western Station and corner arcade"* in High Street, the Castle Cafe in Castle Street *"near the Post Office"*, the Midland Cafe in Wind Street *"opposite the Theatre"* (the New Theatre & Star Opera House), the Dot or Rutland Cafe *"at the L.N.W.R. and Steam Tram Terminus"* (Victoria and Rutland Street Stations). The sites were carefully chosen, and, beyond the coffee taverns, competition was small. By 1895 he had moved his home to Swansea, giving his address, when joining the Royal Institution in that year, as "Southend". Beyond the George Hotel in Southend, Mumbles, he had opened the Yacht Cafe, open only in Summer, but very close to the tempo-rary terminus of the Mumbles Railway — the pier and the line to it were under construction, horse drawn landaus tak-ing the trippers on from this point. A directory of 1899 lists R.E. Jones as con-fectioners —

YACHT CAFE, MUMBLES

LUNCHEONS, TEAS, &c.   PARTIES CATERED FOR
C. H. SUTTON, Proprietor.   Telephone—Mumbles 12.

From a 1920s advert.

PIC: SWANSEA MARITIME AND INDUSTRIAL MUSEUM.

"...a special feature in Mr. Jones's business is that he himself manufactures the confectionery, sweet-meats and bread for his cafes, and also for an extensive retail trade.."

The familiar idea of a cake shop-cum-cafe was then quite new. He had a bakery in High Street Arcade, near the Angel. In 1893, the Angel Hotel, just four years old, was described like this —

"...two entrances and and several large plate-glass windows, fitted with handsomely decorated window screens in ground glass and polished mahogany. ...the restaurant, with its fine buffet, excellent gener-al furnishings, and beautifully ornamented ceiling...luncheons and dinners are served in the best style at all hours of the day...On the first floor is the coffee room...and the commercial room... well adapted to the requirements of commercial travellers...a fine large billiard room lighted by electricity..."

He was a man who knew the market, was ready to put in plenty of money, and understood the value of advertising.

He had further plans for the Angel. By 1894 he was planning an extension, including a grand new entrance. At, the beginning of 1895 this was complete, involving the purchase and demolition of some houses. Then he turned his attention to Capel Seion, which fronted on to Orchard Street, immediately behind the Hotel. This was a branch of nearby Ebenezer Chapel, the pastor since May 1891 having been Rev. W.Gibbon. In that year they had celebrated the 50th anniversary of the original chapel by raising funds for a new organ, organ gallery and vestry. But on 25th April 1895 they sold up to R.E. Jones, using the money to relocate to Henrietta Street, and worshipping in the Higher Grade School (Dynevor) while building went ahead. For the demolition of Capel Seion was under way by August 1896, the hotel being extended on the existing elevation, with *"a wine bar, a shop...dining room...stock rooms for commercial travellers..."* all costing £3-4,000.

The new chapel in Henrietta Street.

At the very same time he was changing the name, as he announce in a front page advert —

> *"Mackworth Hotel. Removal to High Street — R.E. Jones (Ltd.) beg to announce that, the Site of the above hotel having been acquired by the Government, they have purchased the Name, Licence and Goodwill...which will be transferred to High Street.."*

The huge new Mackworth building, at the top of High Street.

His Midland Cafe in Wind Street is on the right.

The old Mackworth Arms in Wind Street, on the corner of Green Dragon Lane, had been one of Swansea's foremost inns since the eighteenth century, and was still popular in the nineties. However, it was chosen as the site of the town's new post office, and it was typical of R.E.J. to spirit away the familiar name for his own purposes.

As the new century came in, he was installing an *"Automatic Cafe....the Greatest Novelty in the Kingdom"* at the new Mackworth. (By 1902 the London, Gloucester and South Wales Automatic Machine Company had premises in the adjoining arcade.) By then his empire stretched out again to the Marine Hotel, Porthcawl and the Central Hotel, Cardiff. A week's stay at one of his hotels, or split between them, cost 2 guineas — what he called *"affordable prices"* were another of his guiding principles. By 1901 "R.E. Jones" was a limited company, (Secretary, J.A. Goode), which comprised only his Swansea interests. He kept nearly all the shares, and it seems that, though R.E. had travelled all over Europe and North America, Swansea at this time was the family home. On 12th November, 1896, his son Parry was 21. He

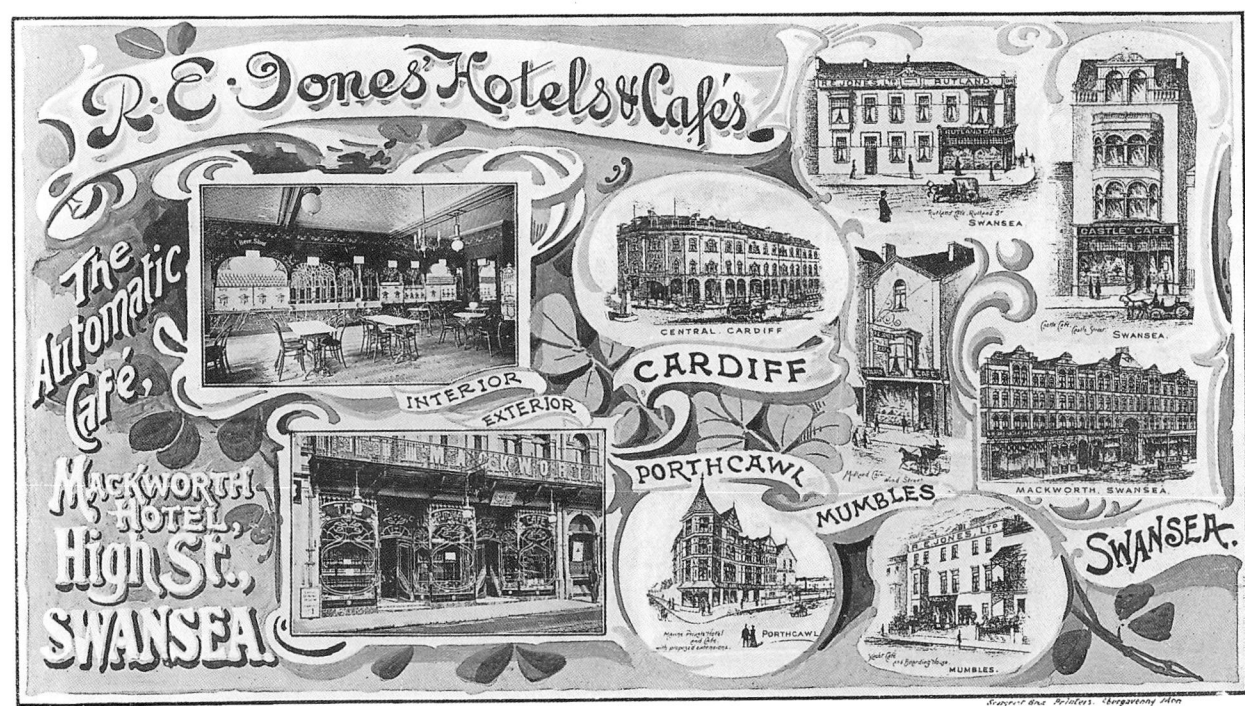

Unique Facilities for Visitors.

A VISITOR may stay a whole week of seven days at the CENTRAL HOTEL, CARDIFF; MARINE HOTEL, PORTH-CAWL; MACKWORTH HOTEL, SWANSEA; YACHT BOARDING HOUSE, MUMBLES; or may divide the week between any two or more of these for **Two Guineas.**

Restaurants are attached to each Hotel. There are also in Swansea—

Castle Café - - - - - CASTLE STREET
Midland Café - - - - WIND STREET
Rutland Café - - - - RUTLAND STREET

Billiard Rooms.

CENTRAL, CARDIFF - - - - 12 TABLES
MACKWORTH, SWANSEA - - - - 6 TABLES
CASTLE, SWANSEA - - - - - 2 TABLES

The Automatic Cafe, HIGH STREET, SWANSEA,

Is the Greatest Novelty in the Kingdom, and should be seen to be appreciated.

was a very keen swimmer and water polo player, and invited some of the Swansea Swimming Club to a formal dinner at the Mackworth. The club gave him a travelling bag, the hotel employees a dressing case, and there were formal toasts and speeches, with talk of swimming matches of the past and future, and the newspaper account concludes *"the rest of the proceedings were of a convivial nature"*. The club met at the Swansea Baths, St. Helens Road.

By the way — the baths, the laundry and the lady swimmers

The Swansea Baths and Laundry Company began in 1884. The firm provided public bathing facilities and laundered clothes on a large scale. It was housed in a range of fine gabled buildings, at the junction of St. Helens and Mumbles Roads, opposite the Bayview Hotel. In 1892, the laundry offered —

"...carpets beaten by steam power. Weather no hindrance. Curtains cleaned, tinted...by Manlove's unrivalled Curtain Decoudum...Cretonnes and Chintzes cleaned and reglazed..."

To be a laundress was often the back-breaking resort of a poor widow, like Margaret Macdonald of Princess Street in 1891, working by hand at home with wash tub and dolly. But the laundry had *"Machinery from the Best Laundry Firms"*, it was *"conducted by a number of neatly clad girls"* and was *"widely patronised by the inhabitants of the town and the suburbs"*. Charlotte Davies of Williams Place near the jail was one *"laundry worker"*, and Hester Williams of Paxton Street the laundry manageress. T.H. Taylor was in charge of the whole concern, and also in the new building worked Charles Way of Fleet Street in the Sandfields, just 16, a *"public baths attendant"*.

(By 1897 there was a rival Model Steam Laundry in Clarence Street, advertising steam carpet beating *"in all weathers"*.)

In 1890, it was decided to keep the swimming baths open through the winter, — *"the water will be kept at a temperature of over 70 degrees"* — and offer a family season ticket for 10 shillings. The Turkish and salt baths were thought to be a cure for colds and rheumatism. There were also *"pine, alkaline, hot and cold needle baths"* in 1897, as well as massage. The swimming pool was 70 feet by 30, its depth going from 3 feet 3 inches to 6 feet 6. It was full of heated seawater. Professor Morris *"gave special lessons in plain and ornamental swimming..."* In 1893 he organised a gala —

"Lever Brothers, the well known manufacturers of Sunlight Soap have presented a silver cup..."

In 1897 the baths were closed for a while, for the building of an extension, giving room for 4 to 500 seats for use *"during aquatic festivals"*. The architect, Alfred Bucknall was a man of note — he designed what became the Palace Theatre, the Working Men's Club in Alexandra Road, and much else. By 1900 Professor Loates was training women in life saving — they gave a demonstration in the baths that August. On the same day his son was the first to use something *"likely to prove a source of great amusement to swimmers"*, what was called *"a shoot"*.

From 1897 at least there were special hours for ladies, and over the next few years female interest in swimming and water polo grew enormously. One of the founders of the Swansea Women's Water Polo Club was Mrs. C.L. Bath of Uplands House,

"...a charming Canadian lady, daughter of Mr. George Grant Francis the mining expert, and grand daughter of Colonel George Grant Francis..."

She married Charles Lambert Bath in 1893, but was tragically widowed by her husband's suicide in November, 1899. (See Jubilee Swansea, I, p.11-12, but with thanks to Sandra Thomas for putting me right on the lady's descent.) She was captain and a leading player, before returning in 1900 to Canada. Lady Llewelyn was President, but an ever present support was Amy Dillwyn. Miss Dillwyn was vice president, and chairing the 1901 annual dinner at the Mackworth decided to dispense with all the toasts, indeed all formality, though afterwards deciding that perhaps *"the club"* ought to be mentioned. The members responded with "For she's a jolly good fellow", rather in line with the Chamber of Commerce which termed her "chairman".

The atmosphere of the time was not in tune with swimming for women. A periodical called "Truth" called women's water polo

> *"a farcical ...sheer waste of time...the women were utterly ignorant of the game...it is a sport like football suited to men alone..."*

Amy Dillwyn.

Referees were men, and Ivor Evans was the *"blushing"* secretary, treasurer and coach over the first two years. But women's galas at the baths did not allow male spectators until 1901, and then only gentlemen. The problem of distinguishing gentlemen could only be solved, one person suggested laughingly, by making the Hon. Odo Vivian the doorman. The reporter for the "South Wales Daily Post" was a lady, pen name "Gwen". For competition, costumes of black or navy blue stockinette were compulsory. It was said that red aniline dyes, for example, in the *"cheaper woven garments...[essential]...in working girls clubs"* would run, and might even cause blood poisoning. Coloured embroidered rosettes, though, were allowed.

> *"...The minimum amount of costume is carefully laid down and stictly enforced. It is to be cut straight at the neck and reach within three inches of the knee..."*

That gentlemen and other males had some interest beyond water sport is suggested by the experience of a Swansea artilleryman during the Boer War.

> *"I was riding my horse to water, and on the wide veldt saw a piece of paper lying on the grass, which I thought was a despatch dropped by one of the orderlies. I dismounted and picked it up, and to my great surprise found it contained pictures of the Swansea Ladies Water Polo Team..."*

The champion lady swimmer over the next few years was Gladys D. Wyrill, almost certainly daughter of the Borough Engineer, Ralph Wyrill. In 1899, she was *"by far the fastest swimmer in the baths"*, among the women anyway. Accounts of matches repeatedly describe her beating all opponents to the ball, and she must have scored about half the Swansea goals over the period 1899 to 1901. *"Racing since early childhood"*, and still in the Girls Intermediate School when she represented Swansea, she tended to win races, even costume races and candle races (holding a lighted candle) and diving competitions. Very often second, and commended for her dribbling skill at water polo was Daisy,

Ralph Wyrill from Scarborough.

youngest daughter of H.A. Chapman, the photographer. In 1901 it was said she *"had undergone a hard course of training"*, but Miss Wyrill still beat her by 5 or 6 yards. Her older sister Eva was a captain of the club, and the first female representative to the Welsh Swimming Association. (She afterwards married Stanley Bassett Jones, son of R.E., and also a swimmer.) Both were considered *"smart players"*. The daughters of Talfourd Strick and R.J. Sails took part, but some of the other names seem far less distinguished, and perhaps there was a minor degree of social mixing in the team.

The team was so successful that by 1901 it was difficult to find opponents — they had to play games among themselves. On the national stage they entered the Ravensbourne Cup competition at Westminster baths in 1900. The pool was twice as big as Swansea's and in 1901 there were 3,000 spectators with 1,000 turned away. There were races —

> *"...white arms threshed the water in man-like style and the limelight man followed their course with absolute devotion...[they were spotlit?]...A neat maid robed each as she left the water. At the end of the first heat the winner won a cheer by diving neatly to the bottom and recovering an umbrella which had slipped out of the grasp of an excited lady spectator..."*

In 1900 Swansea won the water polo, beating Jersey 4-1 in the final, all goals by Gladys Wyrill. These were the first water polo matches ever played in London by ladies. In 1901, the finalists were the same, and Swansea won 5-2, Daisy Chapman this time scoring 3. When they won again in 1902 they were allowed to keep the Ravensbourne Shield.

In January, 1901, the club general meeting was at *"Mr. Chapman's house in High Street"*.

Henry Alfred Chapman, artist and photographer

Samuel Palmer Chapman was born in 1809, 15th of 17 children. His Christian names cannot be to do with the painter Samuel Palmer, as he was only born in 1805, but there was certainly aesthetic flare in the Chapman family. They came of farming (*"yeoman"*) stock in Lincolnshire — the father, William, died in 1866, and was buried in Waddington churchyard. S.P.C. was self taught, leaving the village school at 13 with only limited reading skills. He educated himself between the ages of 17 and 22, keeping a dictionary and a piece of slate for jotting things down always to hand, in his hat! He travelled in Europe. He became a teacher who gave adult lectures on electricity and magnetism, subjects he is said to have discussed with Michael Faraday. He was an amateur astronomer, becoming a Fellow of the Royal Astronomical Society. He wrote poetry — two sonnets written as late as 1894, inspired by revisiting Redbourne Park in Lincolnshire after a gap of fifty years. In 1877 he had published "Stolen Minutes with the Muses", 250 pages of his poems, most written in the thirties and forties, printed for private circulation, but properly bound and with an interesting introduction. Samuel Palmer Chapman must have been a fascinating man, with an open and lively mind, at a time of many new inventions and discoveries. He was drawn into photography at a very early stage, and is said to have met William Henry Fox Talbot of Lacock Abbey, one of the pioneers of the craft. He experimented with pictures of leaves on silver sheet and an inch and a half square minature photographs.

H.A.Chapman, 1897.

His son Henry Alfred was born at Coningsby in 1844 and educated at Lincoln Grammar School, where he won the title of *"best good boy"*! The family migrated to South Wales, living briefly at Llandeilo,

Llanelly then Carmarthen, until they settled in Swansea in 1860. S.P. opened a photographic studio in York Street, at a time when the area around the Royal Institution and Cambrian Place still had some pretensions as the fashionable part of town. He later moved to premises in High Street, nearly opposite the later Mackworth Hotel, not far from the station — it was his son who moved further down to set up shop, studio and family home at 235. He is said to have helped with daguerrotypes as a boy in Lincoln, buffing the copper plates, and in Swansea he cleaned the glass negatives for his father. The two Chapmans were among the first commercial photographers in town. James Andrews, originally in Victoria Road, opposite the museum, called himself *"indisputably the pioneer of art photography in South Wales"*, and Gulliver was another early rival.

H.A. Chapman always made great play of his painting, which suggests he thought it the superior art. Perhaps his unusually long moustaches were part of the artistic image he preferred, although his

approach to everyday life was certainly not affected. He supplied artist's materials from firms as familiar as Rowney and Winsor & Newton. He offered a framing and restoration service. He painted portraits, which seem to have aimed, in the spirit of the time, for a careful realistic portrayal of each sitter. His oil paintings included a large picture of a council meeting in the Guildhall in 1890, with Sir John Dillwyn Llewelyn, the Mayor, centre stage, and the unmistakable William Thomas of Lan also to the fore. There are instances of parliamentary paintings of this type, and the time spent on sittings with each man must have been very considerable...it is difficult to believe such a painting could be done purely from a photograph. In 1893 he donated an oil painting of Lewis Llewelyn Dillwyn, M.P., who had recently died, to the council. For years he was a member of the Free Library Committee. A newspaper reporter remembered how John Deffett Francis, aged, active and eccentric, would seek out and donate artworks to the collection there

PIC: SWANSEA MUSEUM

Chapman in 1893.

"...accompanied by withering references to the ignorance of the town's representatives...Imagine...[he wrote]...the lacerated feelings of a chairman, [H.A.C.] convinced he is an artist from the crown of his head to the soles of his feet..."

One of his advertisements puts it like this —

"...Mr. Chapman is not only at the Head of his Profession as a photographer but his OIL PAINTINGS for Presentation, Family Portraits, etc (without the aid of Photography) have obtained him a name second to none in Wales for correctness of portraiture and artistic effects..."

As suggested here, there were techniques where paint and film were combined. In his early years he turned out 1,500 *"oil painted photographs"* annually, when *"the old collodion process of photography was in vogue"*. In 1870 he was appointed Government photographer for Glamorgan. His adverts were full of the prizes he had won — all *"the Principal Prizes offered in the Principality over the last thirty five years.."* (1902). In 1901 he took 6

first prizes at the National Eisteddfod at Merthyr. In 1908 he became President of the Professional Photographers' Association of Great Britain. Another advertising ploy was to attract attention to his studio building. In December, 1895 he announced *"...the Extensive Alterations are just completed..."*

The *"fine new premises"*, now took in number 236 as well, formerly the offices of Mr. Norton — perhaps this was when the well known metal decoration was added to the frontage. Thereafter his very effective catch phrase was *"under the verandah"*. For a while he called it "the Royal Studio", having had custom from the Queen and her family. As well as waiting rooms and studios, he built up a showroom where *"...an hour can pleasantly be spent..."* Over the years, he must have taken many thousands of photos of people of the Swansea area, and he knew how important it was to keep *"...prices as low as possible consistent with...high class work..."* He was a good businessman —

"It was in 1857 that I earned my first shilling. And I've kept on earning them ever since..." (1915)

HENRY A. CHAPMAN,

Artist and Photographer,

235, High Street,
... SWANSEA.

Winner of the Principal Prizes offered in the Principality during the last thirty-five years.

MR. CHAPMAN is not only at the head of his Profession as a PHOTOGRAPHER, but his OIL PAINTINGS for Presentation, Family Portraits, etc., (without the aid of Photography), have obtained him a name second to none in Wales for correctness of portraiture and artistic effects. Terms on application.

THE LATEST AND BEST STYLE OF POSE IN CABINETS AND CARTES-DE-VISITE.

Prices Moderate ...
Cartes-de-Visite from 3 for 2/- ; 6 for 3/- ; 12 for 5/6.

1902.

In his early years, basic technical changes were regularly transforming photography, and he always remained an experimenter. His card backed portraits, *"Cartes de Visite"*, were 2/- each, 6 for 3/- and 12 for 5/6 and remained so for at least 13 years. A carte de visite measured two and a quarter inches by three and a half, on backing of two and a half by four. Very many middle class families had an album to take them. He boasted of *"softness of tone and clearness of detail...unexcelled"* and examination of his surviving work cannot belie this. A team of "spotters and finishers" worked on the prints, "retouchers" on the negatives, their job to remove blemishes, whether technical or personal, as was then the custom. By 1908 Chapman had an almost unbelievable stock of 350,000 glass negatives. He was a very industrious man over a very long career. A story of 1899 also shows how quickly he could work. Between 1 and 2 p.m. on 1st May there was a crowded ceremony beside the then entrance to the Prince of Wales Dock — a brand new dry dock of the same name was being opened, the largest in town. Chapman was present, and was then spotted driving off *"post haste from the scene"*. At 3.00, *"the company were at luncheon"* in the Mackworth, on the other side of the street from 235, and

> *"...were surprised when a large and beautifully framed photograph of the opening was shown round".*

As he prospered, he bought shares in shipping and industry. He was a part owner with Mr. Henessy and others of vessels, "Arctic", "Antarctic", "Pacific". The last foundered in a cyclone in the Indian Ocean in June 1893. (The co-owner was almost certainly Bernard Rudkin Henessy of 8 Wind Street, a watchmaker who diversified into several other areas, and by 1877 owned more than 2,000 tons of shipping. Bernard M. Henessy of 43 Walter Road in 1891, *"manager, ship office"*, was probably the son.) He had shares in metalworks — Birchgrove Steel (which closed in 1899) and Ynispenllwch Tinplate. It was a normal practice for men who made money in trade to invest locally in this way, and Chapman viewed it seriously enough to attend the metal exchange in Fisher Street on behalf of the Birchgrove works. In the 1870s he became the principal artist for the local

The ornate back of a Chapman "Carte de Visite".

monthly the "Swansea Boy", largely drawing political cartoons, and it was probably this that eased him into *"public life"* in the old phrase. He was elected to the Council in 1881, and served as a councillor and Poor Law Guardian for twenty years. On the council he represented the West Ward, then Alexandra, then Castle. His speciality was the Watch Committee, of which he was chairman for some years. In 1890, the ample Mr. Holland was retiring as Inspector of Weights and Measures, and Chapman commented.

> *"We will save money as one of Mr. Holland's suits will make two for David Jones."*

He was gradually relaxing into the demands of local politics. He seems to have been hard working, persistent and efficient. He fought a battle with the Glasbrooks and others to rate collieries more highly, and eventually won about £700. He was prominently in favour of the street tramways. He was a conventional progressive. He had come to consider himself a Welshman, and asserted unequivocally that Swansea was the metropolis of Wales. When the Boer War came in 1899, he was a strong patriot; his sons Samuel and Bert both went to South Africa to fight.

He was, however, more than a commercial photographer who became a local politician. He was a well rounded character, with a range of interests, which enabled different people to warm to him. By March 1893, the "Swansea Journal" was ready to say —

> *"Really Mr. Chapman is not such a bad mayor after all...I saw him with some bits of fishing line and hooks and things around his hat..."*

He loved fishing — *"few amateurs can boast of being able to throw a better line than he can"*. An early interest was the Volunteer movement, the militia forces which thrived in the 1860s. He first joined during the family's brief stay in Carmarthen. Lewis Llewelyn Dillwyn was his colonel, and Henry Hussey

A selection of Chapman portraits, unnamed.
Notice the ornate furniture, rich draperies...and the best clothes!
(There is another example on page 90).

Vivian too *"had the honour of commanding him"* in the 4th Glamorgan Rifle Volunteers. He was a crack shot. He was involved in rugby, though he just called it *"football"*. He watched regularly. He was president of the Brynymor club which went two years unbeaten, and then merged with the Swansea team in 1886. A number of the players became internationals. He used to pin up rugby results in his shop window in High Street. In October 1892, Newport beat the All Whites and a reporter from the "South Wales Argus" gave the message, via *"the operators of the National Telephone Company"*. The newspaperman recalled —

> *"No sooner was this said than I could hear the strains of 'the Dead March' from 'Saul' being played by the worthy alderman's charming daughter. Laugh! I could have died."*

H.A.C. was captain of the athletics club at the Y.M.C.A. and of their unbeaten tug of war team! He was a keen swimmer, credited with saving two people in Lincolnshire and an Aberdare man on Swansea beach — characteristically unhesitating, he just jumped in and dragged him out. In May 1893, Mayor Jones of Newport, reported to be *"of cut water shape"*, challenged him to a race in Newport Baths. Though *"broader of beam"* Chapman jumped at it, and offered a family contest. It was not the Swansea side that backed out.

Chapman was a strong temperance man; in 1890 he was chairing a meeting of the hard line Total Abstinence Society, and commented —

> *"They had one object in view, the Glory of God and the suppression of the drink traffic"*

In October 1893 he went to a meeting of teetotal mayors at the Mansion House in London. His speech was full of self deprecating humour. For him the fight against drink must not be too self righteous, but he believed firmly that

> *"Sunday closing in Wales has been the greatest blessing for social and moral welfare of the inhabitants of Swansea"*

Mayor Chapman

On 10th November, 1892, H.A. Chapman became Mayor of Swansea. He had long hoped for this, and when he stood at the Town Clerk's table in the council chamber, with Albert Mason, Richard Martin and Edward Rice Daniel, and put on the chain and robes, he must have been filled with simple pride. There is some suggestion that he had been passed over before but was now chosen because a less testing year seemed on the cards. This was rather unfair. He was thought impetuous, — *"headlong"* was another word used — and "The South Wales Liberal" said he *"talks precipitately, his meaning difficult to fathom..."*, but the same Cardiff paper praised his inaugural speech for its sound political sense. In many ways his year in office brought the best out of him. He was not a man of considered thought and ordered programmes, but Alderman Richard Martin (who was) praised his *"activity, energy and honesty of purpose"*. He worked. The day after the mayor making he was on the bench at the Police Court, which was considered unprecedented. And he did not hold back. Ten months later he was again officiating when Samuel Thomas, a lad from Baptist Well Street, was charged with trespass on G.W.R. land. He pleaded that he was looking for a job as a station porter. The mayor told the railway company there were never enough porters at High Street, fixed the fine at one shilling — and paid it himself.

A man who could advertise his work as

"...Paintings and Studies that have received the warmest encomiums from people of approved taste and standing..."

obviously had a regard for his social superiors, but at the same time, he was often able to get on with the leaders of labour who were gradually becoming more important, and for good measure, he was a trader, and was at ease with his fellows. To mayoral functions like the inaugural luncheon in the Royal Hotel in High Street came Lewis Lewis and Richard Lewis, drapers, P.G. Iles and Isaac Gale, grocers, and R.E. Jones, hotelier, all trading in that same street — there were 150 people there, double the normal number. In October 1893, there was a proposal to build assize courts next door to the library in Alexandra Road, where the police station was later (1912) sited. The visiting justices had complained of

"cries of newsboys, clanging and resounding noises of dry docks, clatter of traffic on land and water"...

Ben Evans, founder of the famous store.

breaking their concentration in the existing courts at the Guildhall. Thomas Freeman brought the proposal to council, but the mayor welcomed the elected leaders of the drapers and the grocers, Thomas Yorath and Seymour Arthurs, who came to back the move. He made a great fuss of their civic mindedness, and lamented the unreadiness of tradesmen to enter politics. He was an unqualified backer of the schemes of Ben Evans. When his huge store extension was a building site in September, 1893, Sir John Talbot Dillwyn Llewelyn, owner of the buildings on the opposite side of Caer Street, applied for an injunction to halt progress — he seems to have been worried by the height of the new edifice and narrowness of the roadway. On behalf of Mr. Evans, H.A.C. instantly plunged into a noisy and undignified newspaper correspondence with Thomas William James the solicitor, but took great care to utter no word against Sir John himself. Henry Hussey Vivian had a real liking for the photographer-mayor, attending his installation, although given very little notice, and teasing him for not obeying orders in the Rifle Volunteers, — *"my discipline was not always pleasing to him..."* — long years before. Vivian's long life of dutiful service, — he had managed the Hafod Works for 58 years — albeit cushioned by wealth, was almost done, and the functions he attended over the mayoral year saw him relaxed and jovial in the company of the townspeople. It was fitting that he should be made Lord Swansea, and be welcomed to the town in that guise by H.A.C. in July, 1893. Every window was crowded as the new peer was processed from High Street Station to the Guildhall to be made a freeman of the town — *"enthusiasm could go no further"*. Even the Conservative Club in Wind Street had a banner proclaiming *"Welcome"* to this Gladstonian Liberal. At the inevitable dinner, Vivian modestly made quiet fun of himself by describing, but not mocking, the odd ceremonial of taking one's place in the upper house. He was asked to be the next mayor, but declined. Victorian newspapers will often paint pictures of the love of ordinary people for rich employers, but there can be little doubt that the old man really was popular, and Chapman fitted in to the picture perfectly.

Henry Hussey Vivian.

A little gentle fun was poked at the photographer who had become mayor. At a council meeting in June 1893, chaired of course by the mayor, the case of J.Harrison Goldie, portrait photographer of Temple Street came up. He had not been paying his water rates. Rhys Edwards, a Morriston member suggested

"Photographing was all profit, for it pandered to the vanity of the people, so that photographers could well afford to pay for the water they used".

This was not barbed, and in fact the mayor was in the social middle ground and acted as a very effective conduit between aristocracy and the unions. That first autumn, for example, the slump in the Swansea copper industry, and other factors, put many out of work. H.A.C. grasped the nettle without a moment's hesitation, and used every contact he had. Oscar Snelling was probably his closest ally, a non-denominational minister who we shall meet properly later, but there was also the Anglican Church, in the persons of A.A. Matthews, new Vicar of Holy Trinity near the library, and E.J. Wolfe, who ministered from St. Nicholas's Seamen's Chapel in Gloucester Place. There were Dockers' Union leaders like John Burns, and there was James Wignall. The last mentioned said —

"...he could not help feeling that he [Chapman] had been kept back by the Almighty until the year the unemployed would require the assistance of him and his good wife..."

James Wignall.

Mr. Wignall was a copperman at Morfa and was to be the first Labour member on the School Board in 1899. (By 1903 he was vice chairman, and laying the foundation stone for a new Board School at Pentrechwyth — the inscribed ceremonial gavel is in the Glynn Vivian Art Gallery.) The Plymouth Hall where much of this action started was the meeting place of the local socialists. There were Poor Children's Breakfasts, Soup Kitchens, Food Vouchers. Fellow tradesmen gave bread and meat. Ben Evans donated £100 in clothing. Vivian and Sir John Llewelyn donated £50 each. Chapman's wife Eliza was at the heart of it, running the soup kitchen at the Corn Exchange for three months. A Barnstaple girl, a Miss Beor, she remembered playing on the Devon sands, never dreaming of being a mayoress. H.A wrote to the press to appeal for clothing —

"...socks and stockings, undergarments, trousers, coats and waistcoats...any sizes, patched or whole... men's shirts, singlets or pants..."

Then Eliza wrote with thanks for all the donations received (*...paper bags, Howell Watkins...*) A few months later she had the confidence to address the first meeting of Morriston Women's Liberal Association, speaking in favour of votes for women. For three months the effort continued unabated. On 21st April, Sir John Llewelyn invited the whole committee to Penllergaer as a celebration of their achievement — he organised carriages from Heathfield Street to fetch them.

Oscar Snelling did suggest that, on the example of Birmingham, their poor relief association should be converted into a permanent agency. This sort of idea, as well as the way well-organised charity cut across the established system of poor relief and the workhouse, and the constant accusation that there were *"loafers"* who just took advantage, caused some criticism, but the mayor never gave the critics a second thought. He just accused them of looking for excuses for not helping. Chapman, too, went further than free food. The Council owned land in the Dyfatty/Waun Wen area, the Baptist Well Estate — and he pushed ahead plans to lay out streets there as a way of creating employment. What he called the *"red tapeism"* of the Local Government Board meant the council had not yet been given the go-ahead to borrow £6000 for this, but the mayor said he would pay for it out of his own pocket if necessary.

Chapman and Snelling went back a long way. Oscar Snelling proclaimed himself no Anglican, though that was his mother church, and no Nonconformist, though he admired their good works. He preached

Oscar Snelling.

practical Christianity, first in Hafod in May 1865, later in the Gospel Hall, and most famously in the Albert Hall, where some reckoned he brought in the largest congregation in Wales. His services were known as "Snellings", and he attracted those groups of young men who did not go to other chapels. And his Watch Night services drew in those who *"openly admitted it was the only religious service they attended"*. On New Year's Eve 1889, 2,000 squeezed into the Albert Hall. He never took a collection. Hymns had to be sung with gusto, or he would call a halt and insist *"you will have to sing that through again...and this time sing"*. He would beat time loudly with his foot, swing his arms, and carry everyone up by the force of his personality. He was immensely popular — in April 1893, he topped the election for Poor Law Guardians by a clear 600 votes. His work was supported by families like the Michaels, the Tunbridges and the Marquisses, who you will meet elsewhere in this book. H.A. Chapman was a very early convert, the preacher's leading supporter, and superintendent of the Sunday school at the Hall, not missing a single sabbath through a

very busy mayoral year. He and Eliza were *"Brother and Sister Chapman"*. There was pressure to take his inauguration service to St. Mary's, but Chapman never considered it. With Vivian and R.D. Burnie, (also an M.P.) at his side in the Albert Hall, he heard Mr. Snelling preach, as he put it, *"at the mayor and corporation"*, his text the feeding of the 5,000. His advice was quite concrete — *"do not be mean with your library rate."* He spoke with *"earnest, practical eloquence"* and told a congregation which included a high proportion of the successful that

The Albert Hall today.

> *"...all men were not prize winners in the race of life...let Divine compassion flow into your souls, and flow out to those around you. Bring Christ into all your work..."*

The hymns were sung

> *"with great heartiness...Mr. Snelling started the singing in each instance, never once starting the wrong key note".*

In April 1893 H.A.C. threw a fancy dress ball in the same hall, the afternoon for children, the evening for their parents. It was novel, lively and very well attended.

Chapman's religion was practical too. Each Christmas he gave food, beef in particular, to hundreds of poor families. On becoming mayor, he distributed 15,000 queen cakes to orphans and others in paper bags inscribed *"With the compliments of the mayor"*. For all his simple pride in the mayoral procession through the streets in November 1892, himself in robes and chain, the ancient halberds of the town in evidence, and the police band in the van, he considered

> *"...Politics are destined to have little influence in ameliorating the lot of the working man..."*

Education and religion, he thought, would do that. Anyway, the pageantry was rather spoiled by a downpour.

While he worked with union men, he was not one for strikes — he recounted how one (perhaps at Birchgrove Steelworks) had cost him £1,000. In 1899 he was to thoroughly lose his temper with Morgan Hopkin, one of the representatives of labour starting to be elected to the council and other bodies —

Chapman called him a *"dirty dog"* and there was almost a real fight. In August 1893, a coal strike in the deep mines of the Rhondda evoked a big response among the colliers of Neath and Skewen. In numbers estimated between 500 and 3,000, complete with brass and fife bands, they marched west, aiming to bring out the men of Swansea and its valley. They moved through Glais to Clydach, then south to Ynysforgan, where they were met by a certain Mr. Chapman, who had dashed out of town in a hansom cab. With him were less than 20 police. It was very hot. He parleyed with, cajoled, persuaded and bluffed the colliers' leader, a Mr. Jones, bizarrely mounted on a pony and bedecked in military medals. The legal basis of the mayor's claim that a grouping of more than 12 needed permission to use the roads of the borough of Swansea was very dubious, but he persevered, keeping with them to Morriston Cross, trying to shepherd them back east across the Wychtree Bridge, then finally buying them off with promises of pardon near the buildings of the Copper Pit, at the bottom of Martin Street, while Glasbrook's colliers worked deep underground directly below them. The meagre force of police, some on horseback, acted with great discipline, and the

Councillor Fender who replaced him in the Alexandra Ward.

marchers finally dispersed. (Councillor John Hopkin John was also present, and exchanged a few words in Welsh with the leaders.) In later years, these dramatic events were what folk remembered of Chapman's mayoral year, and his self possession and unheeding courage very likely prevented bloodshed. At the Pentre Pit in Brynhyfryd, hundreds of miners and coppermen had been given blue armbands and staves to act as special constables. If the two forces had

Fairground equipment 1999 on the site of the Copper Pit.

met....Very conscious of this, Chapman strove to ensure they shouldn't, and then characteristically posted back to town and told the press of his success. In the meantime the other magistrates had met and petitioned the government for troops. The 6th Eniskillen Dragoons arrived the following day by train. The mayor was very angry.

On July 6th, 1893, the Duke of York married Princess May of Teck — later to be George V and Queen Mary. The mayor immediately proposed to devote £500 to *"high jinks and bunting"* on the day, both in loyalty to the crown, and to *"boom"* the town, advertise its attractions and draw in thousands of pounds worth of business. This lavishness drew criticism from councillors of all brands and had to be forgotten. It was even suggested, quite unfairly, that he was thinking of the trade of his own shop or even a knighthood! One reason for the opposition was the level of rates in the town. In January that year, he asserted boldly that Swansea was lower rated than Cardiff, an argument based on a use of figures which was at least debatable. Councillors like James Jones, Chairman of the finance committee, took issue, and so even did Mr. Vivian, who spoke of the new Weavers Flour Mill as a marvellous development, and warned *"don't you*

John Brader, 1897. (See overleaf)

The shop and family home in High Street still bears the name.

over-rate them!". Needless to say the mayor did not back down. At a medical dinner, he was full of bouyancy and humour —

"...his adverse critics [should] *understand that their criticisms simply showed they did not understand the question...*[and]*...those who backed him up seemed to be gentlemen of wonderful intelligence..."*

And townspeople did subscribe for a present for the royal couple. It was decided to buy a piano, chosen by Averil, Lady Vivian, and purchased through the agency of John Brader, Chapman's nephew, whose shop at 9 Wind Street on the corner of Green Dragon Lane had long been <u>the</u> place in Swansea for musical instruments. At the end of June H.A.C. joined a distinguished party on the train to lunch with Lord Swansea at Belgrave Square, and go on to White Lodge, Richmond Park, to bestow Swansea's gift. But what they actually gave was a crescent hair ornament, bought hurriedly at Garrards in Haymarket. When the train reached Bristol, Chapman had received a telegram from Vivian to say that the happy couple had already received four pianos, and that more were on the way!

The Chapman Family

H.A.C. was thoroughly active right up to his death in November, 1915. In his last year he was interviewed for a piece in "The Professional Photographer". He sounds relaxed, avuncular...

"I don't believe in having to ask my sitters to walk upstairs...nor in climbing too much myself...

Why should I advertise? Everyone in Swansea and for miles around knows me...

I do not care how stiff and prim a sitter is when she comes in, I like to make her smile before taking a negative..."

He was 71 when he died. He had been bronchitic for some years. and

"...with his black skull cap and long, iron grey moustachio... [was] ...one of the most familiar figures in Swansea...

...apt to blurt out the excessively frank word, and to do his thinking too audibly, H.A.C. is all the same full of generous impulses, and a gruff manner conceals the workings of a soft heart."

Up to nearly the last he had made no will, and was persuaded to leave his whole £7,804 to Daisy, his youngest daughter. Oscar

1902.

Snelling, who called him *"a faithful, loyal and loving friend"* officiated at the funeral, and he was buried at Danygraig. (By the time Eliza died in 1919, it was Basil Snelling who preached at the service.)

H.A.C. was very much at home in High Street, then vying quite successfully with Oxford Street as the main shopping area. In February 1893, Musgrave's basket shop near the Cameron was burnt out, and mayor Chapman was quickly on the scene. His was a big house, with five rooms on the first floor, incuding a billiard room (at least in later days), a nursery and a sitting room. The first of these looked East, over the garden and the tenements of the Strand to the ships in the North Dock. The drawing room had a mass of paintings, irregularly hung, some perhaps H.A.'s collection of Turner, Etty and David Cox. Photos from the nineties show a grand piano and a bookcase quite as ornate as the mirror and the rest of the furniture, large plants in pots, a heavy brocaded tablecloth, and a mass of ornaments. If you had visited them on census night, 1891, you might have met the man himself, his wife Eliza (46, Barnstaple born), children Samuel P. (24), Margaret L. (22), Albert H.L. (16), Eva R.G. (14), Odo A.K. (12 — one of Hussey Vivian's sons was Odo) and Daisy S.(11). They all got involved. Maggie (so described) presented Lady Vivian with a bouquet at the station, on the day the town celebrated her husband becoming Lord Swansea. All but Margaret were at the Royal Hotel in March 1893 for the winding up of the unemployment relief scheme. One of the daughters went with him to the Hafod Bible Christians sale of work in April 1893 and spoke *"gracefully"*. The four eldest were at the fancy dress ball later that month. They had a cook, Catherine Morris from Aberavon, and a general servant Mary Edwards from Ystradgynlais.

As time went on Albert (Uncle Bert to the family), even though trained as a mining engineer, took to portraiture — he was good looking, got on with people, and even learnt a little Welsh to make folk feel at ease. He became the principal in the business. Samuel did outside work — press photography, sports teams, businesses, schools and so on — and some of the developing. He took the first pictures of the "Lusitania" disaster, the first air passenger in a Wright biplane, and the first football "snap" for the "Illustrated London News". Odo married young, lived in Mumbles and ran a garage. Margaret managed the staff at High Street. Eva Rhoslyn Gwladys married Stanley Bassett Jones, son of R.E. Jones the hotelier, in 1902, and in later years they lived in Parkmill. Daisy was Daisy St. Clair (born on Christmas Day, — "Aunt Day" to the family). She was famous for taking football and aerial pictures. These two younger daughters were great swimmers in the family tradition.

Chapman's sons married late. Bert moved to Gore Terrace near the old Grammar School on Mount Pleasant in about 1907. The aunts went to a new bungalow at Pennard in about 1923. This left only Samuel and his family at High Street, and they moved out to Murton in 1928. The shop closed when Albert, Sam, Margaret and Daisy retired in 1950. The two ladies had not married.

Lewis Lewis of Llanegwad, Draper

In 1866, Lewis Lewis became a tenant of 27, High Street. He was

> *"...a man of middle stature with a young man's beard, twinkling grey-blue eyes, and a smooth intellectual forehead...[and]...an ambition to start a business Swansea and South West Wales would be proud of..."*

In later days he opened shops in Llanelli, Neath, Briton Ferry and Aberavon, Cardiff and Rhymney, and even London, but it was the one which jutted out into High Street at the bottom of what was then called King Street (Kings Lane) which lasted, as a business, and in the minds of Swansea people. In terms of business practice, he was one of the first in town to end "chaffering", bargaining between shopkeeper and customer; he felt fixed prices made for a more dignified atmosphere and quicker transactions. He was meticulous, his buying being analysed to the sixteenth of a penny. He began a delivery service to Swansea homes and to stations. Purchases were despatched in horse-drawn vans, and boys were employed to race up and down the platforms shouting *"Lewis Lewis!"* The five horses kept in a stable

Lewis Lewis.

behind the shop were *"the apple of his eye"* — he used to exhibit them every year at the Swansea Agricultural Show. By 1890 he owned £111 worth of *"traps, horses and harness"*.

With success he expanded. The original shop has the look of a converted house. In 1873, Messrs. Thomas, Williams & Son of High Street, were employed to remove this and other *"dilapidated buildings"* and create a shopfront 75 feet long. To mark the reopening, he offered 2,000 "Dolly Varden" hats at threepence-halfpenny each. By 1891 he was leasing the original 27 High Street, plus 28 and 29, as well as 9-15 King Street, behind the frontage. The King's Arms, on the opposite corner, was also his. (After his time 90 and 91 Orchard Street were added). In 1893, he bought up two pubs, the Antelope and the Leviathan, possibly both in High Street. His ledgers still exist. In 1890, for example he paid Pugsleys £35 for painting a new mantle showroom. He employed Billings and afterwards Bennet Brothers for building work, Marquis for decoration, J.S. Brown of Oxford Street for plumbing, and bought furniture from Downs across the road. He makes no distinction between the business and his private dealings.

 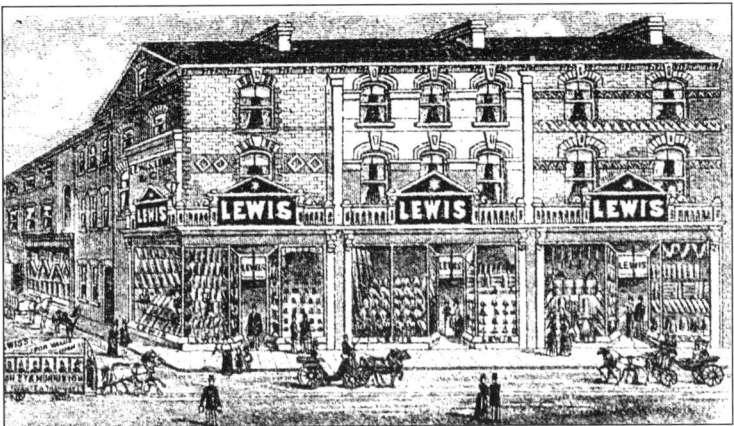

The original shop, and the rebuild of 1873.

He owned three houses in Anne Street, and had an interest in the Market Coffee Tavern. By 1890, he no longer lived over the shop but at "Southville", a fine house where the Uplands end of St. James's Crescent meets Walters Road, perhaps in fact the corner house of this terrace, which has outbuildings and yards, (some modern), stretching some little way up the Crescent — though the house at the opposite end, on Belgrave Lane is another possibility.

Like many successful men of the time, he gave to those less well off —

> *"...Every Friday people in need filed past his cash desk and were given money by Mr. Lewis himself, and if he noticed that a pair of crutches changed hands a number of times outside the shop, he smiled..."*

We can meet quite a few of his staff through the 1891 census. Some of the writing is very difficult, not to mention a whole batch of mistakes and crossings out, but there were certainly 36 *"drapers assistants"*, 7 *"milliners assistants"*, a *"clerk"* and one *"drapers apprentice"* living on the premises, together with a housekeeper and nine *"servants"*, presumably to look after them all. It seems a huge number considering either the living space or the size of the shop. Ben Evans vast store in Castle Bailey Street had only 100 living in, though it is difficult to tell how many "outside staff" either shop had, or how far either ran other nearby hostels — at 36 High Street were 11 more men and women described exactly like these, with Mary Morgan as their housekeeper. It was very close by! No matter how strict the regime in the living quarters, at Lewis Lewis were 54 people aged 14 to 36, all but three under 27. All were single; in fact married women were largely banned from such employment for many years after this. Mary Davies the housekeeper from Cwmtwrch, presumably in charge, was only 26, and cannot have had an easy job! They were all drawn in from a wide area, though very likely the writing on the census sheet, added to the ignorance of the ennumerator, not to mention that of the present author, has led to some rather odd West

A delivery cart.

Wales villages! Just four were Swansea born — Jane Davies, 17, Sarah Harries, 19, Julia Sandbrook, 18 and Maggie Jane Davies, 18. Alice Mary Williams, 22 was from Liverpool, and the two Cardiff girls below may have had to do with his former business. The following came from Glamorgan-

David Davies, 26, and William Losker,
    19, Neath
Henry Williams, 21, Briton Ferry
Hannah M. Jones, 30, Clydach
Ruth Jones, 36, Ynysmeudwy
Barbara Ann Pritchard, 31, (Whitchurch) and
    Lilly Thomas, 23, Cardiff
John Lewis, 20, Treherbert
Emily Jones, 21, Abercarn
A few more from mid Wales —
John Parry Davies, 21 and Daniel Jones,
    25, Brecon
John Hamer, 20, Newtown

Just look at the Carmarthenshire contingent —
Isaac Clayton Jones, Llanngarud
Thomas Thomas, 22, Llansaint
Catherine Jones, 19, Ammanford
Daniel Harries, 22, Cilycwm
John Bennet, 23, Llanelly
Thomas H.Francis, 19, Carmarthen
Alice Davies, 15, Pencader
Thomas Parry Edwards, 24, Ferryside
Thomas Maddocks, 22, Golden Grove
Fanny Thomas, 18,??Aberbaule
Angeline Lamb, 20, and Jenkyn Davies,
    26, Llanllawddog
David Arthur Williams, 14, Llandovery
Sarah Jane Lewis, 19, Llanergors

Morgan Price, 20, Llanfynnydd
Jessie Hannah Rickards, 22, Pontardulais
    (but presumably across the bridge)
Jane James, Sarah Evans, 22, and David
Arthur Williams, 14, Llandovery
George Benjamin Richards, 17, Nantgaredig
William Jones, 20, Llanegwad
(Remember Mr. Lewis haled from Llanegwad
    near Nantgaredig.)

…those from Cardiganshire —
Ebenezer Davies, 17, and Isaac Clayton
Jones,18, Aberystwyth
Joshua Owen Jones, 17, Measllyn
Mary Elizabeth Harries, 22, Cardigan
Ebenezer James, 24, Penrhiwllan?
Benjamin Jones, 21 Strata Florida
John Thomas Phillips, 21, Newquay
Mary Margrette Davies, 20, Llandyssul
Evan Evans, 26, Newcastle Emlyn

and Pembrokeshire —
Sarah Davies, 19, and David James,
    20, Llanfyrnach
Elizabeth Evans, 22, Penrallt
William Henry Lewis, 18, (placename illegible)
Elizabeth Ann Lamb, 16, G. Evans, 20,
    and John Havard, 18, Fishguard
Florence Jane Adams, 16, Saundersfoot

The staff lined up outside the 1873 shop. Very likely some of those in the lists above are present.

A strong link was always kept with West Wales — not only the owner and many of his staff had been born there, but so had many of the customers. It has been said that all the employees were Welsh speaking. This was true of 95% of the shopworkers listed above, though all spoke English as well. So a farmer's wife from rural Carmarthenshire could alight at High Street Station and very quickly find herself speaking a familiar sort of Welsh in a friendly setting — it created a lasting bond which made for good business.

A feature of the shop over many years was the outing, all paid for by the firm. An account of the 1889 trip has survived. 200 went by train, mainly staff, but also a few friends of the owner — J.S. Brown the plumber and his wife, D.C. Jones and his wife — another Swansea draper *"native of an adjoining village"*, — and Thomas Powell of Morriston. Employees were all allowed to take one friend. Mr. Lewis had arranged for them to visit *"the well wooded grounds"* of Cothi Hall, where refreshments were served in a large marquee. They went on to Alltyferin, formerly the mansion of Swansea's Edward Bath, who had died in 1885. The house was described as *"...one of the best specimens of the Thomas, Watkins and Jenkins style of architecture..."*. (see page 44-45 for "the Firm"). Some then made

> *"...a pilgrimage to Llanegwad, the burial ground of which is largely occupied by numbers of the Lewis family..."*

For it was here that Lewis Lewis had been born in 1843, one of eight children, 7 of them boys.....and to his own birthplace he was taking his friends and employees. Proceedings ended with singing, and

> *"a special saloon train...dashing along at extra express speed...[which]...arrived in Swansea somewhat after ten..."*

When he died in January 1911, Lewis Lewis did not go back home. His last house was "Corrymore" the former residence of Ben Evans and of Thomas Freeman on the road between Uplands and Sketty; his last resting place was Oystermouth Cemetery.

> *"High Street tradesmen closed their premises...[in]...warm esteem...the Lewises being quite a household name in the drapery trade...of South Wales..."*

His widow Mary was to have another 21 years.

An undated Lewis Lewis outing, but very likely from our period.

MAP: SWANSEA REFERENCE LIBRARY

Notice the the bedrooms, kitchens, dining room, workrooms and stables.

PIC: WEST GLAMORGAN ARCHIVES

This chemist was next door up ("drugs" on the map), and 31 is Henry Broughton, watchmaker.

The Kings Arms today, across what is now Kings Lane — notice all the houses shown on the map, then in the narrow alley behind it. (Houses are marked "D" — domestic).

Temperance and Coffee Taverns

The town of the nineties had some certainties that we have lost. In 1901, Christchurch in Oystermouth Road issued a little booklet listing the Bible class members. As a space filler, it lists the significant inventions of mankind, with those of the 19th Century comparing very favourably with *"all preceding ages"*. It goes on to give total worshippers in all the Christian denominations, ending with a list of *"Heathens"* including *"Jews 7,186,000... Hindoos 190,000,000..."* Temperance campaigners had a similar self confidence. In March 1890, G.T. Cook *"the Popular Temperance*

Christchurch.

Advocate" came to town on an 11 day mission. The newspaper drawing shows a bearded, tousle haired, heavy browed man, who had *"worked in temperance"* for seven years, having visited Swansea previously in 1888. He could boast that 52,000 pledges to abstinence had *"been taken through his instrumentality"*. Born at Wisbeach in Lincolnshire, he worked as an auctioneer's assistant and a showman in a menagerie before he *"passed through the dark scenes in a drunkard's career himself"*. He was near suicide. So when

> *"...Mr. Cook was induced to speak ten minutes of a mission in Manchester, the effect was electrical. Out of the fullness of his heart did the reclaimed drunkard address the large audience...[and]...moved the people to tears"*.

He was little educated, but built on his personal experience of drink a powerful and passionate delivery, laced with anecdotes of Ireland and the north. In these there was a quiet humour which created an appealing backdrop to the emotional message. Of the expansion of the police force in St. Ives (probably the one in Huntingdonshire) from 1 to 5, he remarked that they were now *"ably assisting each other to do nothing"*. Attendances to hear him in Swansea were described as *"vast"* and halls and chapels were *"full from top to floor"*. He spoke at the Albert Hall, the Drill Hall, and five chapels — Argyle (St. Helens Road), Wesley (top of Goat Street), Tabernacle (Morriston), St.Andrews (St. Helens Road) and Mount Pleasant in Gower Street. Most of these folk needed no convincing; one chairman actually asking why they had bothered to come, for Cook was literally preaching to many of the converted. However, it was claimed that, between 1st and 19th March, 325 people were newly persuaded to sign the pledge to abstain from drink. No doubt funds were boosted too — Mr. Cook urged them to contribute to the cost of the mission, and give to the Bands of Hope.

Prominent local men took part, — for example the mayor Thomas Freeman, a zinc works owner *"who takes a most acute interest in temperance work"*, Alderman Fred Rocke, partner in a woollen mill in the Strand, Frederic Sillery Bishop, copper works manager, John Adams Rawlings, G.P., councillor and hospital doctor. The Mayor of Cardiff Alderman Sanders came to St. Andrews, boasting of his own physical fitness at 60, and referring to *"debt and destruction"* caused by alcohol. Drink wasted money and caused crime. Rev. Gomer Harrison of Morriston, told the weekly meeting of the Gospel Temperance Union the week before the mission that

> *"if...[alcohol]...took its proper place...in the chemists shop labelled as a poison...they would all be satisfied...If we look in the streets in the late hours of the night, we might see the signboards of the public houses lying in the gutters...in the shape of drunken men and women..."*

John Adams Rawlings was a doctor and councillor (see "Jubilee Swansea" I pages 34-5) who carried his uncompromising beliefs into the Council Chamber. He was a gifted speaker, in 1894 voted in a newspaper readers' poll easily the best on the council. In 1892 he suggested, perhaps with justice, that the police

Tabernacle, Morriston.

St. Andrews.

Mount Pleasant.

were just tolerating the eight brothels in the town. (In Orange Street behind the market was a pub incongruously called the Royal Albert, said to be a *"house of ill repute"* in 1896. In 1897, the police admitted to knowing of 98 prostitutes in the town.) In 1893 Dr. Rawlings wanted the Watch Committee to advise magistrates not to permit licensing extensions at Christmas, allowing *"men and women to go home sober on Christmas Eve"*. Councillor Viner Leeder thought the bench would take this heavy handed advice amiss. (He said he represented no interest group. Alderman Daniel replied *"Perhaps you represent the sinners?"*. Actually, on the same committee sat Frederick Bradford, probably the biggest pub owner in Swansea.) That July, Dr. Rawlings criticised the very existence of the police band, then just back from entertaining the passengers of the paddle steamer "Velindra" on their trip to Ilfracombe.

Yet the main use of the police seems to have been the enforcement of the nonconformist code, and the maintenance of a town peaceful and safe enough for its middle class citizens. In March 1897, Captain Colquhoun reported that his force of 102 men had taken action over 300 robberies, 640 cases of drunkenness and 59 of Sunday drinking over the previous year. In May 1896 the police court fined boys 5 shillings for playing cards on the sands, and fined John Wilson of 73, the Strand, for playing pitch and toss on Oystermouth Road. In December 1892, Studt's fair wanted to make use of the empty site next to the library in Alexandra Road, offering £15 for a week. Some councillors were against because it reduced the chance of building development there. Dr. Rawlings, though, railed against

"...the incalculable...evil...of such amusements...especially roundabouts..."

Argyle.

The library. The hoardings to the left are on the site Studts wanted for their fair.

The following January, the plot was let to the Swansea Bill Posting Company at £20 a year. Some members disliked theatres and music halls, and fought against their getting drinks licences. When Andrew Melville of the New Theatre and Star Opera House in Wind Street appeared before the assembled councillors in November 1891, he remarked genially that

Andrew Melville.

> *"...he had not, like every other manager who had come to Swansea gone into bankruptcy...*[laughter]*...even though a small minority of the council were continually sticking pins in him..."*

And there is no doubt Dr. Rawlings could drum up majorities on occasions — in February 1892 the Pavilion (later called the Palace) in Prince of Wales Road was closed, having been refused a dramatic licence.

All the newspaper reports of the police courts include drunkenness. In October 1890, William John Brown of Bond Street in the Sandfields was excused drunken behaviour in Oystermouth Road, on the understanding he signed the pledge. Alderman Freeman as mayor, ridiculed magistrates who delivered

> *"homilies...upon the curse of drink...*[and then] *...called on their way home for a glass of wine or spirits to raise...their fatigued natures..."*

In 1903, Richard Watkins wrote a history of temperance in Swansea — *"...70 years ago there was no Temperance Party, only a dire need for it..."* Open air meetings began in the 1830s, on the Quay, the Sands and especially on a piece of vacant land in lower Goat Street. The pioneers were Joseph Rutter, Valentine Clutton and Mr. Moyse, all Quakers in the ship supply trades. Other notables were William Rosser, Philip Rogers and Joseph Rosser, the last still alive, and in office in temperance bodies since 1840. The author was a Rechabite, full of fire, but uncertain of success. Yes, the Bands of Hope were thriving, but

> *"...Workers excepted they are usually made up of children from five to fifteen years of age. Even before the last mentioned age, the boys attend, for various reasons, in fewer and fewer numbers..."*

In the 1870s an American technique called Grand Templary had been brought in to stop this *"leakage"* of youth. Now its impetus was spent. What other orders called lodges were "tents". So, by 1892 the Swansea area had six, the author being prime mover in the Waun Wen Tent, based at the Congregational Schoolroom in Carmarthen Road. Three more were launched that year — "Sobriety" in St.Thomas, the Park Tent (Trinity Schoolroom, Park Street) and Ebenezer in Llansamlet. Then came a spell of

> *"dangerous stagnation and deathlike calm...this modesty on the part of the Rechabites will be their undoing".*

In January 1897, the St. Helens Tent at the Methodist Schoolroom, Rhyddings was founded, but after more than 6 years, membership was only fifty. In August came the Pride of Morriston Tent, but this fell into a lifeless state. Brother Watkins called for tighter organisation, constitutions, rules....all a way of keeping the ship afloat when individuals fell away.

There was a range of anti-drink societies and organisations. The Swansea Gospel Temperance Union met weekly at the Albert Hall. The Rechabites we have met, their motto — *"banded together are we for the God-like purpose of banishing the drink curse from our land."* The extreme Total Abstinence Society had met at the Ragged Schools since 1857. The President was Charles Davies —

> *"Whether Mr. Davies is a product of the Society, or the Society a product of Mr. Davies, it is hard to say...ever full, bubbling over with talk, grave and gay, wise and witty,...without doubt he is the youngest 'old man' in Swansea, and his spirit is unfailingly infectious..."*

From 1894, temperance groups had a fine new meeting place, what was later called the Central Hall being opened on the corner of Gower Street and Orchard Street. It seated 1,200. The secretary was Thomas Eynon.

You could join the Blue Ribbon Gospel Temperance Army which came to Swansea in 1879, or the British Women's Temperance Association — *"weekly cottage meetings... house to house visitation"*. There was a Roman Catholic League of the Cross, which held a rally in Swansea at August Bank Holiday, 1896 — contingents from all over South Wales marched to St. Joseph's Greenhill. And there was the Church of England Temperance Society. Richard Watkins thought all churches should do more, but, excepting the labours of Mr. and Mrs. F.S. Bishop, he was hardest on the Anglicans

"...the indifference of the Church calls for tears, tears such as the heart weeps..."

Thomas Freeman attacked Anglican leaders who held shares in breweries, but C.H. Glasdcodine of Cae Parc in St. Helens Road retorted —

"...the beer drinking Englishman can do more hard work than any other labourer on the face of the globe...our beer drinking nation has risen...to be the premier nation of the planet..."

Frederick Bradford.

Here spoke a committed churchman. The problem was that among the burgesses of the town, and indeed the pillars of the church, there was a frame of mind at odds with passionate temperance. Some of the mayors are clear examples. Two directors of the Swansea United Brewery Company, formed in 1890 to take over the Orange Street and Glamorgan Breweries, were Albert Mason (mayor 1890-1) and John Aeron Thomas (1898-9). H.A. Chapman, mayor in 1892-3, declared *"they had one object, the glory of God, and the suppression of the drinks trade"* and Alderman Richard Martin (mayor 1899-1900) chaired Temperance meetings, but Frederick Bradford (1895-6) was a brewer and licensee.

Further down the social tree there was a similar tension. In the nineties, the North Dock was still busy, and the pubs along the Strand, which ran beside it, were the lodging, singing and drinking places of sailors from all over the world. In the higher part of the Strand were lodging houses for some of the poorest — the whole place had a wild reputation. In 1868 Argyle Calvinistic Methodist Church of St. Helens Road built Bethany Mission in the Strand and in 1899 they counted 162 on the Sunday School register. George Challenger was involved from 1898. (He was manager of Vivian's Patent Fuel Works beside the North Dock. When his employer was made Lord Swansea in 1893, he had two immense 3 hundredweight patent fuel blocks made, by way of celebration. In 1896 he suffered the sad loss of his daughter Lily, just 22. She had a boyfriend called Elliot Hermann Muller, a clerk with Hancocks the brewers, and it looks as if she died as a result of a botched abortion, though the newspaper account is predictably vague.) George Challenger taught in the Sunday School and also started a successful Band of Hope. It was not easy —

"...such was the rough behaviour of the boys that the leader usually carried a riding whip. The police had frequently to be called in."

One of the biggest public houses was the Cardiff Arms at the bottom of Morris Lane, but larger still was the Bluebell, just 2 doors up. Across the road was a Church Army Mission Room, built into the stone arches of the Great Western Railway's Docks Branch. That October its Captain, Edwin Abel, protested before the court because *"women of ill fame came out in company with men..."*, and used the dark arches either side of his mission for immoral purposes. He referred to an occasion when a fight led to a Frenchman being pitched into the dock. He told how he had gone for a policeman, and the comment was made, *"...have you ever seen a policeman in the Strand?"* The earnestness of the opponents of drink was easy to ridicule and it tended to blind some to the fact that their basic point, that drink had awful consequences for many people, could hardly be denied. The licensee of the Bluebell, William Francis O'Brien, found plenty of defenders. Swansea's senior detective, Frederick William Morris, visited the place and considered it *"well conducted."* A clerk from Goldsworthy's, Ships Chandlers on Broadquay, was one who reckoned himself respectable, but frequented the Bluebell. In 1900 a sailor called John Campbell Shaw drank himself to death in the same pub, but this man was destitute, the landlord, by this time Lane Wilton, befriended him, and it might be said that poverty was the real problem.

There were practical consequences of the temperance movement. Huge efforts were made to prevent the sale of liquor on the sabbath or outside proper hours. In March, 1897, Thomas Sullivan of the Cork Stores, Greenhill was charged with selling a pint and a half of beer on Sunday, but there was not enough evidence. In January that year, a sergeant and constable were on watch at 2 a.m. to spot David Oliver Jenkins of the Brewery Tap in Mysydd Street selling drink. He asked the magistrates if they could not *"look over it"*. The police were still more painstaking later in the month when two P.C.s watched the Ropemakers Arms in Emma Street from 8.15 to 2a.m. and saw 19 women, 2 men and 2 girls go in and out, carrying jugs or tins. In May 1892, Constables Bowen and Williams recorded 40 visits by ten different people to the Dublin Arms, Bridge Street, on a Sunday. The defence council, Charles Slater, contended these were visitors and nurses for the children who were sick — and he carried the day. It was legal for bona fide travellers to be served drink on a Sunday, and that is what five men from Glais and St. Thomas claimed they were when caught by P.C. Thomas in the Vale of Neath Arms in January, 1890.

A Western Mail cartoon comparing sober Sundays in town with heavy Sabbath drinking in Mumbles. The Mumbles train took 1,300 "bona fide" travellers to the village, one Sunday in 1889.

The court considered the publican should have been more sceptical. That same week, John Williams of the Singleton was charged with selling a small bottle of whisky to a woman — on Sunday. She claimed it was for her sick mother. The magistrate John Coke Fowler thought *"the doctor's medicine was much better than the defendant's whisky"* and no doubt chuckled to hear that *"just as the constables were leaving the house, a little girl came up...and asked the landlady to spare her a quart of beer."* All this attention given to the pubs of the town lends some weight to the comment of Alderman Walter Monger, when he stood for Parliament against Henry Hussey Vivian in 1892 — on Sunday closing,

"...he thought the restriction should apply equally to the rich as to the poor, and that the rich man's club should not be on a different footing to the public houses"

Also, the proportion of a force of 101 (1900) employed in enforcing drink laws seems a bit disproportionate. And they were not immune themselves. On New Year's Day 1890 Sergeant Johns and P.C. Elston started a free fight in the public street over Irishmen and soldiers in the force, — a fight fuelled by drink! In March 1890 there was a protest over the intoxicated state of some witnesses in the courts in the Townhall. Left waiting for hours at a time, they made for *"the numerous public houses which abound in the neighbourhood of the Townhall"*. On the opposite side of Somerset Place, numbers 4 to 7, 12 and 19 were all licenced — the Harbour Inn, the Somerset Inn, the Centre Hotel and the Christopher Hotel. In Ferryside was the Vivians Arms and the old Beaufort Hotel by the site of the ferry itself. The call was for a refreshment room within the building, to be supplied by the Coffee Public House Company.

Coffee Taverns

The concept of a cafe was only gradually emerging. The Bovega Restaurant, a longlived establishment at 9 Castle Street, offered:

> *"Snack of Ham or Beef Roll, Pickles and glass of Ale, 6d. Hot Dinners Daily, 12 noon to 3 p.m. 1s. Chop or Steak (at any time of day) with bread 10d. Teas from 6d....Wines, Spirits, Ales and Cigars...F.A. Glover, Proprietress."*

This was unusual. Far more common were the temperance coffee taverns. A guidebook of 1897 lists hotels and then *"cafes and restaurants for those who dine out"* — the compiler mentions the Oxford, the Welcome, the Alexandra and the Market, all of which banned drink. He also refers to the Grand Hotel, on the High Street/Alexandra Road corner, opposite the station yard — the owner, J.E. Fitt, was a tee-totaller, his hotel was "dry", and he ran *"Fitt's Coffee Tavern"* in High Street. The hotel boasted 60 bed-rooms and 6 lavatories by 1897. It was a massive, curving, five storey building with a protruding porch, claiming to be the largest temperance hotel in South Wales. It boasted *"all the delicacies of the season...in the larder...[and]...a marble-top bar counter forty feet in length..."* By means of food and home comforts, it seemed to attract commercial travellers despite the lack of alcohol. The hotel had been founded by Davies & Fitt in 1882. (The later Grand Hotel was across High Street, at its junction with Ivey Place, on the site of what in the nineties was Butt's Hotel, or the Black Cock, proprietor William Butt, 56, Gloucester born. This was a large establishment, and was not concerned with temperance. There was also the Upper Cock, above the station.)

The Grand, looking down High Street, with Alexandra Road to the right. There are adverts for Cadbury's Drinking Chocolate on the windows. Mr.Fitt went bankrupt in April 1900.

The Market Coffee Tavern was *"Opposite the top Market Gate...Hot Dinners..if you want a Good Chop or Steak..."* At least from 1891 (when he was 37) until 1900 it was managed by David Jones — his place of birth, according to the census, was *"Powell Dyffryn."* Louie Cousins, a waitress at the tavern got into the news in 1892 because she won £100 on a six-penny ticket in an Irish Sweepstake.

The Alexandra Coffee Tavern was at 238 High Street (see title page), under the Curtis family at least from 1891 until 1900 — *"...private entrance to Dining and Ladies' Rooms..Breakfasts, Dinners and Teas at moderate prices..Excursionists, Tourists and the Travelling Public will find every comfort..."* It is inter-esting that in 1891 George, the husband, is called a *"painter"*, with his wife Hannah in charge of the cof-fee tavern. It looks as if, as was the case with many town centre pubs, the business did not bring in enough money for a family to live on, though George seems to have taken over in later years. The couple were only 30 in 1900. In 1891 there were two men staying and a staff of five, including Matilda Beard from Tregony in Cornwall.

By 1900 *"the most modern and up to date Temperance House"* — its own claim — was the **Grosvenor** at 23/24 College Street. It had a large dining and commercial room, billiards, a room for ladies and was also an hotel. It advertised *"First Class Pastries and Confectionery"*. The owner was A. Howell.

The Albert Temperance Hotel & Restaurant was on the corner of Cradock Street and Pell Street — *"Commercial, Dining and Ladies' Rooms...Billiards...Tram Cars pass the doors every few minutes to all parts of the town"*. The owner from at least 1894 to 1900 was C. Lockley. In October 1898 the Swansea Amateur Athletic Association celebrated their successful season with a *"social and smoker"* at the Albert, with Mr. Lockley providing a *"splendid repast"*.

An 1894 advertisement is for **The Central Restaurant and Temperance Hotel**, owner William Rowe. No address is given, and it might be guessed this was somewhere near the Temperance Hall on the corner of Orchard Street and Gower Street — what was alternatively called the Central Hall seated 1,400. It was opened that year and extended in 1897. The 1891 census shows the Rowe family running a coffee tavern just below the Cameron Arms in High Street, premises called the **Welcome** and afterwards the **Waverley**. This was a corner building at the top of Welcome Street (our Welcome Lane). Mr. Rowe was from Pudford in Devon, and the family had lived in Birkenhead before reaching Swansea. Elizabeth Rowe was manageress and her daughter Lavinia (16) a waitress. On census day there were two men staying, plus a live-in staff of nine — waitresses, cook and even boots and two billiard markers! (These two lads were William Doherty from Manchester and David Hallow from Liverpool, who perhaps followed the Rowes to Wales.) In 1890 the annual supper for the choir of Holy Trinity Church was at their new schoolroom on Alexandra Road, and catering was by the Welcome Coffee Tavern.

In 1903 there was also the **Devon Temperance Hotel and Cafe** in Castle Street, *"Close to all Railway Stations and Pleasure Steamers, Good Accommodation for all Travellers, Visitors and Cyclists."*

Even in the Strand you could visit James Rupert Mountain's coffee room by 1906 —at number 24, quite

The Albert is on the Pell Street / Cradock Street corner, on the right. Notice the porch in front of the Albert Hall, further up.

likely the former Crown public house — and Ada Fox's coffee rooms, definitely taking over the Troubadour, opposite the Cornish Mount in Anchor Court. In 1896, David Rogers, for a long time cashier to the Cwmfelin Tinplate Works, joined the **Swansea Coffee Public House Company** as secretary. His predecessor was probably Thomas Lloyd Davies, additionally described as general manager, who based himself at the Welcome. This firm operated the Waverley at 243/4 High Street, the Lifeboat, 1 Quay Parade, the Oxford (78 Oxford Street), the Castle in Dunns Place, Mumbles, the Woodfield, 100-101 Woodfield Street, Morriston and the Station Hotel & Coffee Tavern in Pontardulais. Apart from the normal billiards, they advertised bagatelle! **The Oxford** was managed in 1891 by Thomas Oliver from Llanfihangel, Carmarthenshire, assisted by his wife Mary and three others, including a cook. **The Lifeboat** was next to the Arches Hotel, facing the stone railway arches which led towards the river — William Jones the manager was helped by his wife Mary (as cook) and one waitress. The Mumbles branch had been there since at least 1891, when it was run by Edwin Michael.

By 1899 there was also a Mumbles Temperance Hotel at 1, Southend — perhaps just beyond the yard of the George Hotel,... and the Victoria in Station Road, Gowerton by 1902.

Aerated Water

It was presumably the growth of temperance which enlarged the market for commercially produced soft drinks. **Bett's Mineral Water Works** was established in 1851, the oldest in the trade (they said) in town. In 1898 they sold

"Lemonade, Soda Water, Ginger Ale, Zolkakone, Orange and Champagne Cider, Quinine, Potash, Lithia and Seltzer Waters... [some]... in syphon... Picnic Parties and School Treats Supplied ..."

The *"works"* was in Northampton Lane, with premises also at 22 Caer Street. The owner at this time was Charles Llewelyn Watkins, and just after the turn of the century he re-equipped with modern steam machinery. Mr. A. Hurn worked at Bett's for thirty years, organising production, but then in April 1892 left to set up **Hurn's Mineral Waters** in that same Northampton Lane. **Hansard's** Aerated Water was set up in 1871. They offered

"The Best Beverages for the Million!...Gingerade, Raspberryade... Champagne Cider Orange Champagne, Lemonade, Soda Water... Hop Bitters and Stone Jar Gingerbeer... All made from pure Spring Water"

They had *"manufactories"* at Llanelly (Spring Gardens), Bridgend (Coity Road) and Swansea (Wassail Street), with *"stores"* in Neath, Carmarthen and Llandeilo. H.A. Hansard, son of H. Hansard of "Glanmor" in the Mayals died in March 1897. He was buried in Oystermouth Cemetery. His employees were present. **Swansea Aerated Water Company** was an offshoot of the Orange Street

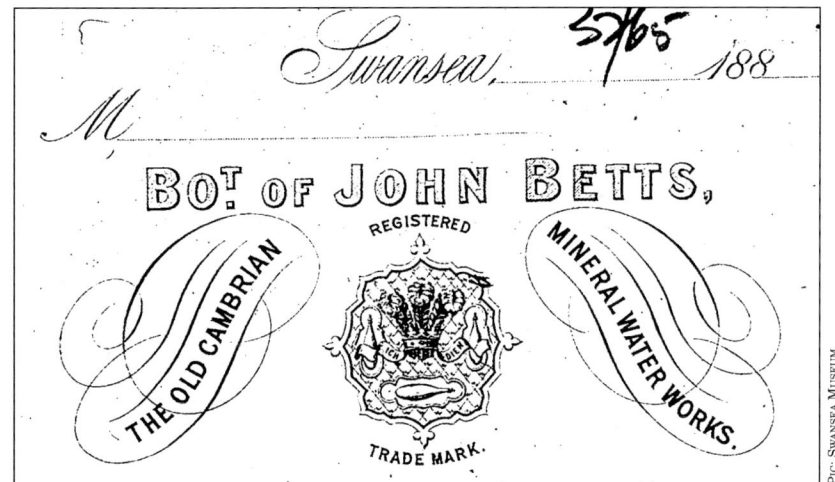

Betts' Mineral Water Works,

Northampton Lane,
. . . SWANSEA.

Manufacturers of all classes of...

Aerated Waters, Stone Ginger Beer, and Hop Bitters.

Soda, Lithia and Potash Waters in Syphons, a Speciality.

Prompt attention given to orders *of any extent.*

Re-fitted with new and modern Steam Machinery.

The oldest Firm in the locality.

ESTABLISHED 1851.

C. LL. WATKINS, Proprietor.

DRINK . . .

HURN'S

High-class

Mineral Waters

and

Hop Bitters

(See Analyst's Report).

Works:

NORTHAMPTON LANE,
SWANSEA.

EMANUEL THOMAS,

Mineral Water and Fruit Cordial Manufacturer, -

Mineral Waters,

Soda, Potash, Seltzer, Lithia, Quinine.

Aerated Waters,

Ginger-Ade, Ginger-Ale, Raspberry-Ade, L i m e , Lemon, &c.

Fruit Cordials,

Ginger Brandy, Ginger Wine, Hot Tom, Hot Toddy, Lime, Lemon, Raspberry, Strawberry, Peppermint, Elderette, &c., &c.

Agent for Wheatley's Hop Bitters and Taylors' Dandelion Stout.

SYPHONS

a speciality.

Families waited upon at their own residence on receipt of post card.

Niagara Works, Alexandra Road,
. . . SWANSEA. . . .

Mr. Thomas was a cyclist — see page 121.

Brewery, founded in 1848, and boasting of its on-site supply of spring water. Both were owned by Messrs. Crowhurst and Benyon Winsor. Its premises were a three storey building of 70 feet in frontage, across the road. In 1889 it was advertising:

"...Mineral Waters...made from Essences prepared entirely on the Premises... guaranteed to be of the finest quality, and perfectly free from impurities...Supplied at the usual prices".

A more specific list of 1888, soon after the firm opened, included ginger ale and beer, champagne cider and lemonade. **Emmanuel Thomas** ran the Niagara Works, and as well as the mineral and aerated drinks listed above, he could boast of *"Ginger Brandy, Ginger Wine, Hot Tom, Hot Toddy, Peppermint, Elderette..."* (1900) He delivered — *"Families waited upon at their own residence on receipt of post card".* So did the **South Wales Hop Bitter Ale Company**. Their non-alcoholic brews were despatched in the company's carts within a five mile radius, at a rate of 27 shillings a hogshead or two shillings a dozen pints.

Castle Square

The tower of the old post office faced down Temple Street, with its decorative frontage reaching south. Linked to it were two shops, with the round tower of the castle rising between and behind them. There was one more building before you reached Castle Lane, a pub. This was the Lion, and in 1892, it was *"reconstructed"* by Mr. Evans, a new landlord. By 1893 more new tenants, Mr. and Mrs. James, were said to be fast making it *"the most popular theatrical house in town".* Beyond the lane was Castle Square.

5th November in Castle Square was, for some years, chaos. It all started in 1872, when someone in the Castle Hotel threw what were called *"bedroom slops"* from an upstairs window on to the crowd below. It caused riot. A surging crowd threw missiles until all the hotel windows were shattered. The mayor, John Glasbrook and Chief Constable, John Allison, both imposing men of some confidence, could make no impression. Over the next few years it became accepted practice for *"thousands of young men"* to gather and indulge in *"pyrotechnic sport",* with the police being content to hold the ring.

By the nineties all this was just a memory.

Who might you meet if you strolled through the Square?

In October, 1891, **Henry Maliphant** was one of the two councillors for Castle Ward — he lived in Castle Square. In 1899 he is listed as a bookseller there. He was a member of the Working Men's Club in Alexandra Road.

In 1865 **John Taylor** from Lincolnshire took over Mathew Brothers at 6 Castle Square, which was already 20 years old. He was only 22, but had such enterprise that by 1885 that he made it a limited

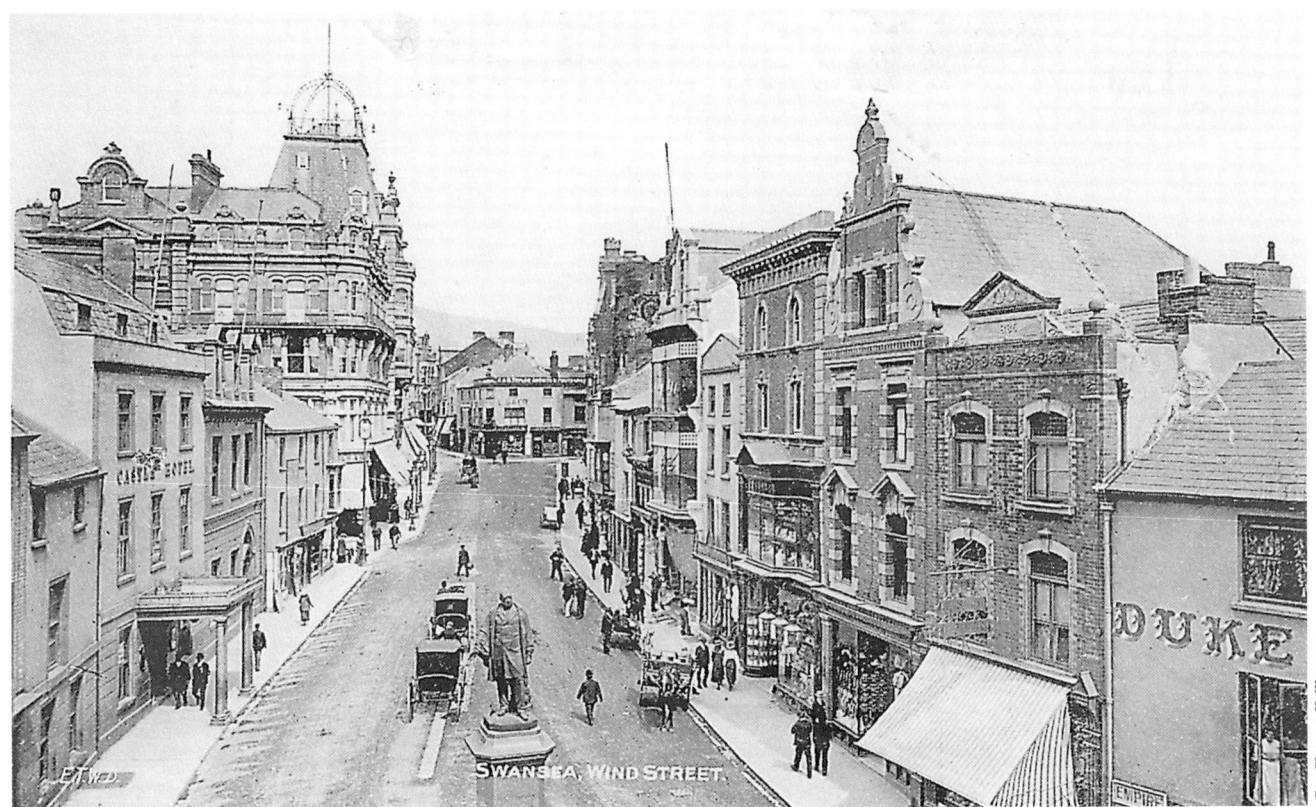

*Castle Square in about 1900. Next to the Duke is number 8 (Phillip Jenkins), then 7 (D.C. Jones), 6 (John Taylor), then 5 to 1.
On the left, 9 is this side of the Castle Hotel, with 11-14 running up to the fine block of Ben Evans.*

company, directors William Stone, J.P., R.D. Burnie, Julius Smith and Henry Hunt, with Taylor himself as managing director. It was registered that November, with a capital of £100,000. The premises of B.R. Henessy, jeweller, at 5 Wind Street, were then taken over as an outlet for glass, china, — services by Minton, Doulton and Wedgewood, other china by Worcester and Derby — as well as clocks watches and jewellery — *"brooches, lockets, necklets, rings, bracelets, bangles, chains, charms, pins, studs, sleeve links..."* A Mr. Davies was manager by 1893. By the nineties Taylor's had branches in Mumbles and five other areas of Swansea, as well as Aberavon (2), Taibach, Dover, Weymouth, Stourbridge and Kidderminster. At a guess, Messrs. Smith and Hunt had links with these more distant areas. Castle Square was still the main shop. The *"noble frontage"* on Castle Square was four storeys, and the premises extended to the Strand, a depth of 250 feet. Apart from things already mentioned, you could buy general groceries, cigars and brushes, and hire tableware of all sorts. They also became sole agent for Mappin & Webb electro-plate and cutlery. New in the late eighties was...

"a saloon in which customers can partake of light refreshments...a resting place for ladies who have extensive shopping to do...tea, coffee, cocoa and other light refreshments of the best kind...".

On the second floor patent medicines and stationery were sold, and there was *"...a tea-blending room, personally supervised by the experienced managing director..."* Taylors were known for their tea. A lift ran from the cellar to the top floor, and the shop made use of *"Lamson's patent cash railway"*.

John Taylor lived at a house called Northway in Bishopston. By 1888 his son John Henry was taking some of the responsibility.

John Taylor, 1897.

S.C. Guilmont was secretary of the Swansea Club opened in 1871. It was for army navy and militia officers. The club was at number 11, next to the Castle Hotel.

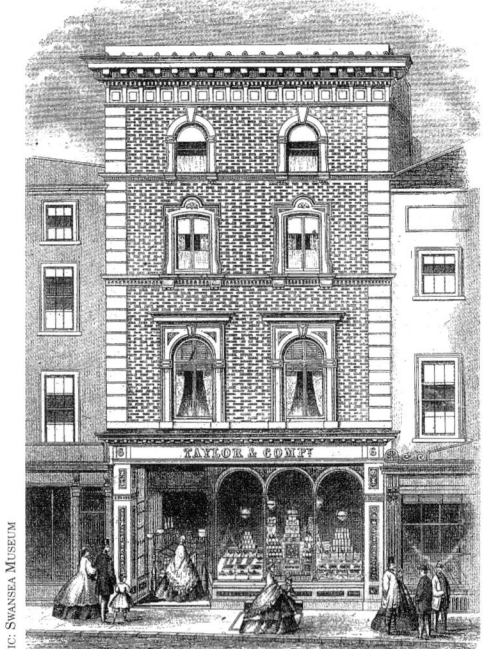

Taylor & Company, inside and out, 1860s.

Edmund Leigh Morgan of Fernhill, a large house on the Mumbles side of Blackpill, died on 28th October, 1899 and was buried at Oystermouth. He had run a wines and spirits business at Castle Square. He had given the clock in the tower of the new St. Mary's Church — the Victoria Tower. He gave this in memory of his father Samuel, owner of the wine stores for many years, a place generally known as "Dirty Dick's". Many of its customers had been "early nippers", sailors boarding or leaving vessels first thing — the licencing laws then did not prohibit this. So, when one morning in the early seventies, Samuel's doors remained fast shut, the police thought it best to break in, and indeed he had passed away in his sleep.

In 1891 **E.E. Rowse** lived at 12 Castle Square, next up to the club. He was Exeter born. His wife Ann was a harp teacher. They were 62 and 70 respectively. He had been headmaster of the Royal National Schools at Windsor, and then editor of the Swansea Journal and the Herald of Wales. He still considered himself a journalist by trade. In 1890 he had published a pamphlet protesting against Swansea still being on a branch off the main railway (change at Landore) and urged the re-opening of the little G.W.R. staion which had been in the railway arches beside Little Wind Street. In 1896 he wrote something more ambitious, 106 pages called "In and Around Swansea". It does wander a little, even worse than this book! About half is concerned with the Celtic people the Silures, who lived in this part of Wales in Roman times. He relates how Caractacus and the Archdruid Bran were converted to Christianity after long *"discourses"* with St. Paul in Rome. He describes in detail — all imaginative — the Silurian settlement called Abertawe —

> *"On high festival days the villagers of the valley would trudge down to Abertawe to see the sports on the river and watch soldiers from the encampment exercising themselves in their chariots, throwing the dart, casting the javelin, wrestling..."*

Nor is his style of writing over restrained! He greets the reader with —

> *"Long before the Adamic race first appeared on the vast plains of Asia the Atlantic waves had preyed with incessant and remorseless fury upon the Western shores of Albion..."*

E.E.Rowse.

He is quite ready to defend his *"romantic"* inclinations, and beside them he records a great deal of Swansea history which was alive in the folk memory of the nineties — without his labours, it would have perished. He was a great supporter of William Thomas of Lan, who he called in 1897, *"my old and esteemed friend"*. From 1896 he was living at 53 Trafalgar Terrace, Oystermouth Road.

From his shop at number 7 might come David Cornelius Jones (always known as **D.C. Jones**). He was born on 19th June 1843. He was the son of a Methodist minister from Llanfynydd, a village in the Towy valley, and began work at John Roberts's drapery in Llandeilo. He progressed to Meekings & Co in Holborn, then to Thomas Richards's business at 7 Castle Square, a shop founded in the thirties. He took over on the old man's death. He kept *"fancy drapery, silks, millinery, hosiery...a speciality is made of dressmaking..."* The shop was four storeys high on a frontage of 30 feet, and 60 deep. Showrooms workrooms and warehouses

were upstairs. He *"furnished funerals"*, arranging John Glasbrook's funeral in May, 1887. He made a new set of mayoral robes of scarlet West of England cloth in 1897 for £40.

From about 1887 he also had a high class gents silk mercery at 3, Wind Street, only three doors down, under Mr. Roberts, but this had gone by 1891, when George Garbutt from Hull lived there, and sold boots and shoes.

"Mr. Jones...[it was said]*... is held in high esteem...in social and commercial circles"*, but was also reckoned *"a charming personality"*. A late photograph shows a striking man with twinkling eyes and a neat white beard and moustache. He was a friend of Lewis Lewis, an exact contemporary from very much the same neck of the woods. In 1891 he lived on the premises with his wife Sarah, daughters Ester (already called his *"book keeper"* at 14) and Ethel, and son Graham. One milliner and two domestic servants lived in. Later he moved to Ernald Place in the Uplands, and by 1899 Ernest E. Jones, secretary of the Drapers' & Clothiers' Association is at Castle Square — perhaps he was shop manager. D.C. Jones died in 1911 and after a service at Argyle, St. Helens Road, was buried at Danygraig.

Phillip Jenkins was at number 8 in 1892. In 1888 he had been at number 5 and this earlier shop and showroom were 4 storeys high, on a 30 foot frontage, and 150 deep. It was a business established over a century. He was a linen and woollen draper and funeral furnisher, under the sign of the Golden Key. At the end of January 1890 he advertised an 11 day sale of *"Winter Drapery — Black French Merinos, Black Cashmeres, crepe cloths, costume cloths, black and blue serges"*. In 1892 he offered

"...Silks, Dress Goods, Flannels, Sheelings, Linens Calicoes, Blankets. Largest stock of Woollens in Swansea. All Tailoring done on the premises...first class cutter.

Depot for all the latest designs and novelties in Cricket, Football, Bicycling, Running and Gymnastic Requisites..."

His drapery came, he said, from the best British firms. In 1890 at the chamber of trade meeting, where he was a frequent speaker, he advocated re-opening the station in the arches beside Little Wind Street. In 1898 he was Chairman of the Drapers Association, and was vocal and prominent in a meeting of town tradesmen to push for a new townhall and a mainline station. Mr.Jenkins was said to be *"well known in commercial circles...[and]...the general patronage of this establishment is drawn from the middle and better classes in the town and district..."* In 1901 he announced- *"for the Autumn Trade...Ladies' and Gentlemen's wear"*. From1888 at least until 1892, he got the contract to supply the clothing for officers of the Harbour Trust. In 1891 it netted him £190/2/11, even though his tender was £8 higher than the lowest London figure.

In 1891 he lived at 35 Carlton Terrace. Born in Llanmadoc he was 62, had a wife Ellen, and they had 5 children at home. By 1906 he lived at Goetre House, 11 Belle Vue Street.

The North Dock and some caring doctors

Dr. E.B. Evans.

Dr. E.B. Evans M.R.C.S. was born in 1848 in Aberdare. He was Welsh speaking. He went to school in Cadoxton, then to Swansea Normal College and Guy's Hospital. In about 1872, he got the job as deputy medical officer to the Swansea Poor Law Guardians and police....and the next year married the daughter of his boss, Dr. D.H. Thomas, — the police *"presented him with a handsome timepiece"*.

"In the same year he commenced practice in St. Thomas, then a small hamlet with a very limited population. The increase......was, however, very rapid, and Dr. Evans by his genial manner and ever ready attention to calls upon him soon reached among the members of his profession, and there is no one more popular, among rich or poor....as he has always taken the greatest interest in the welfare of the working classes."

He became a J.P. in 1893, and was concerned with St. John's Ambulance, but concentrated on the east side, as surgeon to railway companies, works and friendly societies from Llansamlet to Port Tennant. He lived at 18 Mackworth Villas, St. Thomas, next to the Nancarrows, with his wife Mary, two daughters, cook, housemaid and another servant, Jane Davies, who was 50 and deaf and dumb. Mary was sister to John Thomas, Town Clerk. He was churchwarden at St. Thomas's church. He became Honorary Curator of Geology at the Royal Institution in 1894, and was very active in museum display.

Dr. W. Morgan had a surgery in Adelaide Cottages, Adelaide Street. A 37 year old Ystradgynlais born bachelor, he lived there in 1891 with his housekeeper Margaret Roberts from Llandyssul. That November it was reported that dockworkers were making a collection for him.

"' You see", said one of the men who are raising the fund, to a reporter, "go there with an accident when you like, at mid day or mid night, Dr. Morgan never asks, 'Who is he? What is he?' or 'Does he belong to a society?' he simply asks 'What is it?' and then does his best for him.'"

Dr. James Griffith Hall, M.R.C.S., L.S.A. was 76 in 1891. The son of James Hall, harbour master, layer keeper and corporation treasurer, he was at Guy's Hospital in the thirties. He became a conscientious magistrate and had been a visiting or consulting surgeon at the Hospital since 1857. He was surgeon to the 3rd Glamorgan Rifle Volunteers from 1859, as such being presented at court in 1881. In

A full rigged ship alongside the Beaufort Basin, North Dock.

November,1899 he gave a detailed lecture on his work at the Royal Cambrian Deaf and Dumb Institute on Mount Pleasant, and on the training of doctors for such work. In 1891 he lived at 7 Prospect place with one servant Susan Mitchell. By 1899, his address was given as Mount Street, so near by that it was probably the same house!

The North Dock and its basin were very close. It was Swansea's oldest floating dock, but still busy. In July 1890, the 4,000 ton ship "Tosco" arrived, the largest vessel ever to enter. On 22nd May that year, George Sackville sailed out in the yacht "Sunbeam" which he had bought from John Player, the Clydach tinplate owner. July also saw the arrival of the "Vanguard", a steam seal fisher under Captain Pike. It had been a hazardous voyage, her boat and deckhouse washed away by heavy seas, but very profitable — she was averaging 50,000 seals a trip! In July 1891, Henry Hussey Vivian charged Captain Turtle, master of his steam yacht "Eothen" with swindling him out of £3/4/6 by false accounting over dry docking. The vessel was under repair in the Albion Dry Dock, on the eastward side of the dock.

The dock was the scene of many an incident. In February 1893 a missing colliery manager, David Williams, was presumed drowned, when his bowler hat was found floating there. In April 1891, the same conclusion was come to over the hat of Captain Kerandren of the 49 ton dandy "Yvonne" of Morlaix. On 22nd December, 1895, the S.S. Chatsworth, loading coal at the Cobra wharf in the main North Dock, caught fire. It was eventually put out by the horse drawn fire brigade, with Captain Colquhoun the Chief Constable in attendance. Deck planking had to be ripped out.

In February 1891, a 16 year old lad from nearby Powell Street, larking around on one of the cranes at Cory and Yeo's fuel work, fell into the main dock. A French sailor from S.S. "Cambria" jumped in *"with his clothes and clogs on"* to save him. This works was near the top of the dock, on the site of the old Cambrian Pottery (1764-1870). In January 1890 two detectives caught Eldred Jones and Patrick Roley, who was just 10, sleeping on the works boilers. It seems they had stolen sweets and nuts from a house in nearby Pottery Street. Eldred was said to be one of *"a gang of junior thieves"*. They received 10 and 14 days in prison, followed by five years in reformatory school! The Beaufort Basin opened off the lower eastern side of the dock, from which it was separated by a boom. In January 1890 a drunken fireman from the steamer "Salient" fell off that, but was rescued. At midnight on 2nd June, 1891, two dock police were chatting on the New Cut Bridge when they heard a cry — Thomas Jennings a fireman of S.S. "Dromeda" had fallen in. He drowned. There were no accessible steps, no life saving equipment. This bridge over the New Cut was in some ways a frontier post, dividing the town proper from the Eastside. There had been tolls, and their abolition was a cause of huge political uproar. In 1893, George Nancarrow, who lived in St. Thomas, complained of the decrepitude of the bridge — swinging it back into place once a vessel had passed often meant two men pushing and shoving. Another councillor had seen a tug and two railway locomotives in concert used to try and close the gap. In February 1890, a woman may have been trying to dodge the toll on the bridge. Boilermakers working on repairing the Liverpool steamer "Montague" heard a splash.at about 7.30 a.m.. They dragged her out, and then to Dr. Hall's surgery, but it was too late.

His reputation as a caring doctor was universal. In the year 1851 he had made 1,380 house visits. When the hospital adopted a new motto in 1890, "Pity and Need make all flesh Kin", the man depicted with the words was Dr. Hall. He died on May 27th, 1901 and was buried at Danygraig. He left £500 towards a new operating theatre at the hospital. People made mention of his help of poorer people, his readiness to give time and money — he was *"genial and straightforward"*.

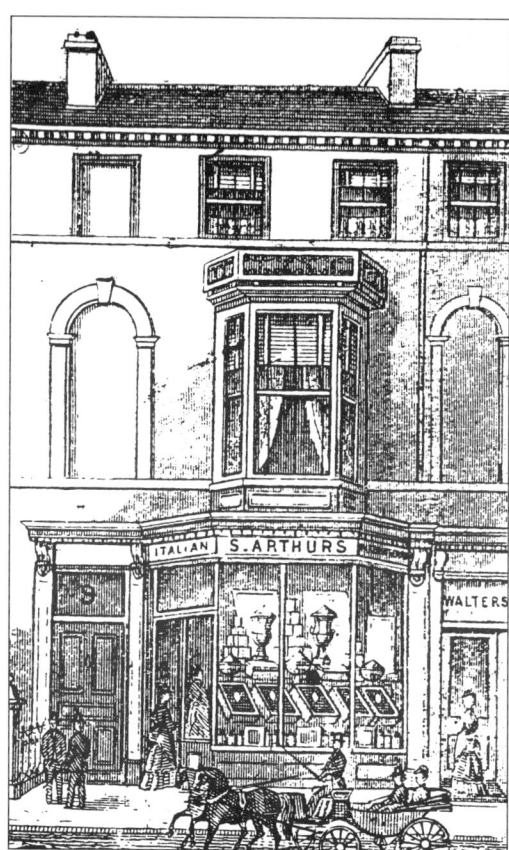

*Seymour Arthurs ran this grocery shop in
Tremont Terrace, Walters Road (see page 106).
It dated from the 1850s.*

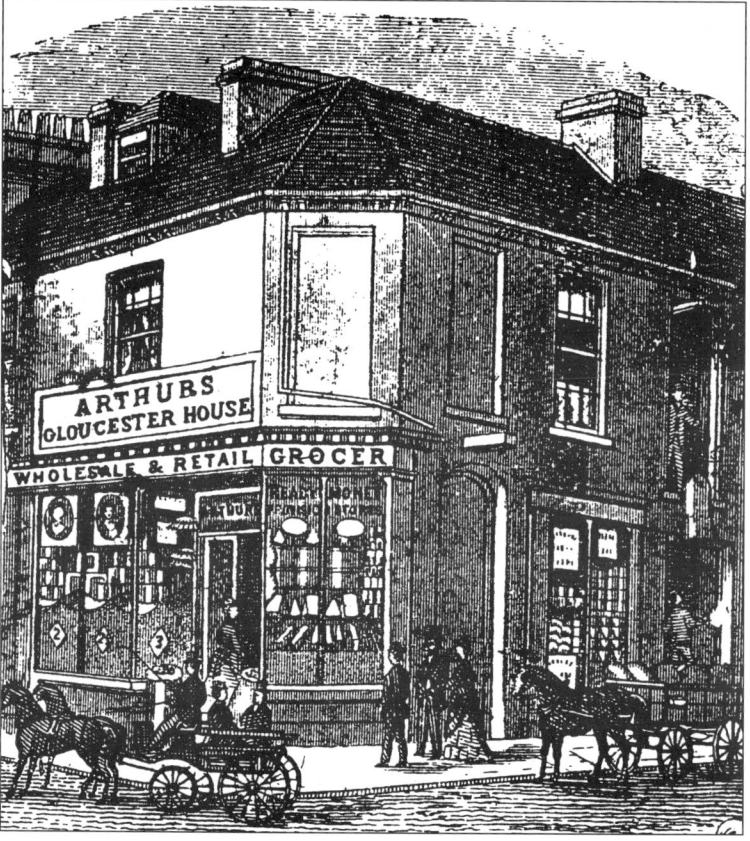

*By the nineties Mr. Arthurs also ran this shop at 66 High Street —
above the station.*

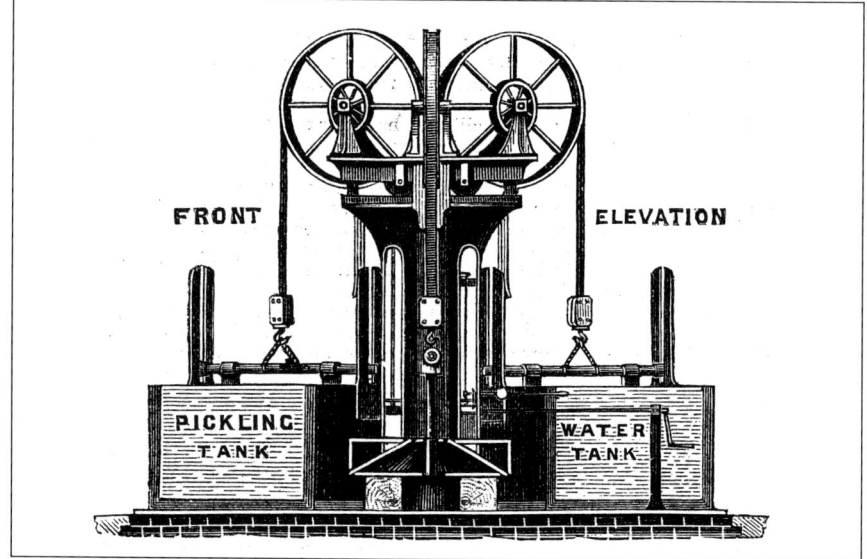

Tinplate pickling machine manufactured at the Millbrook Foundry, Landore, (see page 29).

A great deal of information is from the 1891 census, as should be obvious from the text. Guidebooks and directories too have been very useful; they are not always listed below. The aim is to give an idea of from where the information comes, but prizes will not be given to readers who find errors or ommissions!

Newspapers are coded thus - C - Cambrian...CDL - Cambria Daily Leader... Gaz - Swansea Gazette & Shipping Register...HoW - Herald of Wales...IW - Industrial World or Welsh Industrial Times...SGH - Swansea & Glamorgan Herald...SJ - Swansea Journal... SW - South Walian...SWDN - South Wales Daily News...SWDP - South Wales Daily Post...WM - Western Mail.

The last digit in a reference is usually the page number. Books are described in full the first time, but abbreviated thereafter.

Introductory C/28/10/92/3...C/21/10/98/3

A changing town WM/31/1/95...SW/6/98/474 & 7/99/670... GAZ/30/7/90/5 ...SW/2/97/219...C/10/11/93

A Morriston Wedding Andre Scoville, "Morriston's Pictorial Past", Cowbridge, 1988), p.24...C/29/4/92/8... WM/28/4/92... CDL/28/4/92.

William Williams and Edward Rice Daniel Dewi Glannant Williams, "Morriston Hospital, the Early Years", (Swansea, 1993), 19...SW/10/98/538..."Industries of South Wales", (Birmingham, c.1888), 102...C/1410/98... IW/10/4/96/7...C/5/5/93/3... SW/11/1900/905...Paul Reynolds, "Two Swansea Collieries, Cefngyfelach and Tirdonkin" in "Gower", 1981, p.60-1 and with thanks to the author for some corrections ..."Ports of the Bristol Channel" (1893) 116...C/15/5/96/5...C/18/12/96/8... C/28/10/92/6...SW/6/97/287...T. Marchant Williams, "Welsh Members of Parliament", (Cardiff, 1894), p.67-8...GAZ/10/4/96/7... C/12/3/97/3. A little on William Williams in David Dykes, "The University College of Swansea, an illustrated history", (Alan Sutton, 1992), p.46 & 76. This is excellent on late 19th Century Swansea ...N.L. Thomas, "The Story of Swansea's Districts & Villages", II, 35...CDL/11/7/1919

The McKinlay Tariff GAZ/29/10/90/5...28/10/91/4....16/9/91/6...18/3/91/5... 27/5/91/4 (See "Pluribus" on "Around Swansea Docks")...C/22/5/96/5...6/5/92/5... 17/1/90/6...SW/11/97/373...GAZ/9/3/92/4...9/11/92/5.

The boom... GAZ/17/6/91/6 ("Pluribus")...12/10/92/5...24/6/91/6...C/5/12/90...GAZ/23/7/90/5...25/2/91... 13/8/90... 10/6/91/5...15/2/93/5....13/5/91...12/8/91...15/4/91/5...C17/1/90...GAZ/28/5/90...25/2/91...23/3/92/4...SW/5/99... Glamorgan County History, V, p.144-6.

After the boom... SW/8/96...C/22/4/92/6 "A Workingman's view of the situation...by a Tinplate Worker". (Subsequent articles: 29/4/92/6...6/5/92/7...3/6/92/7)...GAZ/21/9/1892....19/8/1891....& 22/4/1891...C/3/11/99/1... 17/11/99/4

R.N.Cooper, "A Dark and Pagan Place...a history of Penclawdd..", (Cowbridge, 1986), p.57-8...GAZ/10/4/96/11... 4/11/91/5...17/2/92/4...2/11/92/4...SW/6/97/291...

A.M.C. Swansea Guide, 1903, p.27..."Industries", p.74...GAZ/28/1/91/4...

"Times" letter quoted from GAZ/3/2/92/4...15/7/91...15/7/91...SW/6/98/478

SWDP/14/3/93/2...C/5/3/97/8...6/11/96/7...5/3/97/5...SW/12/96/186-7...C/7/8/96/4...IW/13/11/96/10...6/11/96/1... 13/11/96/3...20/11/96/9...27/11/96/11....16/12/96/9....27/11/96/9....10/4/96/1...5/6/96/1...25/12/96/10...Stan Awbery, "Labour's Early Struggles in Swansea", (Swansea. 1949), p.27...

Tinplate workers IW/30/10/96....19/6/96/1...an excellent book for this whole topic is Paul Jenkins, "Twenty by Fourteen, a History of the South Wales Tinplate Industry", (Llandyssul, 1995).

"The Swansea Gazette & Shipping Register" Most of this is drawn from the newspaper itself, but see also SW/11/1900/916.

William Thomas of Lan J. Alun Owen, "Swansea's Earliest Open Spaces, A Study of Swansea's Parks and their Promoters in the Nineteenth Century", (Studies in Swansea's History, Swansea City Council, 1995), especially p.43-48. SW/8/1902/116... 5/97/285

Swansea Museum has 6 scrapbooks of materials on the life and career of William Thomas of Lan. Much in this section is prompted by Scrapbook G, which covers 1876-1902, e.g., copy of letter, William Thomas to G.L. Morris, 5/10/1894...C/30/1/90/4... CDL/19/11/90...For the new political atmosphere, see Stan Awbery, and a little in Gerald Gabb, "Some Cracks in the Fabric of Victorian Swansea" in "Gower", XLIV, 1993, p.50-56...CDL/15/2/91... C/28/8/91...CDL/4/6/91...GAZ/6/5/91/4...C/27/3/91... CDL/15/2/91...SWDN/19/3/1891...C/1/1/92/3...Wright's Guide, 1906, p.41 & 58.

W.C. Rogers, "A Pictorial History of Swansea", (Gomer, 1981), p.50.

Cwmgelly Cemetery D.M. Bayliffe and J.N. Harding, "Starling Benson of Swansea", (Cowbridge, 1996), p.135-152...C/28/10/92...CDL/2/1/92...18/2/92...WM/23/1/92...CDL/29/9/95

The Squire of Lan Wright's Guide, 1906, p.37-77...For the sale of the estate, "Brecon & Radnor Express", 8/8/1901...C/14/2/90...CDL/29/11/90

Last days "Ports", (1893), 135..."Industries" 90-1...Richard Davies, Lower Swansea Valley Factsheet 8, "Tinplate" (Swansea Museum), p.8, 22 and bibliography p.39...Also Factsheet 10, "The Morris Family", p.51-53. Letters to George Lockwood Morris, 5/10/1894 and 12/9/1894 in museum scrapbook... SW/11/1903...Letter from G.L. Morris, 8/10/1894.

Thomases and Morrises Wright's Guide, p.42-3...SW/12/99/754

On the Bevans, Helen Hallesy, "The Glamorgan Pottery, Swansea, 1814-1838", (Gomer, 1995), 7-8...N.L. Thomas, "Districts & Villages..", I, 76.

The Statue of William Thomas Wright's Guide, p.68...An account of the meeting was printed and circulated - copy, Swansea Museum, 51/20...SW/11/97/374... 6/98/475...5/97/284... Wright's Guide, p.69 & 78-9...CDL/22/1/1909...With thanks to Ronald Austin for information on memorial masons.

A.C. Wright Swansea Museum cuttings book, 1879-1923. 131 St. Helens Avenue is a solid two-storey terraced house, contrasting with the larger residences across the road. It has no outbuildings of any size or age. Perhaps the numbering has been changed!

SW/11/96/cover...9/99/cover...9/96/151...9/99/707...Kilvey Men's Bible Class, 8th Annual Report,(copy, Swansea Museum, 81/8) - "This report is a specimen of the Printing executed by A.C. Wright." The Swansea Museum copy of the 1897 Guide (81/12) belonged to Alexander Moffatt. Examples of far better printing, admittedly on higher quality paper, and probably therefore far more expensive: Swansea Harbour Trust, "Visit to Swansea of the Incorporated Law Society.." October, 1898 and Burrows, "Official Guide to....Swansea", about 1903. Swansea Museum has an incomplete run of the "South Walian" up to August 1902. W.H. Jones, "History of the Indefatigable Lodge, No.237, and of the advancement of Freemasonry in Swansea", (Carmarthen, 1923), p.169... SW/1/97/208...Wright's Guide, p.70...SW/12/97/380... 8/1902/117.

W.H. Spring SW/1/97/209-210...A.M.C. Guide, 1895, advert...There are many terse adverts for the concern, e.g. in Wright's Swansea Reference Book, 1897...Insurance Maps, 1887, 1897... W.C. Rogers, p.161-2...C/18/9/96... SW/7/1900/864

W.T. Mainwaring Hughes, "Swansea's Mayors and Civic Events from 1900 to 1973", p.12-13.

John Dixon moves on GAZ/27/7/92/5....14/9/92/4-5....12/10/92/5...11/2/91/4

Floating the river Walter Lewis, "The Floating of Swansea Harbour", ("The Cambrian", 1894) - SM boxfile 19/3... GAZ/11/2/91/4...CDL/19/11/90...WM/13/5/94...SW/6/1901/995...GAZ/13/4/92/4...SWDP/14/5/1901/3...CDL/14/5/1901/2 ...C/17/5/1901/5...GAZ/25/2/91/4...6/5/91/4...SW/11/96/169...GAZ/13/1/92/5

Rossers and tugmen GAZ/14/5/90/4...12/11/90/4...30/12/91/5...16/7/90/4...A.M.C. Guide, 1903, 55-59... Directories, including Wright's 1889-90, Cambria Daily Leader 1887 & 1894, Town & County, 1899...Swansea Harbour Trust tidetables, 1887 onwards..."Ports" 122..."Industries" 98...SJ/14/12/94/4... 5/11/98/2...C/14/10/98/3...10/1/90/6... GAZ/21/9/90/4...C/24/1/90/5...GAZ/22/4/91/6...31/5/91/6...SW/1/97/212...GAZ/18/5/92/4 & 8...GAZ/15/10/90/4...Carl Smith, "Gower Coast Shipwrecks", (Clydach, 1993) throughout, e.g. on "Wasp", p.64, with thanks to the author... Tom Nicholson, "Taking the Steam, the Alexandra Towing Company and the British Tugboat Business, 1837-1987".

Oystermouth Cemetery opened in 1883, and the top picture shows it about 20 years later. It quickly became a fashionable burial place for notables from Swansea and Morriston, especially near the top of the yew avenue.

Here are the graves of...
Left: William Phillip Ching, the tug owner (page 36).

Below left: David Villiers Meager and his family, including Kildare Stucley Meager, the pottery expert (page 41)

Below centre: John Corfield, Amy Dillwyn's trusty works manager who died in 1917.

Below right: John Trevillian Jenkin of Mirador — 1809-1880 (page 98).

David Mansel Glasbrook, colliery and tinplate owner who died in 1933, aged 76.

John White, manager of Ben Evans.

Lewis Lewis (page 142), who christened his son Lewis Egwad after the village where he was born.

John Roberts the engineer, leading light of the Scientific Society (left), and John Taylor the grocer (right).

William Williams of Maesygwernen (and near him James Burchell, coach builder and William Watkins of "the firm").

John Samuel Brown of the cycle shop, who lost a son — killed in the Royal Flying Corps in 1917.

W.H. Stone the timber merchant who lived in Ffynone (pages 98-99)

Edward Towers the dry dock manager.

William Westlake and Constitution Hill GAZ/11/2/92/5...A.M.C.Guide, 1894, advert...C/3/1/90/1...SW/2/97/ cover...SGH/10/9/90/7...GAZ/2/5/91/6...14/1/91/5...SW/12/97/383...GAZ/1/10/90/5...7/1/91/4...12/8/91/5...9/9/91/1... "Ports" 35... C/28/8/91...Nigel Robins, "Homes for Heroes, Early 20th Century Housing in the County Borough of Swansea", (City of Swansea, 1992), p.1-2...C/6/4/83 & J. Alun Owen, "Open Spaces...", p.55...Letter from William Thomas to George Lockwood Morris, 5/10/1894...SW/11/97/364...C/18/12/96/3...14/7/99/4..."Contemporary Portraits and Biographies, Men and Women of South Wales and Monmouthshire", (Cardiff, 1897), Vol I, xxiv, xxix, xliii, 41, 36, 184...CDL/11/1/1913...The story of the line is drawn squarely from J.H. Price, "A tramway fiasco", in "Modern Tramway", December, 1979, p.410-417.

Houses and Builders With thanks to Nigel Robins for advice. N.L. Thomas, "Districts & Villages", I, 50...C/3/1/90/3 ..Report of the Swansea United School Board, 1888, quoted in Sandra Hawkins, "Brynmill School Centenary", 1896-1996, (Brynmill Primary School, 1996), p.5..."Terrace Road School, the first hundred years", (1990)

Goskar Parish of Swansea, Grand Bazaar at the Albert Hall, 25th-27th October, 1893, p.16, (SM/boxfile 66a)... SW/6/96/99...11/96/181...12/96/197

John Davies Wright's Swansea Annual,1897...Carnival Programme, 1901, p.38.

The Marles Wright's Illustrated Swansea & Mumbles Guide, c.1897...Town & County Directory, 1902-3, p.9

Bennet Bros. C/7/8/96/1...7/10/98/1

T.P. Jones/Aaron Boundy C/6/5/92/1...Wright's Swansea Annual...for 1897

Thomas Davies SW/8/1902/117...C/7/8/96/1

Thomas Richards SW/12/96/199.

Joseph Gwyn C/3/1/90/8...C/6/5/87/4

Thomas, Watkins & Jenkins There is a little about William Watkins in W.T. Mainwaring Hughes, "Swansea's Mayors and Civic Events, 1900-1973", (Swansea, 1974), p.8...C/3/1/90/1..."Industries" 101...Kelly's Directory of South Wales, 1891, p.481...GAZ/31/8/92/4...C/10/11/99/4-5...W.H. Jones, "...the Indefatigable Lodge" 170...though he does seem to attribute the work to Thomas White of the Strand on p.96-7 ...W.H. Jones "Port" 290... GAZ/31/8/92...Wright's Directory, 1889-90, p.50...Mainwaring Hughes, p.8...C/6/5/92/1...Ben Evans & Co., the Swansea Improvement, 24/11/1894...SW/12/97/379...8/98/512...C/5/3/97/4

Thomas Evans C/8/1902/117.

J.&F. Weaver C/17/1/96/5...Purrier's Swansea Directory, 1913-4, (South Wales Daily Post), p.14...HoW/30/5/1931 - he died there in 1931, aged 83...Royal Institution report, 1894/5, p.10-11.

Gustavus Brothers Parish Church bazaar handbook, 1899, p.15... C/13/5/92/5... 1/7/92/6...SW/11/97/364... C/12/3/97/5.

Pugsleys Contemp Portraits xxiii...Kilvey Men's Bible Class report, 1900. (Swansea Museum, boxfile 81/8)... GAZ/2/12/91/4 & 7...SW/12/96/188...C/1/7/92/5

Marquisses "Industries" 91..."Ports" 122, 131...C/30/1/90/4

The building workers C/7/8/96/3..."Ports", 135...C/15/5/96/2...Awbery, 109...C/5/3/97/8...C/12/5/99/5...1/11/01/5... 8/11/01/3...HoW/18/4/1933/6

Demolishing St. Mary's With few exceptions the information is from the West Glamorgan Archives, including some plans and drawings blackened in the fires of the blitz of 1941. Kim Collis, "The rebuilding of St. Mary's" in the Annual Report of the County Archivist, (1994-5) is very useful. It concentrates on the architectural side, and I avoided rereading it until I had been through the documents! Swansea Museum has photographs taken by (or for) Col. Morgan and a red covered album, with loose prints also interleaved, chiefly photographs of St. Mary's, but also St. Mark's Waun Wen, St. James's, St. Thomas's and Udmore Church in Sussex. There is also one of Holy Trinity,

Nottingham, where J. Alan Smith officiated before coming to Swansea in 1884. Perhaps this was his album - it is not marked...also SW/12/97/392

The drowning C/9/2/1900/5...SW/5/1902/66...C/30/8/1901/5

The Fever Hospital CDL/15/12.91...C/15/7/92/5...CDL/8/9/97

Minnie Vinter Jill Forwood, "High Standards and Legendary Discipline" in the "Evening Post", 4/11/1988.

John Jones Jenkins W.H. Jones, "Port" 284...Norman Lewis Thomas 144...SW/2/1900/788...SW/6/98/476-7...CDL/12/6/97...SW/2/97/232... SW/7/1900/864...SW/5/1904/77

Cadwalladr West Glamorgan Archives Service/P/123/CW...CDL/18/8/1910

C.W.Slater G.P. Neilson, "Charles William Slater", (typescript)..."1873-1923, Brunswick Wesleyan Chapel...Jubilee Souvenir", 17.

B.H. Morgan Programme of the 4th Annual Lantern Exhibition of the Swansea Amateur Photographic Association, (SM boxfile 39)...C/11/11/92

H.H. Parlby Wright's Directory, 1889-90, 10a..."Industries" 93.

Bishop & Nancarrow... Contemp Portraits ix and 24, C/2/3/94...C/21/10/92...M.E.Chamberlain, "The Grenfells of Kilvey" in "The Glamorganshire Historian", IX, (Cowbridge, 1973). With thanks to Marilyn Jones for help on "Glanyrafon"....P.S. Thomas, "Industrial Relations...in Swansea...1800 to recent times", (University of Wales, 1940), p.73-4...C/1/8/90/3...IW/23/8/90/2... 27/9/90/3 ...4/10/90/3.

The Couches Contemp Portraits xii and 21... "The Mariner", November, 1895, p.56, ...GAZ/19/11/90/5...C21/10/98/3...C/4/11/98/5...N.L.Thomas, II, 189-193...Terry Moyle, "The Mohegan, 1898-1998", (Horton Kirby, 1998)..."S.S. Mohegan", (Planaship Prints, 1979) Direct contacts are 01322/862724 & 01326/312418 respectively. The first is a very thoroughly researched book, the second an attractive poster/chart. Both were obtained through the kind offices of the Shipwreck & Heritage Centre, Charlestown, Cornwall and Captain G.A. Hogg of Padstow.

Lancaster Contemp Portraits xxxix and 9... T.G. Davies, "Deeds not Words, A History of the Swansea General and Eye Hospital, 1817-1948", (Cardiff, 1988), 142-3, 153, 173-4, 182.

William Morgan Contemp Portraits xliv, xxxiv, 224...W.C. Rogers, "Pictorial History" 5,...Dykes, "University" 59...C/20/10/93.

Naerup "Mariner" 54, GAZ/28/9/92/6

Weaver Contemp Portraits lii, 28

Polyblank C/13/5/92/2...C/3/1/90/1...C/6/11/96...C/7/10/98/1...C/6/5/92/1... GAZ/18/6/90/4...SJ/5/1/95/1

Evan Lewis A great deal has been taken from scrapbooks in Swansea Museum, almost certainly kept by Evan himself... SW/12/96/199...and with thanks to Joan Harding for written information and advice.

Livingstone SW/10/98/534...GAZ/14/5/90/5

Crawford Fulton "Ports", 116...C/11/10/1901/4

John Thomas SW/6/98/474, C/11/11/92, C/23/6/93.

Dyers SW/7/04

W.H. Stone GAZ/15/2/93/5...C/5/3/97...Contemp Biog 113...With thanks to Stuart Batcup for information on J.C. Woods and also "Ashleigh" - see also Nigel Arthur, "Swansea at War, a Pictorial Account, 1939-45", (S.W. Evening Post, 1988), p.50.

Albert Mason "Mariner" 58..."Ports" (a copy he actually donated to the RI) 128...SW/4/99/642...SWDP/3/9/94...C/31/1/90...C/11/11/92/3...C/13/5/92/1

A page from A.C. Wright's Guidebook of 1897, (see pages 31-2). For Hansard's see page 155, for the Albert Hotel page 153, for Mr. Seline page 97 and for William Copus page 31.

William Usher C/17/1/90/3...GAZ/22/2/90/5...26/11/90/5...Town & Country Directory, 1899,129...C/28/10/92/8... C/28/8/91

Lindley & Ffynone C/22/9/93...W.C. Rogers, 137.

James Jones "Industries" 65, 87..."Ports" 115...."The Mansion House, Swansea," (Swansea City Council, 1979)... SW/12/99/753...C/22/5/96/5... SJ/10/9/90/2...J.D.W. in HoW/6/6/1931/10

T.W. Williams Newsletter of the S.W. Wales Industrial Archaeology Society, Nos 13 & 16, July 1976 and July 1977.

Alexander Moffat GAZ/24/9/90/5...SM boxfile 49...W.C.Rogers 13-14..."Mariner" 52

William Terrill C/26/7 & 9/8/01, Roy Knight, "A History of the Swansea Arts Society, 1886-1986", (Swansea, 1987),16-41, 105-6.

Horses, carriages and carts SW/1/97/211...SW/4/99/640...C/4/7/99/4...C/6/5/92/8...HoW/14/1/1933/10... SWDP/13/5/01/3...Alderman Chris Thomas, "My Early Struggles", (Hafod History Society, 1997, written, 1972), p.5-6...RSPCA, W. Glam branch, annual report, 1886, p.6....Iris Cavelot, "Taylor's Gower Horse Buses" in "Gower", 1974, 6...C/12/3/97/6...C/13/5/92/6...C/6/5/92/1...C/3/1/90/5..C/7/8/96/6....C/17/1/90/7...CDL/11/3/90/3...C/17/1/96/5... SWDP/2/4/94/3...GAZ/26/11/90/5..."Ports" 120...GAZ/31/5/93/4... GAZ/21/6/93/4...SW/8/96/130

Bullins and more Rossers

Bullins "Ports" 120... "Industries" 73... W.W. Hunt,"To Guard My People, an account of the origin and history of the Swansea Police", (Swansea, 1957), 77.

Rossers GAZ/4/11/91/4..."Industries" 97...GAZ/25/6/90/5...SWDP/20/9/95.

Coachbuilders Advert in Swansea Horse Show Catalogue, 1889 p.635..."Ports" 120...Advert in A.M.C. Guide1894...C/3/1/90/4...SW/12/96/195...C/6/5/92/8...SW/4/99...C/3/1/90/3...CDL/11/3/90/3...GAZ/17/6/91/1... "Industries" 94... Cavelot 57...C/3/1/90/4...C/6/5/92/1..."Ports" 127,...C/3/1/90/4...C/7/8/96/1...C/7/10/98/4... C/7/10/98/1..."Ports" 129...Contemp Biog xxxvi

Or go by bike C/12/3/97/5...SWDP/3/9/94...SW/4/99/641...Stuart Batcup, "James Chapman Woods 1854-1933: Swansea's Greatest Poet?" in Minerva, 1996, 27-29...C/14/7/99/3 &4...SW/6/98/475... "Ports" 133...C/22/8/90/6... SW/4/98/442... 5/99/648...11/99/735....1/97/211... Dan Morgan from Evening Post, 23/2/1951, by which time it was Herbert Morgan's... C/7/8/96/3

J.S. Brown SW/8/96/133-4..."Industries" 75,80...C/12/3/97/5... C/5/3/97/4..."Ports" 119...Oystermouth Historical Association Exhibition, 1993...SJ/5/1/95/3

R.E. Jones Burrows Guide 18...Contemp Port xxviii & 325... SW/7/96/cover... SW/8/96/125...SW/11/96/172... SW/6/97/ cover...C/7/8/96/1 & 6... "Ports" 126.

The baths, the laundry & the lady swimmers C/3/1/90/4...C/17/1/90/4...6/5/92/1... W.C. Rogers 166...C/22/9/93... C/5/3/97/8...The last part is from a charming small format notebook belonging to the Chapman family. It is the story of the ladies' water polo team and swimming galas, 1899 to 1901, in press cuttings, local and national. H.A.C.'s daughters Eva and Daisy Chapman were very much involved, and the notebook may have belonged to the former.

Chapman A certain amount of material has been culled from newspapers, directories, guidebooks, etc., as listed here - C/1/11/92/7...C/27/10/93 supplement...Burrows Guide 10...C/3/1/90/3...C/10/1/90/3...C/4/11/92/5...C/11/11/92/2 and 7... C/5/3/97/1... C/1/5/99/4...C/3/11/99/1...C/20/3/08/8...SWDP/3/9/94...11/12/95..."Industries" 76... For B.R. Henessy, see Joanna Greenlaw, "Swansea Clocks", (Llandybie, 1997), 72-4 and W.H. Jones "Port" 289... C/3/1/90/3...10/1/90/3...4/11/92/5 ...11/11/92/2 and 7 ...5/3/97/1 ..27/10/93...1/5/99/4...3/11/99/1...20/3/08/8... 10/11/99/5... SWDP/3/9/94...11/12/95...SJ/5/1/95/3... Contemp Port 123, xxxii..."Ports" 124...Stephen Rowson, "Early Photography in Cardiff", in "Morgannwg", 1996...TUC guide 1901/135-6, 27... David Farmer, "The Life & Times of Swansea R.F.C. - the All Whites", (Swansea, 1995), p.7...HoW/9/5/1931/6 for J.D.W. on Oscar Snelling...Awbery, 31-2 on James Wignall...However, by far the greater part of what is here derives from three wonderful scrapbooks. They contain cuttings from "the Cambrian", "Cambria Daily Leader", "South Wales Daily Press", "South Wales Daily

News", "South Wales Liberal", "South Wales Argus", "Western Mail" , the national press and a few programmes, invitations and formal letters. All of these are mainly to do with the mayoral year, 1892-3, but there is a little on Chapman's silver wedding, some obituaries, and a few cuttings on the Brader family. With these are pieces from the "Evening Post" March 1931 (some of the memories of the second Samuel Palmer Chapman) and 29th April, 1950 (when the shop finished). It is only surmise, but the cuttings books, "Newspaper Gleanings", may have been collected by "Aunt Mags", Margaret, Chapman's eldest daughter, born in 1868. They are carefully attributed to dates and newspapers in a way which accords with an organised lady who used to welcome customers into 235, and show them examples of photos. There was also a very detailed family tree, "The Professional Photographer" for January, 1915, which is largely about H.A.C., a copy of his father's book inscribed as a gift to his grandson, both donor and recipient being Samuel Palmer Chapman.

Lewis Lewis – almost all the information about Lewis Lewis is from West Glamorgan Archives under D/71 and especially D/85. It should be emphasized that some of the early history has a very second hand feel, being culled from news items, the earliest written in 1873. In at least one case, there is evidence of material being repeated in a mistaken fashion. [That the business was a family concern with a friendly feel and a strongly Welsh character is something I know, as my father, grandfather and grandmother worked for the founder's sons and granddaughter for many years - though these are only impressions gained in the fifties and sixties in the woollen materials department, the "marking off" and the great workroom upstairs where garments were altered. I didn't make notes in those days!]

Temperance for Cook & the Townhall, CDL/28/2 - 19/3/90...C/12/3/97/3...

Rechabites and temperance, AMC Conference at Swansea, 1903, Souvenir Booklet, ed Andrew Mattey...
C/7/8/96/7....C/31/1/90/8...CDL/25/3/90/3...C/28/8/96/7... C/21/10/98/7... "Argyle Calvinistic Methodist Church, Swansea, 1875-1925"... C/5/3/97/7... C/24/1/90/4... C/6/5/92/5 ...C/10/1/90/3...C/3/1/90/3 & 5...C/1/7/92/3

W.W. Hunt, "To Guard My People" 75...SWDP/3/9/94

Coffee Taverns Wright's Illustrated Swansea & Mumbles Guide, 1897, p.30..."Ports" 119...C/10/1/90/5... C/6/5/92/5...IW/18/11/91/6...IW/3/2/92/4...Town & County Directories, Cardiff and District..1899, 49...Kilvey Men's Bible Class, Annual Report, 1900...Unitarian Bazaar Programme, 1900, p.10...SW/10/98/545...Burrows Guide, 1903, 103...Kelly's Directory 1906...Gerald Gabb, "The Strand at Swansea in the 1890s", in "Gower", 1996, p.43... SW/6/96/91...Kelly's Directory, 1891, 9a, 11a...Town & County Directories, Cardiff and District, 1899, p.12...A.M.C. Guide, c.1894, various pages (not numbered).

Betts C/7/10/98/4...Burrows Guide, 93

Hansard Swansea Horse Show Catalogue, 1889... Swansea Regatta Programme, 1893. Wright's Illustrated Swansea & Mumbles Guide, 1897...Wright's Annual Reference Book, 1897...C/5/3/97/8

Swansea Aerated Swansea Horse Show Catalogue, 1889

Emmanuel Thomas Unitarian Bazaar Handbook, 1900 p.22

Councillor Fred Rocke lived at Brynsifi, Mount Pleasant. He was the active partner in a large woollen mill in the Strand. Production methods were not quite this picturesque!

South Wales Hop Bitters C/6/5/92/4

Castle Square C/1/7/92/7...Gazette 7/6/93/6...South Walian Dec 97/379...Gazette 28/10/91/4...

John Taylor Contemp Biog xlviii..."Ports" 116... "Industries" 99

Swansea Club Town & County Directory, 1899, p.26

E.L. Morgan C/3/11/99/5...SW/11/99/734

E.E. Rowse SW/5/99/656... E.E.Rowse, "In and Around Swansea", published by the author, 1896, with thanks to Bernard Morris... "Proposed Memorial to William Thomas of Lan..." pamphlet published May 1897.

Phillips SW/4/99/639

D.C. Jones C/6/5/87/4...SW/12/97/383..."Industries" 87...Burrows 96...Town & Counties Directory 1899, p.49...

Phillip Jenkins C/31/1/90/1...Vaughan's Yearbook & Tidetable,..GAZ/29/1/90/5...C/14/10/98/3...Carnival Programme, 1901..."Industries" 88...GAZ/14/5/90/4... 11/5/92/4...Kelly's Directory, 1906...

North Dock... GAZ/28/5/90/5...GAZ/2/7/90/4... GAZ/9/7/90/4...SWDP/25/2/93/2...GAZ/8/4/91/5... GAZ/25/2/91/4... 3/6/91/4... C/17/2/93... IT/8/2/90/1... SW/6/1901/995

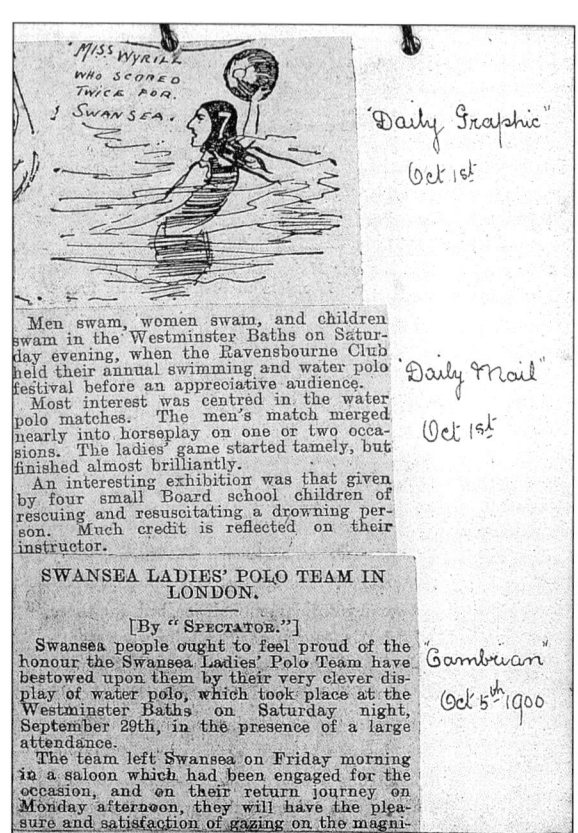

The Swansea Ladies Waterpolo team, 1900, with their secretary, Ivor Evans (see pages 128-30). Pages from the notebook mentioned above.

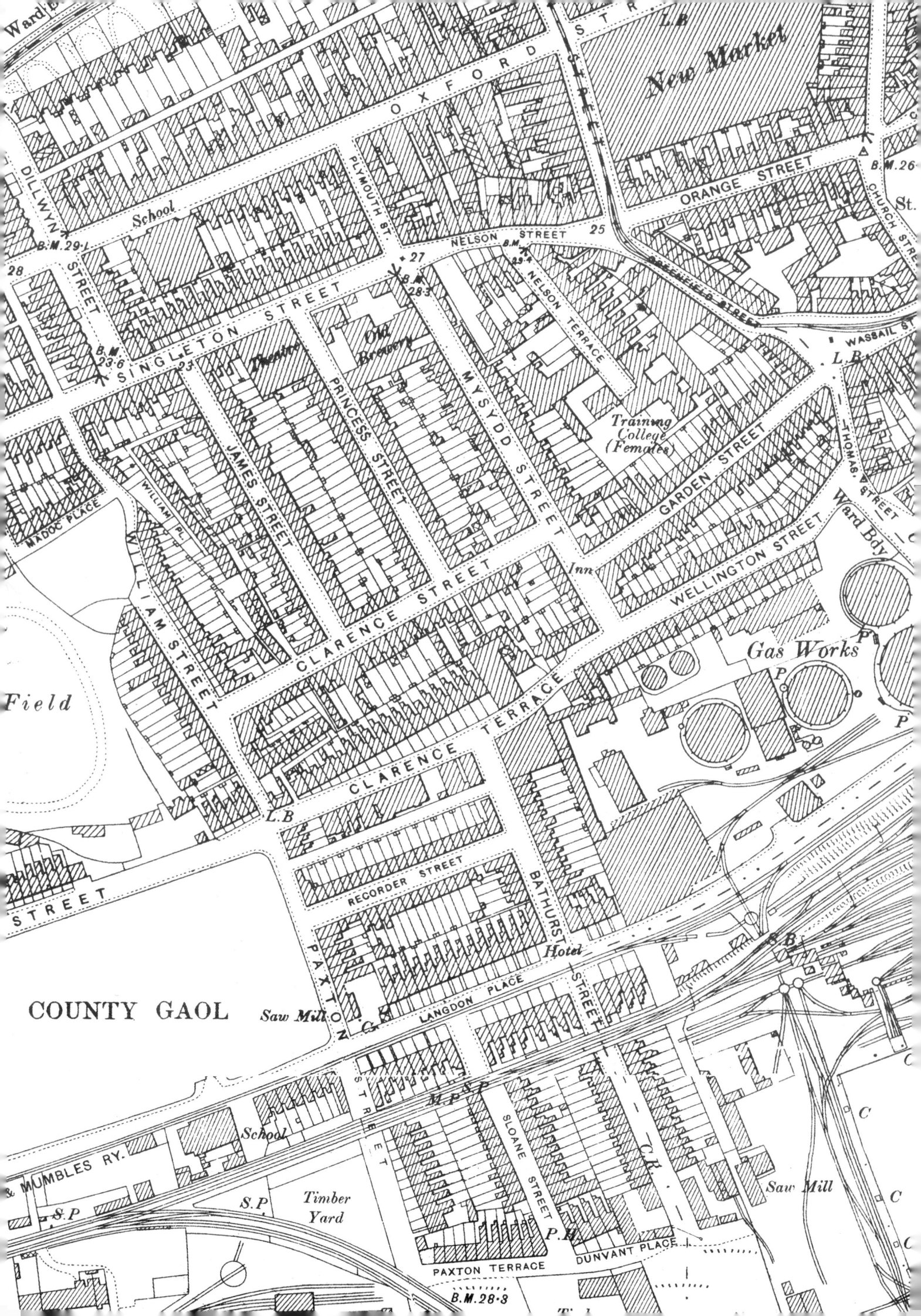